Scrappy

Scrappy

Memoir of a U.S. Fighter Pilot in Korea and Vietnam

HOWARD C. "SCRAPPY" JOHNSON
and IAN A. O'CONNOR

McFarland & Company, Inc., Publishers
Jefferson, North Carolina, and London

LIBRARY OF CONGRESS CATALOGUING-IN-PUBLICATION DATA

Johnson, Howard C., 1920–
    Scrappy : memoir of a U.S. fighter pilot in Korea and
Vietnam / Howard C. "Scrappy" Johnson and Ian A. O'Connor.
    p.   cm.
    Includes index.

    ISBN-13: 978-0-7864-3204-2

    (softcover : 50# alkaline paper) ∞

    1. Johnson, Howard C., 1920–   2. Fighter pilots—United
States—Biography.   3. United States. Air Force—Officers—
Biography.   4. Vietnam War, 1961–1975—Personal narratives,
American.   5. Korean War, 1950–1953—Personal narratives,
American.   6. World War, 1939–1945—Personal narratives,
American.   I. O'Connor, Ian A., 1944–   II. Title.
UG626.2.H69.A3   2008
358.4092—dc22 [B]   2007043938

British Library cataloguing data are available

On the cover: Chris Kenyon, "Scrappy Soars," ca. 1970, acrylic on
canvas, 16" × 24" (Air Force Art Collection)

Manufactured in the United States of America

*McFarland & Company, Inc., Publishers
Box 611, Jefferson, North Carolina 28640
www.mcfarlandpub.com*

To my wife Elena O'Brien Johnson:
partner, soul mate and love of my life.
Elena has been a joy beyond measure.
Her inspiration made me do it.

On the following pages,
I offer nothing more than simple facts
and plain feelings about memories which
are still vivid in my mind, even with
the passing of many years.

—H.C.J.

Scrappy—a living aviation legend. A must read!
    —Robert J. Gilliland, Chief Test Pilot, SR-71 Blackbird

Throughout a rich and rewarding career, Scrappy Johnson demonstrated he is a fighter pilot's fighter pilot. He and his generation taught me and my generation what being a fighter pilot really means. This is his story and it is well worth the read.
    —Ron Fogleman, General, USAF (Ret.),
    Chief of Staff, USAF, 1994–1997

Again and again, Colonel Johnson volunteered to fly Missions Impossible! Our country is fortunate to have patriots like Colonel Johnson, who are the guardians at the gates of our freedom!
    —Ross Perot

Scrappy, your descriptions take me back with vivid memories! Forty years, and those thoughts are like yesterday.
    —Robin Olds, Brigadier General, USAF (Ret.), 1922–2007

Acknowledgments

I would like to thank my college sweetheart and late wife, Dorie Johnson, for putting up with me through forty-three years while this happened.

I cannot say enough by way of thanks to my longtime, now departed, friend, the pride of Texas, Tom Gulick. His help in seeing this project through to completion was immeasurable. I would also like to thank the dozens of others who have contributed to this effort.

I would like also to extend thanks and gratitude to the artist Chris Kenyon for granting permission to use the painting "Scrappy Soars" for the cover of this book.

"Oh Hallelujah! Oh Hallelujah! Throw a nickel on the grass, save a fighter pilot's ass" from a popular song among flyers during World War II, Korea and the Vietnam War.

Author unknown

✈ ✈ ✈

"A Poor Aviator Lay Dying," World War II version, sung to the tune of "My Bonnie Lies Over the Ocean." Original version, circa 1918.

Author unknown

Contents

Preface

"A very impressive feat by a very impressive man."
                                                    Chris Kenyon, 1970

Renowned military portrait artist Chris Kenyon spoke those words of high praise after completing the official U.S. Air Force–commissioned painting of the 1958 Collier Trophy winner. The very impressive man was Colonel Howard C. "Scrappy" Johnson, and his very impressive feat was piloting an F-104A Starfighter up to the dark unknown—up to the very edge of space. Kenyon's photo-realistic painting entitled "Scrappy Soars" captures that singular moment when Scrappy goes over the top, and today it hangs in The Pentagon, a fitting tribute to one of our nation's military heroes.

To put this achievement into a perspective most readers will readily appreciate, eleven years earlier a man named Chuck Yeager was the trophy's recipient for breaking the sound barrier, and eleven years later astronaut Neil Armstrong won the award for the first-ever lunar landing.

This is the official memoir of Scrappy Johnson, an aviation icon whose amazing career is chronicled in this fast-paced—sometimes raucous, sometimes sobering, but always exciting—larger-than-life story that reads like fiction. But a made-up story it's not. His is the world of fighter pilots, of men with nerves forged from steel, a close-knit fraternity of the chosen few. Fly with Scrappy from his days as an aviation cadet during World War II through his tour of duty in the skies over Korea, then later during his more than one hundred missions over North Vietnam as a senior Air Force commander. And during the darkest days of that air war, Scrappy Johnson was instrumental in the founding of an organization that came to be known as the River Rats, or, more formally, the Red River Valley Fighter Pilots Association. What started with a handful of Air Force, Navy and Marine Corps pilots banding together to honor their fallen and captured comrades, and to make sure those brave men would never be forgotten, now, some forty years later, has grown to include five thousand members worldwide. The mission of the "rats" proudly includes the sponsoring of a scholarship fund for the children of dead, missing and captured airmen. Colonel Howard C. "Scrappy" Johnson was the first president of the River Rats.

Prepare to strap in alongside Scrappy for one whale of a ride, starting with his blistering, record-setting flight in the book's prologue, all the way to the last word in the last chapter. You'll climb down from the cockpit knowing you've been riding in the company of a fighter pilot with the right stuff—something Scrappy Johnson has in spades!—I.A.O'C.

Prologue

ONE FOR THE RECORD BOOKS

May 7, 1958. Palmdale, California. The day I flew an F-104A Starfighter into the aviation record books, scores of Lockheed executives were on hand, as were a host of other dignitaries. All were visibly apprehensive, some downright skeptical, because my practice flights had not taken me very high.

I, too, found myself very anxious that morning as I strapped into the cramped cockpit. Minutes later I taxied out, positioned myself on the centerline at the end of the active runway and waited for the "go" from the tower.

In order for me to have sufficient room for a zoom, my track had been meticulously designed so that the apogee of the climb would take place directly over Edwards AFB. This was where the official radar and cameras had been set up to record my exact altitude as I went over the top.

To ensure my success, several things had to happen in rapid sequence and each at the appropriate moment. First, I needed to obtain optimum speed, then burn off just the right amount of fuel so as to be in precisely the right location at the start of my climb. The magic formula was a simple one: The less fuel I had onboard, the lighter the plane, and the lighter the plane, the higher I'd go. But with one very important caveat. I hoped to have enough fuel left in my tanks to make it back to the field and land.

✈ ✈ ✈

I was climbing. The clear, cobalt blue skies afforded Palmdale, California, no cover. Landlocked and naked, the city stood at the mercy of the same sky that now gave my F-104A life. I couldn't help but laugh to myself. Here I was, getting paid to do something a Leonardo da Vinci would probably have given his right hand for. Me, Scrappy Johnson, a Kentucky boy soaring with eagles and not frying chickens. Grandma's "Golden Boy" at the controls of the Air Force's newest and best performing fighter plane ever built.

As I headed for the coast, I gently coaxed the little aircraft up to 43,000 feet, executed a turn over Santa Barbara and made a beeline for Edwards. Nailing the course, I moved the throttle lever to full afterburner and the Starfighter leapt forward. The airspeed indicator moved up rapidly until it showed I was ripping through the air at Mach 2.23. The only sound I could hear was my own breathing.

I carefully eased back on the stick and pointed the plane's nose to the recommended 52-degree angle of attack. The F-104A hammered the air from 50 to 60 thousand feet, then, just as predicted, at 63,000 the afterburner cut out and at 67,000 the engine quit. Not enough oxygen. My partial pressure suit automatically inflated. I was now in a glider. The Starfighter, a rocket whose fuel had been spent, continued to climb.

I blasted through 70 then 80 thousand feet, and still kept ascending. The ailerons, which also act to stabilize the plane, were fast losing their effectiveness: I was now having trouble keeping the wings level. The moment I went over the top I glanced down at my airspeed indicator. Thirty knots. I was barely moving.

The sky was a dark purplish-blue and I could readily make out the curvature of the earth. The engineers later said I could have seen as far as Salt Lake City had my eyesight been good enough—and had I taken the time to look. I didn't. I should have experienced the stick kicker, but it had been deliberately disabled before takeoff.

On my way down the radar operator at Edwards radioed that I had reached 91,249 feet (27,813 meters), which meant I had just broken the world's altitude record by over 14,000 feet!

Continuing my gliding descent, I turned toward Palmdale, and at 47,000 feet I started the General Electric J-79 engine. My pressure suit deflated and I began my dash towards the plant where the anxious crowd awaited the results.

I entered the traffic pattern at Palmdale with less than 400 pounds of fuel, landed without incident and taxied to the ramp.

Tony LeVier, Lockheed's famous test pilot, climbed up to the now-opened cockpit, reached in and pumped my hand. I was mentally and physically drained, but managed a huge grin.

Such an opportunity does not come often in life, and had I muffed it, I would have surely regretted it for the rest of mine.

1

River Rats

By early April 1967 U.S. Air Force, Navy and Marine Corps pilots were being shot down in ever increasing numbers over the world's most heavily defended piece of real estate—an area known as Route Package Six—deep inside North Vietnam. As director of operations for the 388th Tactical Fighter Wing, I was but one of a handful of senior officers flying these missions, and most of us realized that something had to give, and give fast.

Ten thousand miles away in Washington, President Lyndon Johnson, Defense Secretary Robert McNamara and a score of political underlings were not only telling the pilots which outhouses in North Vietnam needed bombing, but they then directed on which day it should be done. On those rare occasions when they actually unleashed our F-105 Thunderchiefs to strike at real, honest-to-goodness high-value targets, we'd find ourselves forced to return again and again because insufficient resources had been allocated to finish the job the first time. The North Vietnamese generals quickly caught on and used the time between strikes to reposition their anti-aircraft defenses so they could hammer us when we returned—as we inevitably did. We were fish in a barrel, we knew it, yet we continued to fly into harm's way.

We felt that a blind man could have spotted what should have been our targets. Every day we saw them from miles away, protected under a dense carpet of black smoke and metal, exploding anti-aircraft fire known as flak. Flak is terrifying stuff, yet we'd be forced to fly right past these high-value targets—airfields, railroad yards and power plants—because our orders were to bomb some dilapidated footbridge near some godforsaken rice paddy. And men were dying as a result of this folly.

To be fair, how the air war was being micro-managed wasn't entirely the fault of the politicians back home. There was plenty of blame to go around, and that included the honchos at Headquarters U.S. Air Force (USAF), Headquarters Pacific Air Forces (PACAF), and even the Seventh Air Force commanders in Saigon. These staff guys were the ones fragging us to fly to our targets in eight separate waves; each wave was a four-ship formation and all were neatly spaced to arrive in precise, five-minute intervals. You could set your watch by those formations, and we all knew it was beyond stupid. Now,

I didn't see combat in World War II, but I sure listened a lot to the guys who did, and the one thing I learned was never make two passes at an airfield—or any other highly defended target—unless you wanted your ass shot down. That lesson had served me well as a young captain flying in Korea in 1950, but now, sixteen years later, I knew I should again be heeding that warning from pilots of a long-ago war.

The biggest problem lay in the fact that all of our strike missions north to Hanoi were being built around the aerial tankers, the jammers and the rescuers: never around the bombers and fighter-bombers, the guys doing the dirty work. Getting us to and from the target was what each mission should have been about, but no one would have guessed that from the way things were being run.

To repeat, something had to give.

On a rainy morning in April 1967, I cornered my boss, Colonel William Chairsell, commander of the 388th Tactical Fighter Wing and suggested we host a tactics meeting with other in-theatre wing commanders and their staffs to do something about the asinine way we were flying our missions. I finished my pitch with a proposal that while we had all those fighter pilots together at Korat Royal Thai Air Base, maybe it would also be a great time to hold a good old-fashioned blast.

"What you got in mind, Scrappy?" Chairsell asked.

"How about a dining-in? That should top off the meeting and allow the men to blow some steam."

Chairsell shook his head. "No can do. Oh, we can have us a big dinner all right, but not a dining-in. You see, according to regulations, a dining-in is an official function which means as the commander I've got to invite every non-flying grunt officer on the base to join us. Is that what you had in mind?"

"Hell no!"

Chairsell laughed at my pugnacious reply. "I kind of thought not. Okay, you've got my permission to invite the other commanders and some of their pilots to come for a conference, and who am I to argue if you want to arrange for what you call a good old fashioned blast at the same time. Just don't go calling it a dining-in."

I didn't give a rat's ass what we called it, so I got on the phone to drum up support. First on my list was Colonel Daniel "Chappie" James, the Deputy of Operations with the 8th Tactical Fighter Wing at Ubon Royal Thai Air Base. Chappie was an old friend from the 18th Fighter Group where we had first served together in the Philippines, then later in Korea. He thought it a super idea and was more than happy to cooperate. I was off to a good start.

Next I formed a committee to hash out the details. Major Alfred "Lash" Lagrue and Captain Frank "Smitty" Smith would head up this effort. Things began to snowball and soon I began to worry. Could we adequately deliver on the promise or not? These fighter pilots we were inviting gave their best everyday, and I felt they deserved the best we had to offer in return. I pestered Lash daily to make certain we were in agreement as to how things needed to be handled, and he assured me time and again that he knew what had to be done. Lash took the ball and ran with it, clinching all the details.

I personally contacted every pilot in the wing and charged each ten bucks, which would cover everything—food, booze, entertainment, the works. I suggested to my committee that we greet the arriving pilots at the flight line, then kickoff the festivities by having some sort of a parade to the officers' club. Which meant we needed a band to lead the way. Then at a meeting a couple of days later I really upped the ante. "See if you can get something for the guys to ride on, maybe a couple of elephants." Then I passed along what Chairsell had said about not calling our shindig a dining-in and asked Lash to come up with another name for the affair.

Lash told me later that he and Smitty had both come to dread going to the club during this period for fear of running into me and my adding to the ever-growing list of things for them to do. They still hadn't figured out what to do with the six elephants and the accompanying attendants they had hired for the big day. Providing food, water and bedding for a half dozen Asian pachyderms was one more problem definitely not included in a fighter pilot's training manual—and it sure didn't appear in any squadron officer's job description either. But that was before they discovered the abandoned horse stable on the base.

Years later at one of our reunions, Lash confessed how a last-minute problem had almost derailed the entire event. He told of how he had sent two fighter jocks to Bangkok to pick up a ton of Kobe steaks for the big dinner and how he had mentally checked off that project as being done. Then, boom! All hell broke loose. Two days before the bash he learned that the pilots he had sent to town had disappeared and that the cook was wondering what had happened to our meat! Lash recounted how he had turned the world on its ear trying to contact those missing pilots, but no luck. No luck? No steaks? No shit! Son of a bitch! Lash was beside himself. And no way was he going to come whining to me with his problem. He finally ended up sending two more guys to town with very specific instructions on where to buy the steaks and to get the hell back to the base, ASAP. We both had a hearty laugh as he relived his nightmare. Funny now, but I know it was nothing short of terrifying for Lash then.

The big day arrived. May 22, 1967. Because of the heightened tempo of air ops that spring, Colonel Robin Olds, the commander of the 8th TFW was the only wing commander able to squeeze in the time to attend. The others sent deputies in their stead: men they had empowered to make decisions. Robin and a bunch of his pilots flew in from Ubon along with the senior delegates from the 355th TFW at Takhli, and they were joined on the tarmac by representatives from a couple of the navy air wings operating off-shore, along with the brass from the tanker outfits.

I had set aside enough time for everybody to greet one another, for old

Col. Daniel "Chappie" James, D.O. 8th Tactical Fighter Wing, atop the number two elephant at the first Red River Valley Fighter Pilots Association meeting at Korat RTAFB, Thailand, 1967 (courtesy of USAF).

friends to catch up on the latest news, then had Robin and Chappie hoisted onto the backs of the first two elephants in line. This was my prearranged signal with Lash to start the parade. And if six elephants lumbering trunk-to-tail alongside the flight line wasn't an impressive enough sight for the cheering and whistling crowd, Lash had somehow cajoled the Royal Thai Provincial Police Band from Korat into helping us celebrate the day with a stirring oompa-pa medley of Souza marches.

The "Parade of Elephants" at Korat RTAFB, Thailand, 1967 (courtesy of USAF).

Forty minutes later I called a temporary halt to the festivities to allow those slated to attend the conference to assemble at wing headquarters. For the next two hours we held a very serious tactics meeting. The most productive item to come from that roomful of air force and navy pilots was the creation of what quickly became known within the group as the "Snoopy" report. Snoopy was to be a daily exchange among the flying wings of their selected targets.

Until then we had all been flying north and hitting our own targets, yet none of us knew what the other wings were doing or where they were going. From now on we would pass this report back and forth among ourselves, eliminating the need to depend on Seventh Air Force for this vital information. It was a good day's work.

After the meeting we climbed back on the elephants and girded ourselves for the all-important phase two.

I had asked Lash and Smitty to come up with a name for this shindig, and they did. As we neared the officers' club, a forty-foot monster of a banner came into view.

Welcome Red River Valley Fighter Pilots

Lash and Smitty had conjured up the name from the Red River that wends its way through Hanoi. In many ways we fighter pilots were akin to the wild, untamed cowboys of yesteryear, men who had run the little doggies through the Red River Valley in the American West, men whom we had learned to sing about and emulate in games when we were kids.

It took twenty minutes for us to dismount, enter the club, clean up, and then find our places in the dining room. The base chaplain raced through his invocation then said grace. This was one padre who knew his congregation. His blessing went something like this: "God bless this food, God bless these shit-hot fighter pilots, let's eat, amen!"

Now I'm not big on being called upon to be a host—and I detest all things formal—but I had nominated myself to be master of ceremonies that night. Without fanfare and like the chaplain, I rushed through my introduction of Chappie James as our guest speaker then scurried back to my seat. Chappie had a well-deserved reputation for never meeting a microphone he didn't instantly fall in love with, and this night would prove to be no exception. True to form, he began to deliver one hell of a rousing speech.

A minute into his talk, though, a tall, skinny captain noisily entered the room and made his way to the head table. Under his arm was cradled a large, framed photograph of Chappie with his head centered inside a white, plastic toilet seat. Apparently Chappie had fallen asleep in the gooney bird on the way over from Ubon and one of the guys had held up the seat while another snapped the picture. The photo was a million-dollar keeper.

And this captain was a man on a mission. He stepped boldly up to a spot right in front of Chappie, paused for several beats, then wordlessly continued on his journey to the rear of the dining room where he whipped out a hammer from one of his flightsuit pockets and began to pound a nail into the wall. Chappie stopped in mid-sentence, jaw slackened in surprise. Every eye in the room was on the captain as he hung his masterpiece, fussed with it for a moment then stepped back to admire his handiwork. The room exploded into gales of laughter, and no one laughed louder or longer than Chappie. The guy was one really good sport!

After several follow-on speeches, I took control of the proceedings and suggested everyone adjourn to the main bar. This was fighter pilot country and within minutes the drinks began to flow. Major Maurice "Moe" Seaver allowed enough time to pass for everyone to become lubricated, then took it upon himself to head up the fun and games portion of the unofficial program. Every fighter pilot knows some of these games can get a little rough, but usually there aren't any lasting casualties. Outsiders might think we become childish and boorish, but I guarantee you, we sure know how to have fun after a few drinks.

The floor of this particular officers' club was made of terrazzo—a polished mixture of concrete and aggregate which becomes very slippery when beer is sloshed all over it. And we proceeded to dump gallons of the stuff that night in order to set the right conditions for a game of "night landings."

Night landings are performed by taking a running dive at a beer-slicked floor while holding a large serving tray tightly to one's chest. The idea is to slide across the room as quickly as possible, riding the tray headfirst into either a wall or a pile of old bottles—and to do so without killing oneself. This, of course, has its limitations. Our particular club barroom was only about 50 feet long, so some quick-thinking captain had opened the door to the adjoining game room thus creating a far longer slide. More sober heads had then grabbed seat cushions and placed them strategically on either side of the door for padding.

One of our younger pilots, in a mad dash for glory, missed the pillow-buffer completely and crashed headfirst into the doorframe, severely gashing his chin. Fortunately, the base hospital was nearby where a flight surgeon sewed him up in short order, and he came back to perform several more times before passing out under one of the tables.

Another game we played was called "Friar Tuck." Here, two opponents faced one another balanced on half-gallon whiskey bottles; each man armed with a cue stick and whose mission it was to toss the other from atop his whiskey bottle kingdom. Imagine the fun. Playing this particular game was always a bartender's worst nightmare.

During a lull in the festivities Robin Olds pulled me aside and whispered, "Scrappy, I've got a game in mind, but I've got to warn you, it usually starts a fight." Somehow I knew this was no inconsequential statement, so I immediately corralled Moe and a couple of others close by and warned them to be on the alert for whatever might happen.

Robin Olds was a big guy, easily 6'2" and 230 pounds. He'd been an All American football player at West Point, and now, two decades later, was still made of solid muscle. I would soon understand why the six guys Robin had brought with him were all bruisers—including Chappie—and what he'd meant by his whispered statement.

Robin and his band of brigands maneuvered their way to the far end of the very long bar, then, without warning, rushed pell-mell down its business side laying waste to everyone in their path. My gang managed to stop them about two-thirds of the way down, but everyone in front of us, including Colonel Chairsell, had been knocked flat on their asses. Robin and his bruisers could have mowed down many more bystanders if the barstools hadn't been in their way.

None of us knew it then, but we had just seen the first of many casualties-to-come from a soon-to-be-world-famous "Red River Rat MiG Sweep."

We all ended up in a pile with Robin and me on the bottom where I managed to get a hold of the scruff of his neck and found myself trying to pound his head into the sticky terrazzo floor. After a couple of seconds it dawned on me, "What the hell do I think I'm doing?" I'm 5'8" (I never had to duck when going through any doors) and on a good day I tip the scales at 170 lbs. Robin was easily six inches taller, and had me by sixty or seventy pounds. I immediately stopped trying to pound his head into the floor. Robin and I were under an ever-shifting pile five or six deep, yet somehow I still had my cigar clamped firmly between my teeth and the smoke was choking the both of us. My arms soon were pinned uselessly to my sides but I somehow managed to make Robin understand that he needed to get the damn thing out of my mouth so we could both breathe.

It was one unforgettable night.

The Red River Valley Fighter Pilots Association was born that May 22, 1967, and was baptized in a lake of liquor. But I'm proud to report that the organization has both flourished and prospered for the intervening forty years. We now have five thousand members and counting. There are so many worthy accomplishments to the organization's credit, and I've often wondered what would have happened if we hadn't looked for a way to define ourselves during that special gathering of Air Force, Navy and Marine Corps officers so many years ago.

For example, what if Colonel Chairsell hadn't said to me that rainy day in April 1967, "Oh, we can have us a big dinner all right, but no dining-in?" What if he had simply given me a silent nod and a gung-ho thumbs up? My guess is military historians would have recorded just another formal dining-in for the 388th TFW that sultry May night, because what fighter pilot in his right mind would join a Fighter Pilots Dining-in Association, then enthusiastically commit to attending reunions for decades to come? And lastly, what if Lash Lagrue and Smitty Smith hadn't come up with that magical name, Red River Valley Fighter Pilots, a name which in an instant forged us into this resolute brotherhood of pilot-warriors during one of the darkest moments in our nation's history?

It was a fraternity destined to endure for a lifetime—and beyond.

2

Growing Up

I'm an old guy now, but I wasn't always. I sure don't feel it and I definitely don't believe it, but every morning my shaving mirror tells me it's true. Inside my skin a youngster nicknamed Scrappy greets the old gent in the glass with an impish grin and a sly wink, then watches in silence as he scrapes away the gray stubble on his cheeks and chin. Some days the kid will chide the old guy that he's missed a spot here, or nicked himself there, but more often than not he just nods his approval. And who knows better than Scrappy what a wonderful life the old guy has lived? His is a life still filled with excitement—though not as interspersed with the huge dollops of heart-pounding danger found many years earlier, but definitely a life lived to full measure. And the kid is still thrilled to be tagging along on this rollicking good ride.

Young Scrappy steps back from the mirror and lays down his towel. Then with a steady hand and beady eye he cocks a thumb and forefinger, takes careful aim and squeezes off a single shot. Bang! The old man staggers for a fleeting moment then pulls himself erect. He smiles, secure in his knowledge that this is the same pistol he's faced every morning since early forever, and it only shoots blanks. The kid smiles back at the old man in the mirror. I'll see you tomorrow.

Scrappy Past and Scrappy Present are still on the same page of the checklist.

✦ ✦ ✦

I was born and christened Howard Carrol Johnson, this all-in-one event taking place in my grandmother's home in Knoxville, Tennessee. The day was Groundhog Day, February 2, and the year was 1920. Grandma Ella (Coker) often told me that both Punxsutawney Phil and little Howard Carrol Johnson both saw their shadows at exactly the same moment that bleak winter morning. But unlike Phil who snuck back into his warm den to snooze for another six weeks, she says I started bawling, the sound carrying from one end of the county to the other. I was letting the world know I had arrived and was ready for my adventure to begin.

Maybe Grandma exaggerated, but I don't think by much.

✝ ✝ ✝

Grandma Ella had a profound impact on my life. I was an only child, and because our home was close to hers, I spent a lot of time in her company. Ella was a strong woman. She was the one who insisted that mom and I move in when dad's job took him to another town. "Maintaining two households is out of the question," she told her daughter. Mom protested, but without much conviction in her voice, obviously pleased with this money-saving arrangement. Ella's husband, John, had died somewhere around the time of his fortieth birthday leaving his widow close to penniless and with four children to raise: a boy and three girls. Knowing now what I know of life, how the woman did it is beyond me. A stern, but very loving lady, she was the only grandparent I really can remember.

Grandma would hold me on her knee when I was what the locals called 'the holding size,' then she'd pull me close and whisper in my ear things like, "You can become anything you want if you set your goal." Or, "You are judged by your friends," and "never tell a lie." The one I heard most often though was "Never take the Lord's name in vain. " This was her line in the sand—for any-one, pauper or prince!

In what devolved into

Grandma Coker. I was her "Golden Boy."

something of a game between us, Grandma Ella enjoyed bushwhacking me in front of her friends. Without warning she would swoop me up off my feet, plant a big wet kiss on my cheek and declare, "Howard's my million-dollar boy!" And this clutch of widows and spinsters—all wearing hats and gloves no matter the season—would cluck and coo a very vocal collective approval. I'd wriggle free and run out of the room thoroughly embarrassed, but secretly pleased that this woman who always smelled of fresh lilac loved me so much. Her million-dollar boy was three years old at the time and I just knew that a million was all the money in the world!

Ella wasn't one to wear her religion on her sleeve; she lived and breathed it every waking moment of every single day. I truly have never met a more religious lady, and she, more than my own mother, insisted I plant my feet early in life squarely on the path of righteousness. Every Sabbath I'd accompany her to the Methodist church—first to Sunday school to learn about our Savior, then into services to pay homage and sing His praises. As I grew older, there were some Sundays she would tell me quietly—but only after class had ended and before services began—that God would understand if I skipped out early today. Maybe Ella knew in advance the sermon's subject for that particular Sunday and didn't relish the thought of having to explain to her million-dollar boy what lechery, debauchery and fornication was all about. Remember, I said Ella was deeply religious. I should also add, smart.

To suggest Ella had strong feelings against alcohol was akin to suggesting there existed somewhere in God's creation a fire hotter than hell's own. Like all genuinely religious people, Ella was slow to see anything but good in most souls, and naively believed what she was told. Let me give you an example.

During Prohibition my father often bought grapes home from Ella's backyard vines. To eat, you might ask? No, I'd reply, to make wine. She never caught on, thinking he was actually turning out grape juice for the family. And when grapes weren't in season my father made beer. I remember one stifling day when some of the bottles he'd stashed away in the back of the hall closet began popping their corks. Pow! Bam! Blam! It was the Fourth of July in spades inside that closet. My mother, who was entertaining the ladies in her church circle at the time, was beyond mortified. As her friends left, she made them all promise not to say a word about this to Ella, but my father sure heard about it when he came home.

For as long as I can remember, Ella kept an old, single shot 12-gauge shotgun in the corner of the kitchen beside the back door. It had belonged to my grandfather. She also kept his loaded Iver-Johnson thirty-eight revolver on a nightstand beside her bed. That revolver lay there for years and I never dared touch it. Indeed, I never remember being told not to, it was just something I knew was out of bounds. Some four decades later I found it in a chest of drawers when I was packing my Uncle Bud's belongings shortly after his death.

When I finally handled this piece for the very first time I was forty-nine years old. I've often thought about that. Now there's so much emphasis on keeping handguns out of the reach of children. The world has sure turned many times since the days of my youth, and in its turning I feel something profound has been lost between the generations.

My mother, Clara Coker Johnson, was a small lady. Petite is probably a more apt word to describe her. This beautiful, china doll of a woman stood maybe 5'1" and weighed all of 105 lbs. But what she lacked in size she more than made up for in persuasive personality, especially when it came to disciplining yours truly. Mother was dead set against me acquiring any bad habits and was constantly explaining to me what it was that gentlemen did and didn't do. One day, while goofing off in a field behind my grandmother's house, another kid and I were smoking the leaves of a gray weed that grew in Tennessee called Rabbit Tobacco, and I'd learned somewhere that the Indians used to smoke it. We'd hardly fired up when my mother suddenly appeared before us like some avenging apparition. This wasn't my mom, but a ten-foot-tall giant who really looked like her. Seems she had spotted the smoke rising from out of the tall grass and hurried to investigate. She told my friend to get on home immediately then proceeded to blister my rear end all the way back to grandma's. It had the intended effect. That first cigarette was also my last. Well, that's technically true, at least until the age of thirty when I was stationed in the Philippines and started smoking cigars.

Scrappy at 3 years of age, Knoxville.

✈ ✈ ✈

During those early years I played marbles for endless hours with a kid down the block named Tommy Goosie. There were kids in the neighborhood I wasn't allowed to play with under penalty of death. Tommy was considered borderline, but mother did make that rare exception, like, maybe right after the first snowfall of August. Anyway, Tommy and I played marbles for keeps, which was very much one of her "no-nos." Tommy was a couple of years older than me and a better player. Luckily, however, I managed not to lose enough marbles so that my mother found out, and those I did lose, I kept my mouth shut about.

One day a group of us from several of the surrounding streets were playing baseball in a vacant lot across from Mrs. Jackson's house. This widow lived alone, save for a mangy cur that looked as old as his mistress. On this particular day her dog was all over that lot, getting in

A future fighter pilot (Scrappy at 9) and "Buddy" in Knoxville, 1929.

everybody's way. He was wearing himself to a frazzle chasing the base runners and fielders, and he even took off after the spectators. One of the kids decided it was time to chase the mutt home, so he grabbed a stick, let out a blood-curdling yell and took off after the animal. The dog caught on real fast that the game had suddenly changed and he lit out for home lickety-split; his terrible yelps of genuine fear filled the air. Both teams stopped playing, all eyes agog in anticipation of the mayhem sure to come. Mrs. Jackson had been following the progress of our game from her front porch and must have thought the kid was hell-bent on killing her precious. She began yelling. Tommy Goosie, who was playing on the other team, decided it was up to him to save the dog from certain death, so he ran an intercept and knocked the kid down. That was the lucky break the dog needed. He flew up and onto his porch, stopped on a dime, turned to face his tormentor, and, I swear, that dog started laughing from his secure sanctuary between his mistress's legs.

Meanwhile the kid on the ground was fit to be tied. He jumped up, and as soon as Tommy was back up on his feet, he wound up and landed a solid punch on Tommy's cheek. Tommy began to howl, the sound of his misery louder than the dog had managed only moments before. Our game ended then and there.

Tommy's older brother, Clyde, standing on the sidelines saw the whole thing, but not wanting to be a twenty-something-year-old bully yelled at the kid, "Get out of my sight, you little son of a bitch!" The kid started crying, and as he headed for home, he yelled over his shoulder at Clyde, "I'm going to tell my daddy you called me a son of a bitch." Most of the neighborhood men were out of work thus at home during the day, so Clyde realized this was no idle threat but one capable of carrying real consequences. That kind of talk in East Tennessee could start a major war, and Clyde reckoned he would be the first casualty.

Clyde was a relatively frail man, and sizing up the kid who was definitely big for his age, assumed the father would be a fully-grown version of the same, so he lit out in the opposite direction, hoofing it hard all the way to his house. He ran inside only to reemerge a minute later. He tore down the front steps, threw himself into an old rattletrap family car and roared off.

Within five minutes the other kid returned to the lot, his legs pumping to keep up with his fire-breathing father, a monster carved out of iron. "Where's Clyde?"

We all started jabbering at once, a dozen kids babbling in tongues, hopping from one foot to another in a display of raw, nervous excitement. Somehow he figured out we were telling him that Clyde had left, so he grabbed his kid by the arm and marched him off in the direction of home. We knew this was not the end of it. No sir, not by a long shot. We began whispering among ourselves, all the while being eyed mischievously by the old dog that had started the ruckus in the first place.

Tommy told me afterwards that Clyde had gone to his brother's house and had gotten a gun. Now armed, he'd driven up the street and parked in front of the kid's house, and with the engine running began to talk to the father who was sitting in a swing on the porch. "I didn't call your kid a son of a bitch," he called out, "I was yelling at the dog."

"That the God's honest truth?"

"Yes, sir, it is. God strike me dead here and now if it ain't."

Tommy said the kid's dad then invited Clyde to join him up on the porch, but Clyde shook his head, said he had errands to run, and drove off. Clyde explained that he'd declined the invitation because the man could have shot him between the eyes then told the cops he thought Clyde was coming towards his house to do him bodily harm. This is but one example of why my mother had plenty of reservations about many of my neighborhood associates.

My father, Roscoe Howard Johnson, was known as Howard, never Roscoe. Not even Ross. He loathed his name. And since he was known to all as Howard and my name was also Howard, for about my first ten years I was called Howard Junior, or Little Howard, although, technically, I wasn't a junior.

My father had been raised on a farm about ten miles north of Knoxville, and he was the youngest of thirteen. When he was little more than a toddler his left leg was run over by a wagon wheel, permanently damaging the leg to the point it was a good two inches shorter than the right. For the rest of his life he was burdened with a decided limp and a very odd gait. He would swing that bum leg way far out to his side before planting it on the ground, take a step, then repeat the process step, after step, after interminable step. Between the accident and being the baby, dad was coddled and protected by the others, and, sad to say, he never really grew up to become a responsible adult.

Around the time of my fifth birthday grandmother Johnson passed away, and a short time later the family farm was split up. My father immediately sold off his part, and with his newfound wealth bought a two-seat Chrysler convertible, a new hunting outfit and a Remington 16-gauge shotgun. It took only a couple of years until the money from the farm was gone.

Grandmother Ella was a staunch Republican, and this in an era when being a Republican in Tennessee was anything but mainstream. When I was eight or nine she married a man named Tom Eubanks, a well-to-do gent, but Tom was a Democrat. Since they voted opposite tickets, come Election Day he would drive to the polls alone, leaving grandmother to take a taxi. And when

Franklin Roosevelt was elected president she refused to allow his name to pass her lips. She would only refer to him as That Man.

Her new husband was also a devoted foxhunter. Now, foxhunters didn't hunt foxes in East Tennessee by riding horses and jumping fences. No, sir, that was for the sissy Englishmen, not a descendant of Davy Crockett. Tom and his pals went out at night (usually it was a Saturday), released the hounds, built a fire, and sat around listening to the dogs run the fox. They knew the sound of each dog's broadcasting and would say things to one another like, "Old Red's lost the scent" or "There goes my Old Yeller" or "Your Jake is chasing a darn rabbit." I have a firsthand knowledge of this since I was allowed to accompany Tom on more than one or two of these excursions. Looking back, I have a feeling that there was a little white lightnin' of the odorless kind involved in the hunt, because if Tom had come home with alcohol on his breath, grandmother would have sent him packing.

One Sunday when I wasn't able to worm my way out of listening to the Methodist preacher's hour-long sermon I remember him railing in a stern voice, "If some folks among us hadn't stayed out all night fox hunting they wouldn't be dozing off now during my sermon." My grandmother, thoroughly embarrassed, swung to her right and stared directly at Tom, causing a chorus of titters to break out from the pews around us. Tom was both livid and mortified, and if looks could kill....

Tom had a granddaughter from his first marriage and on one of her birthdays he gave her a pony. For me, this would have been the ultimate gift, but Tom's answer to my hints on the matter was to give me a coupon he'd cut out of a magazine. "Send this coupon in for a chance to win a pony," it read. My dream was stillborn.

I had a deep admiration for Ella's only son, my uncle Edward "Buddy" Coker. Despite his small size, 5'9" and 165 pounds, he had been captain of his high school football team and was also a great baseball pitcher. Buddy was offered a full-ride scholarship to the University of Tennessee but had to turn the offer down because he was needed to work to help support his mother and the rest of the family. Buddy never made it to the big leagues but he did manage to pitch for several minor league teams. He was the youngest of my grandmother's children and only fifteen years my senior. When I was eleven or so he'd get me to catch for him while he practiced his pitching. He'd always warn me prior to throwing his knuckle ball, because even he didn't know exactly what it would do. My grandmother would always tell people that Edward— as only she called him—had never taken the Lord's name in vain. I, however, had more than a passing doubt about the validity of that claim.

I attended West View Grammar School, a small, red brick building that housed grades one through six in its classrooms. I recall one day at lunch period when two kids got into a fistfight. About a dozen of us were standing around, yelling and egging them on, when suddenly some kid standing at the back pushed me into the melee. Acting on instinct and adrenaline, I started a turning-swing without looking and caught the offender square on the nose, causing him to bleed profusely. At this point one of the teachers broke up the fight, and since the kid with the nosebleed was yelling up a storm, I was taken to the principal's office where he was warming up a paddle in preparation to warming my behind.

Mr. Simcox was our school janitor. He and his wife had recently emigrated from England and lived in a small cottage near grandmother's. Since they were not very well off, my grandmother took them food on special occasions, such as Christmas and Thanksgiving. Well, kindness was about to be repaid with kindness. Mr. Simcox rode to my rescue. He told the principal in a loud voice for all to hear that the other kid had pushed me into the fight and got what he deserved when I bloodied his nose.

I will never forget my savior, Mr. Simcox.

For as long as I could remember my father always had a job as a clerk for the Louisville and Nashville Railroad. During the height of the Depression—and as a part of downsizing—his job in Knoxville was eliminated. Of course, the railroad operated on a seniority system, which meant he was able to claim the job of another employee who had less service time. There were no jobs to bump in Knoxville, so he bumped someone in the small town of Etowah, Tennessee, some sixty miles south. We packed up and moved there for a year, living in a cheap hotel near the center of the town, and because we could ride the train for free we visited Ella most weekends. Then when my father was transferred to Corbin, Kentucky—for reasons beyond my knowledge—my mother and I moved back to Knoxville and again moved in with Ella for a year while dad lived in Corbin alone. He managed a few weekends home with one in particular standing out in my mind.

It was Sunday afternoon. A group of us were playing in the yard of the nearby grammar school when a kid kicked a football in my direction. Instead of catching it, I attempted to kick it back, and instead of connecting square on, it slipped off the side of my foot and went arching through a window in a house adjacent to the playground. An enraged crone stomped onto the porch and let it be known that she expected me to pay her fifty cents for the broken pane. I went home and told my father, but his reply was that he didn't have fifty cents. I was distraught until Grandma Ella came to my rescue. She accompanied me back to the woman's house, gave her the fifty cents and told her we were sorry for any trouble I'd caused.

After a year of living with Ella, my mother decided we were moving to Corbin so that we could be a proper family. We moved into a small, white two-bedroom house. Our landlord, Mr. Young, was a local lawyer, and he lived in a grand house adjacent to ours. I can remember my mother and father arguing constantly during this time, the cause of their bitterness being his drinking and coming home late almost every night. And she also accused him of messing around.

Sad to say, I personally witnessed evidence of the latter. Once, while walking somewhere between home and town just after dark, I stumbled heads-on into a couple. The woman was our landlord's housekeeper; the man was my father. As we passed he recognized me and I recognized him. He lowered his head and hurried by. I suppose he figured that since he was sporting a wide-brim fedora he could successfully hide his face from me. Hell, not only would I have recognized him by his clothing, but for him to have dared hope I wouldn't have pinpointed his pronounced limp would have been a joke.

And another time, I saw him wooing the housekeeper with hand signals from a window in a small room in our attic. Unfortunately, mother spotted him also, which resulted in one of their most heated encounters ever.

Sadly, you can count me in as one who can testify to the terrible feelings of insecurity children experience from such free-for-all bouts by their parents.

It was the stuff of nightmares. Too bad I did not remember this in later life, it could have made growing up a lot more pleasurable for my own children.

3

"Louavall"

In the spring of 1933 my father was transferred to Louisville. This was a great move for us, but not for Lawyer Young and the local grocer whom we left in our wake raising holy hell over a mountain of unpaid bills.

Louisville was very much a laid-back Southern town in the nineteen thirties. My father called it a big country town, and in many respects he was right. Even today Louisville retains a special flavor all its own, and when conversing with someone from there you can readily identify him as a native by the way he refers to home as Louavall.

Louisville is where I got the nickname Scrappy, and the honor goes to my Sunday school teacher, Mr. George Stiglitz. This second christening occurred at a picnic when I was thirteen and another boy was razzing me mercilessly. After several failed attempts at warning him to quit, I lit into him. Mr. Stiglitz pulled us apart, and since the other kid was bigger, he called me "Scrappy" for going at him. The name stuck, and I've been Scrappy ever since.

By the time I was ready for high school I had to make a choice. Boys and girls went to separate high schools in Louisville in those days. All of the boys' schools were located downtown; Louisville Male High, DuPont Manual Training High School and St. Xavier. Since I wasn't Catholic, St. Xavier was never a choice, but I ended up going to DuPont Manual for no other reason than Frank Landers, a neighborhood kid a year ahead of me talked me into it. DuPont Manual was supposed to train kids to do shop work, but the shop part of the curriculum was optional, so there wasn't really that much difference between the two. Besides, what I learned in the shop classes at DuPont Manual made me a first-class handyman around my own home in later years.

DuPont Manual was housed in an old three-story building at the corner of Brook and Oak. Decades later it was declared a historical monument, but it should have been proclaimed a relic a full century before I was a student there. I can still remember racing to the weekly assembly which was held in the gym, and almost falling head over heels down the timeworn, rounded wooden stairs only to be saved by the cluster of boys around me.

Ralph Kimmel—who was also a local scout for the Baltimore Orioles— coached our baseball team. One of our players was a kid named "Peewee"

Reese who went on to become a legendary professional player and member of the Baseball Hall of Fame.

Our head football coach was "Ab" Kirwin. He was also an English teacher. Ab was an excellent coach who had come to us after graduating from the University of Kentucky where he had been a star end all four years. The year I graduated he was made head coach at the University of Kentucky, but after a couple of so-so seasons he was replaced and became the dean of men. Ab Kirwin finished a stellar career in academia as president of the university.

Our line coach was Ray Baer. Ray had been a tackle at the University of Michigan. I once read where a reporter had asked "Bronco" Nagurski to name the toughest guy he'd ever played against. He replied, without missing a beat, "Ray Baer of Michigan." When Ab left for Kentucky, Baer became our head coach.

In high school my overriding ambition was to make the football team and star in every game. Alas, that was not to be. My dreams were never fully realized, but I did experience some very limited game-time, playing left halfback, and my good friend Jack Pruitt played right halfback.

Jack and I were fast friends and both of us would have sold our souls to make the team. We, along with Alan Parr, who played end, would often ride home after practice with another member of the team, Bill Bailey. Nothing untoward about this, except Bailey owned the most unusual car any of us had ever seen. It was an Austin. Not an Austin Healey, just an Austin. It was the first really small car that I can ever remember seeing. In fact, some folks actually mistook it for some rich kid's toy. The four of us piling into that car was akin to four teenagers squeezing into a horizontal phone booth.

One day some of the guys on the team carried that little car to the top of the stadium while Bailey was still in the locker room changing. He had to beg a group of us to help get it down so we could all go home that night.

In those days there was no distinction between offensive and defensive football teams. Everyone played both ways. Substitution was limited, and in most formations the quarterback was used as a blocking back. The halfbacks did most of the ball handling, the running and the passing. Facemasks were not to appear on the horizon for many years, and our helmets were made of leather. Which often serves to remind me of some of the more mean-spirited comments that made the rounds about Gerald Ford when he was president. If he did or said something that certain folks disagreed with, they would shrug it off with an all encompassing, and overtly snide, "The man can't help it. He made too many plays without his helmet."

Since Jack and I each only weighed about 135 pounds, the coaches used us as cannon fodder. We could, and did, perform all of the required skills: run, pass, block, tackle and handle the ball; we were just too small to be considered threats. The coaches kept hoping we'd get bigger, and Lord knows, so did we, but it just wasn't in the cards. Every week during practice we two would pretend to be the stars of next Saturday's opponent's team. This allowed the first team to practice with less risk of being injured. Some days we would join the offense, on others we'd huddle with the defense. Of course, we got the living hell knocked out of us, with pummelings which produced an untold number of aches, sprains, and bruises. I also ended up with a broken nose, a fractured cluster of small bones in my right hand and some more in my left foot. It may have been character building but sometime later I had my doubts about it being confidence building. Losing 2 yards a carry, two hours a day, 5 days a week for three months in the fall did not build up a lot of confidence in oneself.

The team had an old-style tackling dummy at the practice field which lay adjacent to the stadium. It hung on a cable, which in turn was attached to a heavy weight, and the harder a player hit the dummy, the higher the weight would rise, and if it were really hit hard, the iron weight would rise up and strike another piece of metal at the top, producing a distinctive clanging sound. One day Fred Davis hit the dummy so hard the weight flew to the top and made one hellava clang: a sound which was never repeated. Not only that, but Fred then took the dummy with him, stripping it clean off the cable!

At seventeen, Fred was a giant of a man, 6'4", 240 pounds, and stood on legs as huge as oaks. Fred was one of the few football players I can remember who could easily compete with today's behemoths.

Oftentimes during practice a play would be called for me to carry the ball over Fred's left tackle position. Instead of tackling me he would just grab me around the middle and hoist me off of my feet where I would dangle upside down, grinning stupidly but glad with all my heart that Fred was on my side.

I also remember being told of the time Fred and a football player from St. Xavier High went to the carnival when it came to town. Wandering from booth to booth they came across a boxing ring where one of those "I'll take on all comers" was shouting his spiel to the crowd. The player from St. Xavier decided to have a go, so he jumped into the ring, and with Fred serving as the referee, raised his fists and headed towards the carnival boxer. The poor kid never knew what hit him. He was coldcocked with one punch. The carny began dancing and shadowboxing his way around the ring repeating his offer to a gathering crowd. "I'll take on anyone," he crowed. Fred tapped the man on the shoulder and said, "How about me, loudmouth?" The boxer stopped dead in his tracks, took one look at Fred who was wearing his football sweater with a big white M on his chest, three strips and a star on his arm, saw he was serious and hightailed it from the ring yelling, "Ain't no way, ain't no way!" The crowd howled its approval and rewarded Fred with a thunderous ovation.

Jack and I were both rewarded for our hard work and dedication. We did get to play for the last five minutes or so in those games that were already won, and at the end of the season a red sweater emblazoned with a big white "M" was awarded us both. We earned those letter sweaters; we gave it our all until the last snap of the last game in our senior year. The fact that Jack and I went through a similar baptism under fire (getting the hell kicked out of us for four or five days a week), cemented our already fast-held friendship.

And, Fred, after packing on more pounds of rock-solid muscle, went on to play tackle for the University of Alabama where he became the captain of the team. From there he went to the pros and played for the Chicago Bears. On one occasion Coach George Hallas remarked that Fred Davis was the best tackle in pro-football. In 1951 I watched a game on TV between the Chicago Bears and the Cleveland Browns. Fred was playing left tackle and he was the only player I noticed who still played both defense and offense. He was the last of a very special class of players.

I've certainly met my share of characters, and some were real standouts—not because they went on to fame, fortune, or infamy—no, it was just because of who they were. One in particular I met during the summer between my junior and senior year. I was playing tennis almost every day and I'd walk or ride my bike to the nearby park to join a group of regulars. He was named Spence Matthews, and he was truly weird. The guy stood a rangy six-foot, was built for tennis, and was pushing thirty. He was also a pretty fair player, but nobody really knew how good he was because none of us actually ever saw him play a game. He would latch on to someone and just hit balls, hour after hour. Most of us suspected Spence sought to portray himself as being better than he really was, and all the while he was hitting those balls he would hum the same damn two notes over and over, *ad infinitum*. This could be rather distracting if you were hitting balls with him.

Those were the days Johnny Weissmuller played Tarzan in the movies, and those movies were a humongous part of our lives. There was no television, just radio. Anyway, Weissmuller wore his hair long and Spence must have thought this was cool because he, too, wore his in similar fashion. Now a man sporting long hair today goes unnoticed, but in 1938 it was unbelievably far out. The only acceptable haircut was short, or a crewcut, and that was it, period.

At about this time I met Elmo Compton. Elmo hailed from a part of Louisville called Portland, an Irish enclave and waterfront community on the Ohio River. Elmo played football, first at St. Xavier, then at Louisville Male. He was what we call today a running back, but like all other players of the day he played defensive back, too. The guy was fairly large for a halfback, and I'd been told how on one occasion Elmo had tried to run through the wooden fence which bordered one side of the Male High football field.

The day I met him for the first time I was part of a group when out of the blue Elmo yelled, "Watch this." He then ran real fast, executed a complete somersault and landed squarely on his feet. And his hands had remained locked to his sides throughout the maneuver. We all looked down at the concrete sidewalk and to a man were all duly impressed.

On another occasion we went to Shawnee Park to play touch football. At the park we threw the ball around for a while to loosen up, then chose up sides. Elmo, four others, and I were teamed together. For the first few plays Elmo lined up against the opposing center and the two of them started going head-to-head in a rough sort of way. Words were passed back and forth. Things were becoming tense.

Finally, someone on our team asked Elmo, "Do you know who that guy is?"

"No, so tell me."

"That's Ted Axton. He's All Falls City (meaning all Louisville, New Albany and Jeffersonville, Indiana) Center for Manual High. He has a full ride scholarship to Purdue."

Elmo went back to the line a changed man. He didn't quite go so far as to call him Mister Axton, but he came close.

The Louisville area had several abandoned quarries, all of which had filled with water long ago. Some had been turned into commercial swimming areas, and Tucker's Lake was a particular favorite because of its exceptionally clear water. Several years earlier a professionally built 10 meter diving tower had been erected with both a low and a high board.

One day a group of us was having a rip-roaring good time when a fellow unknown to any of us started diving off the high board on that ten-meter tower. This showboat would walk purposefully to the edge, pause, then go through a series of gyrations prior to executing his dive. It was obvious he was stalling, waiting until he was sure everyone was watching. After several such performances, Elmo followed him up onto the tower. All eyes were on Elmo, none knowing what he was up to but sure it would be something worth watching. We didn't have to wait long. As the ham was posing prior to his dive, Elmo ran from the back of the tower as fast as he could, sailed right past the startled fellow, sprang off the lip of the board and thrilled us with a perfect swan dive. The showboat lost his balance and entered the water with a high-pitched, "nnnoooooo!" his arms and legs flying in all directions. His landing was not a pretty sight. Elmo's dive elicited a rousing round of cheers, all of us happy to see the unknown showoff put in his place.

Those years flew by. It was time to graduate.

That autumn I enrolled in the University of Louisville, and since I had no idea what I wanted to do with my life I randomly chose English as my major. Because of the times, I needed a job, any job, so I worked swing shifts—from 3 to 11—as a messenger boy in the freight office of the L & N Railroad, and also carried a full academic schedule during the day. By the time I staggered home it was often past midnight, yet I had to be up by 7:00 A.M. to start my day all over. My grades soon suffered, so much so that my faculty advisor suggested my classroom schedule was too much to handle along with a full-time job. I heeded his advice and dropped a couple of courses to lighten the load, but deep down I knew the real problem was a combination of a lack of direction and poor study habits.

My job with the railroad called for me to take waybills and other sundry papers from one office to another. Some were within walking distance; others required me to ride the streetcar. I'd make these runs then come back to the main office where I had nothing to do until the next run. With the brilliance of hindsight I know now I should have used this time to study, but I didn't. My eye was set on a promotion to becoming a billing clerk, a position which required an applicant to type forty words a minute, error free. So I decided to use the time between runs to learn how to type. There was an abandoned ancient Underwood in one corner which I commandeered and began practicing every day for at least a couple of hours, oftentimes more. Day after day I'd copy the morning newspaper, and then the evening edition. After a while I became quite proficient.

And when I wasn't typing I would daydream. A lot. About the future. I would muse about whom I would eventually marry. What would she be like? Would she be pretty? Heck, that was always a non-starter. Of course she'd be pretty! But what would I do in life? You can be sure I never dreamed I would one day become a fighter pilot. World War II would change the course of my life, but I'm getting a little ahead of myself.

Early one evening one of the other messenger boys came over and plopped himself down beside me. He waited until I'd finished the paragraph I was typing then said, "Hey, guy, you know, you're screwing up the rest of us by coming back to the office so fast from your runs. We've had it set amongst ourselves that we take our own sweet time and do a little fooling around a little between runs. You know what I mean?"

He wasn't particularly impressive physically, and I needed the time between my runs to learn how to type, so I just looked him square in the eye and said, "You do it your way, pal; I'll do it mine." That was the last I heard from him on that, or any other subject.

The office clerks couldn't fathom why I wanted to stay in college. To a man they'd wheedle, "You have such a good future here, Scrappy, why would you want to waste it by going to school?"

Maybe I didn't know what I wanted out of life, but I knew damn well it was to be more than a railroad clerk.

During the summer of 1941 I was still working but managed to spend a part of my days and weekends at the Lakeside Swimming Club. This commercial establishment had been built around an abandoned quarry situated on the east end of Louisville, and was a favorite of mine. One Sunday, I spotted two girls walking toward the pool, and as they got closer I could see that, while both were very attractive, one in particular caught my eye. She was Doris Holder. I immediately fell in love, an unrequited love I should hasten to add, but it was a love from afar.

Early in the fall semester of my sophomore year at college I discovered that Doris Holder was also enrolled. She had spent her freshman year at Centre College in Danville, Kentucky, but had transferred to the

Dorie Holder at 18. Louisville, KY.

University of Louisville to be closer to home. I was finally able to introduce myself at the first mixer of the year. It was a life-altering event.

I was standing on the sidelines shooting the breeze with my friend, Bright Harris, when I spotted her entering the gym. My heart flew into my mouth. She was a thousand times prettier than I remembered. I mentioned to Bright as casually as I could that I'd sure like to meet her. He immediately noted the besotted look of one head over heels in love or in lust, so he pushed me to cut-in while she danced with another guy. I took a deep breath and boldly sallied forth. Scrappy was about to meet his future bride.

Doris Holder could best be described by the inscription under her picture in the Atherton High School senior yearbook.

Doris J. Holder

No bigger than a minute and quick as a flash—that's Doris.
She's full of mischief and has a fatal attraction for trouble.
If you want to liven up an occasion just call for "Dorie."

Soon after that encounter I mustered up the courage to telephone Dorie and ask for a date. This was quickly followed by another then another, until we had had several, then our times together became more and more frequent. Years later she told me that some of her friends had predicted nothing but trouble for her if she hooked up with me.

I was a painfully shy young man, totally inexperienced in dealings with members of the fairer sex. And I had two strikes against me. First, I attended an all-boys high school, and second, my father didn't own a car, a must for dating then, just as it is now. Oh, sure, I met some girls in high school, but real dates were very few and very far between. And for those I did manage, I had to scrounge rides with friends such as Bright, or another pal named Billy Francis. I lived in the West End of town and most of the dates I had were with girls in the East End, and since most of my friends also lived east, I would ride the bus back home rather than ask them to drive me so late at night. Those times were different. With crime the way it is today, I wouldn't think of riding a bus late at night; back then, I didn't give it a thought. I would simply catch a nap during the half-hour ride, never once feeling the need to be wary of any of my fellow passengers. I was just glad that I had a home and a bed to ride back to.

I was a child of the Great Depression—an enlightening and sobering experience—and unless one lived it, there's no way to either comprehend it or adequately explain its impact on an individual. There were thousands—no, make that tens of thousands—of homeless people desperately wandering from city to city in search of work, shelter or simply their next meal. Some hopped on freight trains and rode the rods—sleeping wherever they could find a safe spot, which oftentimes meant somewhere near the railroad yards. The majority of these hapless souls were men, but their ranks included a smattering of women and, sadly, even some children. Everyone referred to them as hobos, a name I thought was special to this period of history. Years later Noah Webster taught me otherwise.

The times were hard and although my father always held a job he never seemed able to get out of debt. If he earned ten dollars a day, he'd spend eleven. Let me give you two examples of how desperately close to the edge we really were.

The one girl that I had been somewhat dating on and off in my senior year in high school, Gwen Owens, was going away to Ward Belmont, a women's college in Nashville. Before leaving she gave me a popular recording of the day, "I Don't Want to Set the World on Fire." I was deeply moved by such a sweet gesture, but didn't have the heart to tell her I didn't own a record player.

As for the second example, a couple of months later, at Christmastime, my father told me about a certain coat that mother wanted. It was expensive—about one hundred dollars—and he suggested we buy it together as a present from the two of us.

"You give me the ten bucks for the down payment, Scrappy, and I'll take care of the rest."

I did, and come Christmas morning when we opened our presents, mother burst into tears and said to me between sobs, "You didn't get me anything for Christmas." I tried to explain that I had given the down payment on the coat, my share of the present, but it was impossible. She ran out of the room and my father never said a word in my defense. That little episode did nothing to elevate my father in my eyes. And neither did the fact that he made me pay rent while I was working to pay my own way through college.

In those days the university had some professors who were really a sorry lot, my U.S. history teacher being one. Not only was he a boring drone, but his students refused to sit in the first row because of his disgusting habit of spitting as he talked.

His final exam was held on the afternoon of the last day of the first semester, and Bright Harris, Tommy Ryan and I were wolfing down lunch at the Cardinal Inn across from the university. Bright was enrolled in the engineering school so he wasn't in our history class. Tommy and I told him about this professor and as the meal wound down, we somewhat in jest dared him to come and take the test with us. We explained that this guy was so dense he wouldn't even realize Bright hadn't been in the class all year.

Bright's sense of humor overcame his good judgment and he followed us into the exam room. Sure enough, that egghead professor didn't spot that Bright wasn't a member of his class or that there was even an extra person in the room. This was especially amusing since there were fewer than twenty pupils enrolled.

The last question on the test called for the student to write an essay describing the framing of our constitution. Bright wrote a silly piece, opening with the words, "George Washington cut down his father's cherry tree," and his treatise proceeded to devolve into utter rubbish from there.

When he finished he dropped his test book on the professor's desk and before reaching the door heard a stern voice call out, "Young man, wait a minute, come back here."

Tommy and I thought for sure Bright had been discovered, but when he returned to the professor's desk he was told, "You forgot to sign your paper."

Back at the Cardinal Inn I asked Bright what name he had used to sign the test.

"George Washington," he replied, to our whoops of laughter.

That wasn't the end of it, though. The professor figured out that an extra person had taken his test and came to the oddest possible conclusion that someone was trying to steal his exam. Bright was quickly uncovered as the culprit. He was in a fair amount of trouble for a few days until a well-placed friend interceded and convinced the professor it was only a joke. The matter was quietly dropped, but for a while it looked that Bright was going to be expelled from the university.

And on that sobering thought I began my second semester.

I remember New Year's Day, 1941, as being uncommonly cold and raw; the weather a reflection of the country's angst. The news from Europe was not good. The Nazi swastika now flew over most of the continent, the only exception of note being England. New Year's Eve celebrations had been as muted as any in memory; folks were just not in a partying mood. More and more men my age were being drafted, and many others were volunteering for the Navy, Marines or the Army Air Corps, with the hope of becoming officers and pilots rather than facing life as a conscript.

I found myself joining groups in the student union between classes where we would listen to many of Adolf Hitler's rants. His German audiences were obviously enraptured with the prospect of more conquests, and they thundered their approval as he told them it was their birthright to rule the world. I understood all too well that this madman would soon have a decided effect upon all our lives, and I deeply resented the intrusion I knew was soon to come.

The year 1941 was lived on tenterhooks. Like everyone of a certain age on December 7, 1941, I will go to my grave remembering where I was and what I was doing the moment I heard of the Japanese attack on Pearl Harbor. I was in car with two friends, heading to Seneca Park for a game of touch football when the radio program was interrupted to bring an urgent news bulletin. Needless to say, there was no football game that Sunday.

Four days later Tommy Ryan and I decided to take the Army Air Corps examination. We would become aviation cadets.

Tommy aced it, I flunked it. True, he had been taking flying lessons with the Civil Air Patrol for over six months and had logged about 50 hours plus ground school, but this didn't help me one bit. I began to scheme. I came to the conclusion that I had to sit the test again because my life depended on it, to say nothing of the future well-being of the Republic.

I learned the exam was to be given two weeks later at the University of Kentucky in Lexington, so I pulled out all the stops to ensure my success. A certain girl—a girl who even today must still remain anonymous—purloined a copy of the exam, complete with the correct answers prominently marked. I saw my challenge was simply not to just pass, but to make sure I didn't score too high. I ended up with a respectable 120 out of a possible 150, and I owe everything from that moment forward in my life to that young lady, because without her intervention I would never have had such a rewarding career as a fighter pilot in the U.S. Air Force. And the Air Force made out okay, too.

Within an hour of passing the exam I was sworn into the army as a private and told to go home and await further instructions. The next day I dropped out of school, knowing I would be called up at any moment. A couple of months passed and I still hadn't heard a peep from the army, so I got a job stacking whiskey cases at the Seagram's distillery plant in order to supplement the $22.00 check Uncle Sam was sending me every thirty days.

Dorie and I grew closer, and one evening in June 1942, when I knew her mother and father wouldn't be home, I swaggered up her front steps bearing an engagement ring and a celebratory bottle of Taylor's champagne. We both oohed and aahed at the ring, guzzled all the bubbly, then left, but not before arranging the empty ring box and upended bottle just so on the dining room table. When the Holders came home they thought we had eloped, and were very visibly relieved to learn we had only become engaged. Ruth Holder had done everything possible in her power to see that this day would never come to pass. She was forever beseeching her daughter to date other boys, imploring her not to throw away her promising young life by marrying the likes of me. And while there was little love lost between Ruth and I, Dorie's father, Dewey, was one of the nicest men I have ever known. That gentleman gave us his blessing: an approval which meant the world to Dorie and me.

4

The Army Air Corps

I was ordered to report to the train station at Lexington, Kentucky, on August 7, 1942. From there it was off to aviation cadet training in San Antonio, Texas. Dorie and her mother drove me to the station, barely a dozen words passing between the three of us; each of us was lost in thought. The train's route would take it back through Louisville, so on a last-minute whim, Dorie decided to ride with me. She held onto my arm as if she'd never let go. We had a few minutes to say our goodbyes in the Louisville station where we clung to each other with a desperation heretofore unfelt. In that moment I knew I loved this woman more than life itself.

I re-boarded the train along with 49 others. Our destination was the Aviation Cadet Center at Kelly Field, near San Antonio, Texas. Because of the overwhelming influx of volunteers and inductees, I spent my first week sweltering in a brown canvas squad tent before being moved into a two-story, open-bay, white clapboard building. The days were filled with batteries of tests meant to determine whether we would be trained as pilots, navigators or bombardiers. It was a nervous time for me, but finally my prayers were answered. I was slotted for pilot training. To this day I remember one poor fellow who was tapped for navigator training because he had scored so high on the entrance exam. He was devastated, because, like the rest of us, he only wanted to be a pilot. I remember how he sat on the barracks' steps bawling his eyes out as he waited for the bus to take him away. And I really thanked God that I hadn't gotten full of myself and aced that test the second time around!

I was issued a complete set of uniforms right down to my skivvies, then told to pack up my civilian gear and send the box home. Next, it was off for a haircut at a shop run by civilian contractors. To these men speed was everything, and I'd been warned that when asked if I wanted tonic, the correct answer would be an immediate "yes sir," even though it bumped the cost by a nickel. Say no, I had been told, then I could expect to get scalped.

Later that afternoon I got a really good scare during yet another physical exam. The doctor had lined ten of us up, then had us lean forward and place our hands flat on the floor without bending our knees. No problem for me, except I happened to be eighth in line, and after what seemed like a year playing contortionist, he ordered me to rise. My back suddenly developed a nasty spasm and I winced involuntarily as I tried to straighten out. Old eagle eye decided I had a back problem and ordered me to the hospital for a slew of X-rays. Turned out that that my back was fine, but I almost washed out before I got started.

After two weeks my class was finally granted a one-day open post. This meant freedom, at least for a few hours, and we were all champing at the bit. One of the guys in my little group of friends had arranged for his girlfriend to come to San Antonio to celebrate his few hours of freedom in style. Two days before the big event she called to say that she'd talked five of her friends into coming with her, so arrangements were quickly made for five of us to accompany them to dinner. Everyone had been made aware of the fact that I was engaged, including the girl I was paired with. She turned out to be a charming young lady, real easy to look at, and we had a wonderful time.

Scrappy as an aviation cadet in San Antonio, 1942 (courtesy of USAF).

Our orders were to be back on base by seven. The other guys flagged down a cab and made it, but I found myself short of cash so I had to catch the bus. I was five minutes late. The Officer of the Day, a skinny, pimply faced second lieutenant, stood at the main gate and read me the riot act in a falsetto voice. After standing at attention and listening to his stupid tirade for a good fifteen minutes, he informed me I would receive five hour-long tours on the parade ground in full uniform, one for each minute, said tours to be walked off the following Saturday. Did I understand? Yes, sir, I understood!

I wrote to Dorie and told her about the dinner, about how I was late getting back to the base, and my resultant punishment. I thought she would feel sorry for me, but, boy, was I ever wrong! Dorie wasted no time writing back, her words exploding off the pages in a fit of jealousy, revealing a side of my fiancée I had never before seen. I wanted to brush it off as insecurity and possessiveness, but deep down it stuck in my craw, and as I walked off my tours I began to feel sorry for myself, the anger welling with every step, so much so that the incident became a defining moment in my life. Then and there, sweating like a dog on that parade ground, I decided I would never, ever, tell Dorie—or anyone else for that matter—about my comings and goings when away from home.

This compartmentalizing of my life would become the cause of untold grief in the years that followed. Grief for those I loved; grief for me as well. I now confess from the vantage point of an old man, that if I could turn back the hands of time and live those parts of my life over, I would do so in a flash. Because the decision I made that Saturday in Texas as a callow youth was the root cause of much unnecessary anguish.

$$ \text{✈ ✈ ✈} $$

A hurricane slammed into the Texas coast in late August 1942, necessitating the evacuation of all airplanes from a score of seaside bases and flown to the inland safety of Kelly Field. Well, that was the idea, but the storm was still packing a wallop when it arrived at Kelly, causing quite a bit of damage to a number of planes. It also blew away Tent City, scattering the belongings of four hundred cadets all over the base. The place looked like a war zone for the several days it took to clean up. I was just glad my stuff was safe and sound inside the wooden barracks which only suffered light damage to its roof.

On a Sunday afternoon two weeks later, a cadre of about fifty of us were ordered to assemble on one of the many parade grounds. We had no idea why. Soon, an army staff car arrived and a distinguished-looking gray-headed colonel got out. He was a man of few words.

No preamble, no greeting, just, "How many of you fellows would like to be flying tomorrow?"

Our response was a thunderous cheer.

He allowed a fleeting smile of approval at our good attitudes. "There's a class ahead of you that's skipped primary and is being sent directly to basic training. We don't know if this experiment will pan out or not, but we need you men to backfill them at once. Report back here tomorrow at 0800 with all your belongings. There'll be buses to take you to Ballinger, Texas. Dismissed."

The next cheer was louder and longer than the first. We had no idea how we were selected, nor did we care. We were thrilled to be skipping preflight, a grueling ten weeks of nonstop academics and military training.

Boy, oh boy, I sure knew how lucky I was! Academics was the one thing that could do me in quicker than any ground loop could.

✈ ✈ ✈

Ballinger, Texas, was right out of a seedy western movie set. One hotel, two filling stations, a drug store, a movie theatre and a smattering of paint-stripped homes. This was no place for a red-blooded American to spend his Saturday nights, so I'd hitchhike to San Angelo, the closest town of any consequence. In those days it was easy for a young fellow in uniform to hitchhike, but later it became too dangerous to pick up anyone, uniform or not. Folks simply stopped doing it.

On one particular Saturday I decided to test my luck at finding a girl, so I boldly struck up a conversation with a young lady I spotted in the town square. She told me her name was Betty. I bought us each a coke, then we walked and talked up one street and down another until we were back where we started. I told her who I was and where I was staying, but she seemed preoccupied. I would catch her frowning in the fading light when she thought I wasn't looking. Something was bothering my newfound Betty. About nine we parted company and I headed to my hotel. Half an hour later, lying on my bed and listening to the radio, I heard a muted tapping on the door. I opened it to see Betty.

I was tongue tied, but had enough sense to motion her in and close the door after sticking my head out to check the hallway in both directions. I was truly an innocent at this time of my short life—the most I had ever dared by way of sex was to maybe cop a quick feel of a breast. Betty ended up in my bed where we spent the night, but come morning and first light, I was still a virgin. She confessed to being engaged to a young enlisted guy, but confided they had had a spat and she had come into town by herself. By eight o'clock that Sunday morning, a guilt-wracked Betty got dressed, phoned her beau, made up, and left.

That was my first night alone with a woman. Definitely not the sizzling stuff of dime-store romance novels.

✈ ✈ ✈

The washout rate at Ballinger was extremely high. Any cadet could get pink-slipped for any reason—or no reason—and many did. Indeed, that was almost my fate one particularly hot afternoon.

Flying low in my PT-19, the engine sputtered once, twice, then quit, forcing me to make an emergency landing in a fenced cow pasture. On the way down I remembered a cadet two classes ahead of me saying, "If you ever think you might hit a fence, before you do, just make sure to ground loop the damn plane."

As I set up my approach all I could think about was that fence at the end of the field rushing toward me. I waited for just the right moment then pushed the right rudder full forward. Luckily, the PT-19 slid to a stop, my left wingtip coming to rest within a foot of the fence.

One of the instructors arrived in a pickup truck a few minutes later, jumped out, looked at me, looked at the plane, looked at the fence then back to me. "Son, you're one lucky son of a bitch, and that's a fact. I'll just bet you anything you forgot to switch over your gas tanks."

Sherlock Holmes was bang-on. I lowered my head and kicked a couple of times at a clump of Texas dirt, figuring silence as my best response. There was no doubt in my mind that had I hit that fence he'd be now telling me I'd washed out for sure.

Even with this incident hanging over my head, I still managed to make it through primary because of the good graces of my first instructor, Mr. Vohringer. He was also the senior check pilot and had quite a bit of clout with the civilians who ran the school. Vohringer had instructed five of us for our first 20 hours then turned us over to a guy named Mr. Vandewater. When the time came for me to take a check ride, Vohringer told the man slotted to test me that he didn't want to see those 20 hours he'd spent with me go down the drain. The instructor only nodded then followed me out onto the tarmac.

I passed the ride with flying colors.

The day came for the first group in our senior class to fly an initial cross-country mission en masse. Their outbound leg was uneventful, but during the return to base the wind changed direction by 180-degrees, a fact all failed to recognize. Six of us went out to watch the fun and fireworks as they entered the pattern. They were all trying to land in the direction of their earlier takeoff. To a man they'd fly down final, level off and flare to land, only to find themselves floating a couple of feet off the ground with no hope of getting their wheels onto the runway. All were forced to firewall their throttles and make go-arounds. After several failed attempts, one of their number figured out the problem, came around and landed into the wind. Like a flock of ducklings chasing after their mother, the others quickly followed suit. In the meantime, our instructors had poured out of their offices, each waving and pulling on his hair, just waiting for the accident they knew was inevitable. Luck was with those cadets that day. None crashed.

My best friend at Ballinger was a kid from Brooklyn named Eddie Wilson. Eddie had curly blond hair, a light complexion, and stood about five-eight.

He was a flying New Yorker with a cocky attitude. I met Eddie during an evening softball game. I was playing left field; Eddie was covering center field. On the last out of the game a fly ball came whistling down the left field line, forcing me to run my butt off to make it, which I did, catching the ball with my bare right hand. This impressed Eddie no end, and as I was walking off the field I found him next to me. We discussed the game, and asked each other where we were from. He began ribbing me about my Louisville accent, a somewhat bizarre fact considering he spoke in a near unintelligible Brooklynese. But we became close friends, and remained so until our paths parted several years later. I sure learned a lot about life from Eddie.

Dorie came to visit just after Thanksgiving, with her mother in tow. We managed to spend two weekends together—Saturday noon until Sunday evening—and three hours on the one Wednesday night. To her credit, Mrs. Holder gave Dorie and me our space and a fair amount of time alone, so the visit was everything I could have hoped for. We had decided not to get married until I had completed flight training and was commissioned a second lieutenant, a decision heartily endorsed by you-know-who. We were deeply in love and the parting was difficult.

When I think back to Ballinger, Bing Crosby's "White Christmas" always comes to mind. It was played over and over ad nauseam on the canteen jukebox. Christmas 1942 was the first of many that I would be forced to spend away from home and I felt very alone that holiday season. I missed Dorie, and it ached.

After primary, Eddie and I were transferred to another civilian contract school for basic, this one in the nearby town of Brady, Texas.

When we arrived, the incoming commandant of cadets, Captain Jackson, had not yet reported for duty so the physical training officer was serving in that capacity. He informed us that the syllabus called for all cadets to complete fifteen hours of drill during this phase of training. He went on to suggest that since we had three days before school actually started we could get it out of the way early. We agreed this was a good idea, so, with some padding and fudging on his part, we did it.

On our fourth day, Captain Jackson arrived. He was the most gung-ho trooper in the army, and the first thing he told us was we could expect to repeat our fifteen hours of mandatory drill under his supervision! Jackson was a bullet-headed officer who spoke a language only meant to be written and read in army manuals. In regular conversation he would say such things as: "This is your suit, flying type, issue two. This is your cap, service, issue one, and your belt, web, all-purpose, issue one. Treat these items well, they're the property of the U.S. government." Soon we were all mimicking our fearless leader.

I remember one particular foggy morning when we found ourselves grounded. Jackson ordered an hour of close order drill to fill in our time. He put a cadet named Murray in charge of our formation. Murray began to run us through a short order drill. He wheeled us around smartly, then marched us close to the reviewing stand where Jackson stood alone at attention, his beady eyes following our every move. Then Murray marched us to the rear, and off into the mist. Once we were well out of Jackson's sight—and hidden inside the pea soup—we plopped ourselves on the ground while Murray continued to belt out a series of commands; "column left, column right, to the rear march," and on and on. After about twenty minutes of this we reformed and marched our way back to the ramp where Jackson was still standing at attention. He was never any the wiser.

Brady was no San Angelo, but it was definitely larger and a helluva lot better than Ballinger, so the few times I had off I always headed into town. One Saturday night, while eating in the only decent restaurant, who walks in but Betty, the girl I'd spent an innocent night with some time back. Seems she'd long ago broken up with that fiancé, and had now come to Brady to try and win back the heart of another. No grass was growing under Betty's rounded heels! After a couple of drinks she became all cuddly and amorous, and by ten o'clock was hinting broadly that she was available to spend another night with me.

This sudden bit of good fortune was in dire danger of collapsing before I could manage the main event. When I went to the front desk of the town's lone hotel, I was told by the hundred-year-old doddering night manager that there were no rooms to be had. I remembered that Eddie had reserved a room and was able to wheedle a key from the old geezer. Try pulling that stunt today!

Betty was as eager as I to succumb to the sins of the flesh, so we rutted, not once, but twice. After my initiation and first taste of forbidden fruit, I dozed off, only to awaken some time later with a start. What had I heard? It was Eddie, fumbling at the door. What the hell was I going to do? Betty was out cold, snoring softly, oblivious to the imminent peril, so, like a scalded cat I bounded out from between the sheets and scampered to some imaginary safety under the bed. Eddie entered, threw his key down on the dresser, flicked on the light, jumped almost high enough to hit his head on the ceiling, and let out a startled cry.

"What in the hell…!"

In spite of myself I began to laugh, then crawled out of my hiding place. In a whispered voice I told Eddie what had happened. Betty continued her blissful snoring.

"Are you freaking stupid?" he hissed, all of a sudden transmogrified into a real live adult. "You're supposed to be getting married in a few months, for Christ's sake. What the hell are you thinking?" He looked down at the sonorous sleeping beauty. "Man, we've got to get you to the base infirmary for a prophylactic. There's no time to waste."

Oh, God. I flew into my clothes, caught a bus to the field, reported to the infirmary, was issued a pro kit, did what I needed to do, then hit the sack, praying my heart out that certain parts wouldn't start to fall off. Eddie was right. What the hell was I thinking?

It didn't dawn on me until much later that good old Eddie had stayed behind in that room with Betty.

I started on the wrong foot with the flight instructors at Brady, especially my first. But a higher being must have intervened because instead of washing me out I was assigned to another instructor, a man named Nick Lutz. Nick had been a football and basketball star at the University of Kentucky and I can honestly say I had actually heard of the guy. Seems he had entered the aviation cadet program a couple years earlier when it was harder to get in, and even harder to get through. Folks were being washed out in droves, and for the flimsiest of reasons.

It had happened to Nick, but he was no quitter. Instead, he went back home to Ashland, Kentucky, changed his name and re-entered cadet training. This time he made it all the way to graduation. As was customary then, and still is today, the army sent his picture and a blurb about his graduation to his hometown newspaper. Someone on the paper wrote back to Army Air Corps Command: "Great news, but you have his name wrong. This officer is one of our local heroes, Nick Lutz."

The Air Corps was not amused and washed him out again.

Of course Nick had no difficulty getting a flying job, and that's how he ended up instructing in this civilian school. However, the army now desperately needed pilots, and in Nick's case was willing to let bygones be bygones. They wanted him to join the Ferry Command with the rank of second lieutenant, and fly bigger and better airplanes. The only obstacle in his way was the school. The owners wouldn't let him break his contract, and the army didn't push it. Which meant that by this time Nick Lutz was one pissed-off pilot. If the traffic pattern was being flown to the right, he'd fly it to the left. He would purposely break any of the rules in an attempt to get fired and out of his contract. And when it came to washing out cadets, Nick was known as the Grim Reaper. Nobody wanted to fly with him. Oftentimes he would just look at a cadet and think, "No frigging way this clown is going to make it through, especially after what they did to me." And sure enough, the clown wouldn't make it.

I figured that was why Nick was assigned as my instructor. The Grim Reaper was being asked by the staff to perform his diabolical magic and make me disappear. But this time they were fooled. Eddie and I were the only ones to finish with him: Eddie, because he was a character and Nick liked him; me, because I was from Kentucky.

✈ ✈ ✈

"Red" Lancaster was another one of my classmates. He hailed from Mississippi which meant he had a marbles-in-the-mouth way of talking which was all but unintelligible except to a handful of us fellow southerners.

Red accumulated punishment tours at a pace never before seen by the staff at Brady. The man was a walking disaster: messy, unkempt, unable to march, everything a cadet shouldn't be. Red Lancaster was definitely no favorite of Captain Jackson.

One Saturday Red was scheduled for a solo flight at noon. He knew that the cadets over at Ballinger would be assembled at the base main gate about that time, waiting for buses to take them to town on open post. He decided it would be a great idea to fly up there and buzz the hell out of them in his big basic trainer. He became so engrossed in his buzz job that it wasn't until his third swooping pass that he realized he had an AT-6 tucked in real tight on his right wing. It was the school's commanding officer, Major Tipton, returning from a cross-country flight just in time to catch this idiot from Brady buzzing his airfield.

The brass at Brady was lined up shoulder to shoulder on the flight line to greet Red on his return. Why he wasn't washed out on the spot I'll never know, but he set another school record when the commander awarded him an ungodly number of additional tours to be marched off before he could graduate.

Toward the end of basic we were hustled into a classroom and told we had to make a decision right then and there to either sign up for single-engine or twin-engine advanced. The choice had to be made now, we were told, and those not present would be assigned by the commander, based on the needs of the air corps. I quickly looked around the room. No Eddie. Shit! I signed up for single-engines because I wanted to fly fighters. I then added Eddie's name to the list. He acted pissed when I told him later, but I quickly shut him up when I threatened to go see Captain Jackson and have his name switched to flying twins.

Poor Red. He was held back at Brady to walk off his tours when the rest of us left for advanced training. I never found out if he made it or not, but I doubt that he did. Red could get tours so fast that he probably was still walking them off on VJ Day!

On our last morning at Brady, Eddie and I ran into Nick in the canteen. The guy was wearing a smile as big as Texas. It seems the school had finally relented, allowing him to break his contract and join the army. He was on his way to the Ferry Command, and a commission as a second lieutenant. We were glad for Nick, and we told him so. He wished us luck. "I expect each of you to become famous aces, so y'all don't disappoint me now, hear?"

We both saluted Nick, and chorused, "Yes, sir!"

Our next and last stop on the road to graduation was Moore Field, in Mission, Texas. Eddie and I rode the train together. Moore Field wasn't all that far from Brady, but the route took us through Houston where we had to change trains. With a couple of hours to kill, we made our way to a fancy hotel near the station and ordered lunch: two of the most expensive steaks on the menu. I was thoroughly mortified when Eddie asked for ketchup. Our waiter arched a disapproving eyebrow then scurried into the kitchen, no doubt to inform the chef that a certain cretin was at this very moment darkening the hallowed sanctum of the dining room.

In advanced, we finally got our hands on a real airplane, the AT-6 Texan. The whole atmosphere was definitely more relaxed now, and the washout rate was markedly lower. For the first time I felt confident—I was in my element; this is what flying was all about! My days were filled with air-to-air combat training, low-level work, gunnery practice (both air and ground), and tons of daytime cross-country missions. I couldn't have been happier.

Night flying was introduced later in the schedule.

My first night cross-country was nothing more than a puddle-jump: short and easy. The next was anything but. Here I had to fly to Laredo, Kingsville and Harlingen, then back to Mission. Flight time would be about ninety minutes, and on the day my turn came to make the trip, we'd already lost two cadets, both killed in fiery crashes. I found myself filled with nervous excitement, but anxious to prove to my instructors that I had the right stuff.

I took off for Laredo, then turned east to Kingsville without incident. I was once again my grandmother's million-dollar boy of many years ago. At Kingsville I headed south for Harlingen but within minutes flew smack into a fog bank. It was a big one. And this scared the hell out of me. One moment I was tooling along in the clear, the next I was flying blind. There wasn't supposed to be any fog. No one flying ahead of me had radioed anything about fog! I had never even flown in clouds before, not to mention fog, and certainly never anything like this. The only useful instruments the AT-6 had were the needle and ball, and airspeed indicators. It took all my effort not to slide into an uncontrollable panic attack. My breathing became ragged, and my heart began to pound its way out of my chest. God, I don't want to crash and burn like those other two guys.

Major Boedecker, our group commanding officer, had recently told us in a class on weather, "If you ever get yourselves into a dicey situation, your smartest decision will be to execute a 180-degree turn and get back into familiar airspace. Remember this little nugget, gentlemen, because it will save your life one day, guaranteed."

Although it wasn't easy in my state of mind, I managed to complete a 180-degree turn, and shortly thereafter I broke out of the fog and into the clear. Still rattled, but fast calming down, I flew straight and level, allowing myself time to think through on my options. I decided to fly west for several more minutes then turn back south again. By a stroke of pure luck, it proved to be the right decision. Just as I was beginning to have some serious doubts about my position, I remembered that an instructor was stationed on the ground at Harlingen in case of trouble aloft. I got on the radio and gave him a call then anxiously awaited his answer. He came on the air loud and clear, and told me to turn on my landing lights.

"I see you, Johnson. You're right over Harlingen. Make a 90-degree right turn and proceed directly to Moore Field. You copy?"

Later, I figured out what I had done wrong. I had overflown Kingsville then mistook Corpus Christi for it. Then when I turned south from Corpus, that put me over the Gulf of Mexico and bang into the fog bank. Luckily, I listened to the voice of Major Boedecker talking inside my head, made my 180-degree turn and flew west, which ended up putting me back to where I should have been when I started flying south the first time. I knew how lucky I really was. It was probably a hundred-to-one shot that I ended up over Harlingen. I could have run out of gas far out over the Gulf of Mexico, crashed, and never been found or heard from again. That was a real-world scenario which had played out more times than any of us cared to think about. Many student pilots were lost in training in such mishaps, both in Texas and along the Florida Atlantic coast. It was scary then and even scarier now just remembering it.

That same night, a cadet named Gangami became hopelessly lost, but had the good sense to look for a place to land before running out of gas. He began circling over a small town until the locals figured out he was a student in trouble and came to his rescue. They used automobile headlights and flashlights to assist him in landing in a large field at the edge of town.

The next morning our commanding officer went to fly the plane back. He was in awe when he saw what Gangami had managed to pull off in the dead of night. Gangami had somehow flown his plane under a sagging power line, then skipped over a fence and managed to completely avoid hitting an army of stumps or sliding into a mishmash of ditches before coming to a safe stop just shy of another fence line. The squadron commander had to have both fences taken down and a dozen stumps removed before he dared fly the plane out. He also didn't have the heart to wash Gangami out of the program so close to graduation.

✈ ✈ ✈

Moore Field was also home to a handful of fighters—planes stationed there for the instructors to fly and to remain proficient in tactics. We were often entertained after a long day of training by a man named Lieutenant Colonel Russell Spicer. Spicer was our director of flying, and he cut an impressive figure with his head full of black hair, a white silk scarf, and a fighter pilot's mustache. Spicer reveled in demonstrations of low altitude aerobatics. One evening he took up a newly arrived P-38, and after being airborne for about ten minutes he barreled toward the runway no more than fifty feet up, feathered one prop, then executed a perfect roll into the dead engine. We learned later this was his first-ever flight in a P-38.

To a man we were speechless, each silently wishing he would someday be able to fly like Colonel Spicer.

✈ ✈ ✈

As I mentioned earlier, Dorie and I had agreed to delay getting married until we were sure that I would graduate, become a lieutenant, and be able to support her. Well, that day arrived, and on February 20, 1943, we were married. The wedding was held in Mission, Texas, with both sets of parents attending. This was no easy feat, as members of the armed service had priority for all travel in the continental United States. Seats on trains and buses were scarce.

Classmates Jerry P. Jenkins and J. K. Jordan stood up with me. Why them, you might ask? The answer was simple. The army bunked folks alphabetically, and that's how I had become a close friend with them both. I was sandwiched between them. Of course, I wanted Eddie to be my best man, but when the big day came he was away on temporary duty attending gunnery school at Matagorda Island. On his return he gave us six beautiful crystal champagne flutes for a wedding present. After more than sixty years, and what seems like a thousand moves, I still have four of those flutes.

I graduated on March 20, 1943, becoming a pilot and a second lieutenant all on the same day. The ceremony was held in a hangar. One by one we marched across the stage to be awarded our commissions by Colonel Spicer, who then pinned on our silver wings. I was so proud I could have popped right out of my tunic! Me, Scrappy Johnson, the kid from Louisville was now an honest to goodness pilot! Dorie on the other hand, was thoroughly miffed. She had wanted to pin on my wings. However, she became somewhat mollified a little later when we had our picture taken with Colonel Spicer.

The next day we boarded a bus and rode seventy miles in the airless Texas heat to the border town of Laredo. All our worldly goods we carried in four small pieces of luggage.

5

Laredo

I remember Laredo from sixty-plus years ago as being a dusty border town on the Rio Grande with a population of twenty-five thousand, its citizens mostly of Mexican descent. The land was bone-dry, which meant the scant vegetation was a mix of cactus, mesquite trees, tumbleweed and any other plant foolish enough to try and find a home in the inhospitable sand. And the heat. It sucked the energy right out of any living, breathing thing—even at ten o'clock at night. No one ever mistook this place for paradise.

This was the home of Laredo Army Airfield, where housing was so scarce that the federal government had to step in and control rents to prevent the good citizens of Laredo from gouging its soldiers. Dorie and I moved into the town's only motel and lived there for several weeks until a small, two-room duplex apartment became available. Ours was not a picture postcard honeymoon in a picture postcard world.

Laredo was not chosen for its scenic beauty but rather because its cloudless skies allowed aircrews to fly almost every day of the year. This base was one of several flexible gunnery schools whose mission in 1943 was to train gunners for the country's heavy-bomber fleet of B-17s, B-24s, and B-29s.

My first assignment was flying student gunners in the back seat of an AT-6 (Advanced Trainer) in which the rear canopy had been removed. The gunner sat facing aft, and armed with a thirty-caliber machine gun he would practice shooting at towed banner targets. Some days I alternated flying assignment jobs and towed the targets for the gunners to fire at. These men started out in the AT-6, then advanced to the AT-11 then to the AT-18. The AT-11 was a small twin-engine Beech while the AT-18 was a larger Lockheed twin, capable of carrying five gunner-trainees.

The guys in my squadron made lots of self-deprecating remarks about being tow pilots. This was not the fighter pilot world we had each envisioned ourselves being a part of at graduation. Fact is, a lot of us were embarrassed by the assignment, but that's where the air corps wanted us, so that's where we stayed.

I remember one particularly boring day when the radio came alive with some joker in a mock Texas twang, breaking into song with, "I'm an old tow-hand from the Rio Grande." We all got a good laugh as he continued in a dreadful voice into the second line of the song.

It just so happened that our director of flying, Major Gordon Paulson, was also airborne at the time. Paulson was a no-nonsense, everything-by-the-book kind of officer who was also known by the name Iron Ass. He wasted no time getting on the horn.

"This is Major Paulson. The pilot singing, identify yourself!"

For several seconds there was absolute silence, then a taunting voice let loose with a laugh before replying, "Right, chief, can't wait to comply!" There were about 50 planes in the air at the time so he knew his anonymity was secure! But the rest of us sure admired him for his balls!

I alternated flying schedules every week, first flying from dawn till noon, then from noon till dusk. I usually flew about seven sorties a day, including Saturdays and Sundays if necessary, to meet the demands of the schedule. I flew over one thousand hours that first year and gained a ton of flying experience which went a long way in preparing me to fly the much hotter, faster, more complex fighters later in my career. And that one half-day in which we didn't fly we had mandatory physical training which was comprised of 15 minutes of calisthenics followed by an hour of basketball in the gym, or touch football outside. Playing basketball indoors where the temperature was about 110 degrees really gave me a good workout. I was in the best shape of my life.

There were lots of service pilots at the field, guys whose wings had an "S" stamped in the middle of a similar shield found on our wings. These men had been civilian pilots before the war, so, in the interest of getting them into cockpits as fast as possible, the government sent them to special bases where they were taught military etiquette, commissioned as second lieutenants and presented their wings. Many were older—much older—and it was weird for us new guys to see forty-year-old second lieutenants all over the place. Most of them could have cared less about being officers and gentlemen; they just wanted to fly.

After a few weeks of riding buses everywhere, Dorie and I came to the conclusion we needed a car. We quickly settled on a 1936 Pontiac coupe for

$325.00. We knew that if we balked, someone else would snap it up. It was black, had definitely seen better days, but it got the job done. At least most days.

One day I was driving to the base when it sputtered once and stopped cold. I could have learned how to fly to the moon quicker than I could have figured out how to fix a car. I had the hood up and was staring glumly at the engine when one of the guys in the squadron pulled alongside.

"What's the matter, Scrappy?"

"Hell if I know. It quit on me, Hank," I said to Lt. Murphy.

Murphy came over. "Let me take a look."

A minute later he went back to his car and returned with a rag which he had soaked in water from his canteen. He wrapped it around the fuel pump and commanded, "Go fire it up, Scrappy."

I jumped in, pushed the starter pedal and after a few seconds it caught, and my car began to purr like the cat in front of the cream. I was in awe. "What was the matter?" I called out.

Murphy lowered the hood and grinned. "Your fuel pump got too hot. No big deal. I'll help you fix it properly when we get to the base."

✈ ✈ ✈

It was during these early days at Laredo that I came to learn just how insecure Dorie could be.

One afternoon I sprained my ankle playing basketball. I immediately went to the base hospital hoping to get it taped up, but the doctor didn't like what he saw so he ordered a battery of X-rays. He found a broken bone, which prompted him to order me admitted as a patient. Dorie came by the squadron to pick me up at the end of the duty day only to be told I was in the hospital. Instead of coming inside to see me, she stood outside my window and began wheedling me to come home with her. At first I thought she was kidding around, having fun, so I laughed at her cutesy June Allyson antics. But Dorie then did something that completely startled me. She lay her head against the windowpane and began to weep in deep wracking sobs. Her whole body heaved. This was serious. I hobbled over to the window and tried to explain that they wouldn't let me out, but she couldn't, or wouldn't, understand. After a few minutes she straightened up, passed the back of her hand over her eyes, gave me a feeble half-wave, and walked all hunched-over to the car, got in, and drove off.

The next morning my ankle was considerably better. The doctor now decided that the break showing up on the X-ray was probably an old one. I thought it maybe had happened playing football in school. He released me from the hospital with orders to go home and rest my leg for a couple of days.

I caught a bus and went to be with Dorie.

✈ ✈ ✈

Eddie and I remained close and Dorie and I saw a lot of him over the next year. Eddie was proving to be a very competent pilot, but his heart wasn't in it. His sole ambition in life was to go back to Brooklyn as soon as the war was over and become a fireman. But he was a good pal, and fun to be around.

One day in February 1944, he brought down the house during a squadron meeting. The assistant director of operations, Major Bill Allen, was carping on a bunch of "be no's" (there'll be no more of this; there'll be no more of that) when he asked if there were any questions. Eddie, who was only a 20-year-old second lieutenant, popped up and said in his Brooklyn accent. "How about telling me how to fill out my income tax, sir?"

"You know the meaning of the word sedition, Lieutenant?"

"Doesn't sound like something good, sir."

"It isn't," Major Allen replied, then turned to the rest of us. "What should we do with this clown?"

We all started throwing things at Eddie, which brought the meeting to an end.

Although Eddie was often lighthearted, he also had a serious side. He was bothered by the fact there was a war going on and he wasn't in it, so he started a one-man protest by showing up for work not wearing his wings on his uniform. This caused the other pilots to get down on him hard, but I understood his deep sense of pride and knew he was one of the most honorable persons that I had ever met. But there were times even I considered his actions a little excessive and I told him so. But Eddie would just shrug his shoulders. He could be as stubborn as a jackass when he wanted to be.

After a few months of this, and other minor infractions, a quota request came down for some pilots to go to B-24 school and then off into combat. The commandant placed Eddie's name at the top of the list of volunteers. That was the last time I saw him and I don't know if he got to be a fireman in Brooklyn or not. Years later, when Dorie and I were traveling through the area, we looked in the New York City and Brooklyn telephone books, but no Eddie Wilson. He was a one of a kind. Some days, and after all these years later, I still find myself missing Eddie. He was a good friend.

✈ ✈ ✈

Dorie and I fell into the habit of drinking every night after work, and there were times she didn't hold her alcohol very well. I remember one evening we got into an argument over having nothing in the house for dinner and she got really angry with me for bringing it up. She grabbed the car keys, slammed the door hard on her way out, got into the old Pontiac and roared off. An hour later she came back and told me she had been in a small fender-bender. Our car was not damaged much, but it was sporting some light-colored paint on its left fender. No big deal, I thought at the time, but several days later a sergeant stationed on the base came into our operations room looking for me. He asked me to come outside with him to where my car was parked.

"Sir, the other morning somebody sideswiped my wife as she was going home after taking me to work. The car that hit her was just like this one." We both looked down at the paint streak on the Pontiac's fender.

"Couldn't have been this car, Sergeant. True, my wife was in an accident, but it happened four nights ago, not in the morning. I was home when she left the house, and I was there when she came back an hour later and told me what happened." I pointed at the smear. "That's the paint you're seeing. It's from a different accident."

He looked at me long and hard, said nothing, saluted and walked away. He didn't believe a word I said. Later, I remembered that I had called our insurance agent to pay for the damage to the guy's car that Dorie had hit, and that if need be, he could attest to the fact. By then it was too late. I had no way of finding the sergeant. I didn't know his name or what unit he was attached to. It was a huge base.

About a month later, several of us were sent on temporary duty (TDY) to Eagle Pass Army Air Field, a remote station at the north end of our gunnery range on the Rio Grande River. I was told to expect to be away for a month, possibly longer, news which did not sit well with Dorie. She became deeply agitated at the prospect of being left alone, so much so, that two days before my departure she informed me she was going home to spend the time with her mother. I thought she was acting like a spoiled brat and told her so.

At Eagle Pass, I became friendly with a service pilot, Ray Carson, a lieutenant old enough to be my father. Like me, Ray was a hunter; unlike me, he was a really good one. He and I had gone out several times, but mostly without much success. He was sliding into a funk after so long a dry spell, and began muttering things like he must be losing his edge. One day I took off alone and came upon a passel of ducks on a lake. In short order I bagged fifteen. I would shoot one and the rest would take off only to land on the other side. I would creep around, get another, wait for them to land again, then blast the next one. I brought them back to the bachelor officers' quarters (BOQ) in a large sack, went directly to Ray's room and pounded on his door.

"Hey, Ray, come out here and see how a real hunter operates."

He came out and watched as I removed the bag from the trunk of my car and proudly dumped the birds out in the parking lot.

He took one look and walked away tossing his bone-cutting words over his shoulder. "Some hunter you are. Those aren't ducks, Hawkeye, they're frigging mud hens!"

This became his favorite story for months to come, re-telling it to all who would listen and laugh at my folly.

Most colonels in the Air Corps had been in service for a long time. Promotions did not come fast during the lean period between World War I and World War II, and to my twenty-three-year-old eyes, these guys were ancient. Such a Methuselah was Colonel Bundy, the commanding officer at Eagle Pass. Bundy might have been old to the likes of me—maybe forty-eight, maybe fifty—but he sure knew how to have a good time, and he also sure knew how to fly.

One Saturday he sponsored a rodeo to promote goodwill between the base cadre and the residents of Eagle Pass. There was to be a parade followed by an air show, then a big, old-fashioned, western-style barbecue. Bundy led the procession on a spirited quarter horse, all decked out in western finery and grinning from ear to ear. And he handled his horse as if he'd been born to the saddle.

The main event of the follow-on air show was an aerial dogfight over the field put on between two AT-6s. Bundy had choreographed the event so that he would get shot down, and with smoke pouring from his plane disappear behind a thicket of trees. It went off as planned. The smoke billowed, Bundy vanished, and seconds later we all heard a loud boom!

Now smoke began to undulate up higher and higher from behind the trees and the townsfolk started to chatter nervously. It sure looked like something had gone terribly wrong from where they were standing. After a couple of minutes Bundy popped up from behind the trees and performed a series of rolls down the runway to the delight of the crowd. Only then did they see the "accident" was nothing more than a well-executed stunt.

While I was there the base was hit with a "no notice" inspection by a team from Air Training Command. After they completed their review, the detachment assembled in Bundy's office to brief him on its findings, and I was there representing some of the tow pilots. The team chief, a rah-rah, ring-knocking major, opened his briefing by informing Bundy that a lot of his instructors were seen wearing cowboy boots with their uniforms—a flagrant disregard of the regs. He asked Bundy if he was aware of this breach of good order. Bundy looked at the major as if he had just popped down from another planet then gave his answer by placing his feet on his desk and hiking his pants up to his knees. He was wearing a pair of exquisitely tooled boots that must have set him back a good two hundred dollars. It was all I could do not to laugh out loud. Any further talk about cowboy boots ended then and there.

The field passed the inspection with high marks.

After flying the North American AT-6 Texan for a year I was promoted to the Beech AT-11 Kansan. This was a small, twin-engine trainer with a turret in the upper rear, a modified version of the civilian C-45. This little guy was a real workhorse; more than ninety percent of the forty-five thousand or so bombardiers trained in World War II learned their craft looking out its transparent nose. It was a great plane, and I enjoyed every flight, even though ours were only modified to train gunners.

Some months later the commanding officer advanced me to the Lockheed AT-18 Hudson. This was a larger, faster, more complex trainer, which we nicknamed "Galloping Domino" because of its squirrelly landing characteristics.

The AT-18 carried five student gunners and a sergeant/instructor. It had no dual flight controls for a copilot's position, but it came equipped with an autopilot, a novelty at the time. Oftentimes on the way back from a long mission I would turn on the autopilot then go back to the lavatory in rear. This really got the students' attention when they'd peer into the cockpit and discover that no one was flying the plane. Huge sighs of relief would greet me on my return trip to the front.

One Saturday I was able to wangle a ride back to Louisville in an AT-18 which was taking a group of senior officers there for some sort of a meeting. Even though it was only for one night, and the flight would return the next day, it gave me the chance to see my parents. I rushed home to pack, telling Dorie how I'd just be gone the one night as I stuffed my B-4 bag with gear. She became upset, started crying, then accused me of abandoning her. That was more than I could stomach. I yelled at her to quit acting so damn childish and finished by saying I didn't want to hear any more crap on the matter. I was thoroughly peeved when I left for the base. Her snits were getting out of hand.

One day we had a visit from General Henry "Hap" Arnold, the Commanding General of the Army Air Corps. Our commanding officer was a nervous wreck in the week leading up to the big event, and on arrival day had all his officers lined up on the ramp an hour early to greet Arnold just in case he was ahead of schedule. He and his deputy stood at attention in front of the troops when General Arnold climbed out of his airplane, spotted a major back in the ranks and called out his name. While the base brass stood at attention and saluted, Arnold rushed past them, grabbed this major's hand and started pumping it, his face creased by a huge grin. Turned out the major—our base operations officer—and Hap Arnold were classmates at West Point and had graduated together in the class of 1907.

I never did find out how or why he was still a major thirty-six years later. Our Methuselah had to have been at least fifty-seven years old the day Hap Arnold came to town!

✈ ✈ ✈

I really welcomed my next assignment. Someone at Training Command had decided that the best way to train gunners was to put them in bombers and have them fire cameras at attacking fighters, in place of bullets fired at towed targets. This was far more realistic training. Here they would learn how to pull lead on attacking fighters, which meant some of us got tapped to fly the fighters. One of the lucky few was me. The rest of the pilots would fly the B-17s and B-24s. The fighter we were given was the Curtiss P-40E Warhawk, and after three days of ground school I got to take up the first P-40 sent to Laredo. I needed a crew chief to help me start it.

There are no words to describe how I felt that first time I pulled back on the stick and felt the plane bound off the runway and head for the wild blue as if it was a living, breathing thing.

For the first time in my life I was a no holds barred fighter pilot, and soon I was making strafing runs on B-17s like I was born to the task. One day while making passes on a single B-17 practicing evasive action, I made a steep pull-up from a pass, the idea being to better position myself for another run at him. At the top of my maneuver I rolled the P-40 over on its back and looked down for the B-17. I couldn't see it, but I sure didn't want to start my pass without having that big bomber in sight. I scanned the sky beneath me: no B-17. I looked upward. Nothing. And at this point I made a really big mistake. While inverted, I pushed the stick full forward. Bad, bad move, because a few seconds later all hell broke loose. My P-40 went ass over teakettle, its fuel venting all over the sky. This P-40 rookie had put his warbird into an inverted spin. Luckily, I'd remembered from somewhere in my training an instructor saying, "If you get in an inverted spin, the best thing to do is to kick it into a normal spin, then use your spin recovery procedures." That's what I did, and with the proper controls applied, the P-40 quit tumbling and flew itself out.

A very shaky Scrappy Johnson completed his mission and returned to base still shaking. The B-17 pilot was already in base ops drinking coffee when I entered the room.

"Man, you're really getting hot in that P-40. Sure wish it was me."

I smiled and said, "Yeah, I really like to wring it out." I didn't tell him that all those maneuvers were unplanned and that they had scared the living hell out of me. It was a valuable lesson in what not to do in a fighter you know diddlysquat about.

✈ ✈ ✈

Our director of flying, Major Paulson, was not just a straight-arrow officer, but he was a rugged ex-hockey player from North Dakota as well. Some folks insisted he was really a nice guy once you got to know him, but since I was a second lieutenant, I didn't get to know him at all. In fact, I went out of my way to stay well out of his.

One day a nearby rancher called the base and complained that someone had buzzed his spread, scared the hell out of his cattle, and in general had caused havoc. This guy was a local bigwig and his grumbling was taken seriously.

The base wheels determined from his description of the airplane that it had to have been a P-40, and when they checked the records to see who had been up at the time, they found my name and two others. Paulson called me into his office to question me, but since I knew it wasn't me, I denied it. He decided that since he had me already on the carpet and standing at attention, he needed something to rail on. He looked down at my shoes, then began chewing me out for not having them shined to his liking. I saluted and left, happy to have gotten out of there with my scalp intact. Because if I had been really grilled, I didn't want to have to explain how it couldn't have been me, simply because at the time in question I was fifty miles away, flying in the opposite direction over Mission, raising hell and buzzing the cadets in their AT-6s!

Shortly after this incident, we were ordered to transfer five of our P-40s to Luke Field, a base near Phoenix, Arizona. I was one of the pilots picked, and our flight lead was a newly promoted captain named Pat Patterson.

We flew an uneventful first leg to Marfa, Texas, but things definitely got interesting upon landing when we found out that the base didn't have any one-hundred-octane gasoline on hand—the only fuel our P-40s could safely take. After going over the situation among ourselves, we decided that since we still had some of the high octane stuff left in one of our internal tanks, we could put a minimum amount of ninety-octane into one of the other tanks, take-off on the good tank of one-hundred octane, then cruise on the tank with ninety octane the short distance to Pyote, Texas.

Our perfect plan managed to go into the toilet, and fast. Patterson was the leader, I was flying the fifth airplane and the strategy was to fly north to an east/west highway then follow it to the airfield at Pyote. Simple. But when we arrived at the highway Pat made a couple of orbits trying to figure out whether we should fly east or west. Meanwhile, I was following number four and soon learned that he had completely lost the other three. Number Four kept circling with no apparent new plan in mind, so in frustration I decided to go off on my own, and flew east along the highway. By now I was running low on fuel. Luckily, I spotted an airfield and as I entered the pattern a red warning light came on, announcing I had less than ten gallons left. Ten gallons may be a lot of gas in a car's tank, but in a P-40 it would be gone in less than ten minutes. I landed and found I was at a place called Big Spring. This was the only time in my long air force career that after I'd landed at a base I had to ask where I was!

Number Four had decided to follow me, so after he landed we telephoned Pyote base ops, got Pat on the line and told him where we were. We then refueled, flew to Pyote, rejoined the rest of our group and spent the night. The next morning the five of us flew to El Paso, refueled, then pressed on to Luke.

Luke Field had no runways at the time, just one huge square of black asphalt. With no good reference point to work from, it was next to impossible for me to keep my P-40 straight during the after-landing rollout, but somehow I managed, and didn't hit anything.

I spent an uneventful night in Phoenix and we all hopped a train the next morning for the long ride back to Laredo.

✈ ✈ ✈

Dorie and I lived in one side of a small duplex; Lt. Charlie Dickerson and his wife were in the other. Charlie had been on the flight to Phoenix and he and Pat Patterson had shared a hotel room that night. One day Pat came to visit Charlie when his wife wasn't home and the two began to relive their apparent dalliances on the layover in Phoenix. The walls between our two apartments were paper-thin and Dorie heard them discussing their exploits with the women they'd picked up. When I came home she lit into me, carrying on and accusing me of similar misconduct. The truth was I had shared a room with two other lieutenants that night, and none of us had met anyone or gone anywhere! No amount of denial could persuade her to believe me so she stayed angry with me for days, which in turn did nothing to add to my sense of well-being, or elevate my mood when in her presence.

✈ ✈ ✈

In early 1944 I was able to get some time off, so Dorie and I took the train back to Louisville to visit our parents. It was a long ride, but we enjoyed the change of scenery after spending so many months in the desert. Dorie was also able to spend time with a lot of her friends but most of mine were off to war. Still, I was glad to be home and to catch up on the doings in the Johnson family. Before leaving Laredo we sold the old Pontiac, and with the money from the sale, coupled with some savings, our plan was to buy a better car while we were home. We ended up buying a 1938 Ford convertible club coupe, which we drove back. In those days there were no freeways so we passed through what seemed like a thousand towns, both big and small. The trip took several days, but it was an interesting drive, and it sure was fun riding with the top down.

✈ ✈ ✈

The next plane I flew was the Bell P-39 Airacobra. This was a great little airplane, but under powered and a lot less forgiving than the P-40. Prior to entering aviation cadets I'd seen one crash near Bowman Field, in Louisville. Two guys flying out of Ft. Knox got into a mock dogfight at low altitude over the town hoping to impress the folks gathered on the ground to watch. One pilot racked it in too tight and stalled, but discovered to his horror that he was too low to recover. Even though he crashed in a highly populated area and no one on the ground was injured, he came to his untimely end at the bottom of one hellava hole in somebody's back yard.

Some desk jockey in Training Command Headquarters had decided that to check out in this plane we first had to spend some time in a two-seater model. The cockpit had been lengthened forward, making it stick out way in front of the normal cockpit, thus leaving the guy in front with only minimum controls. We didn't have any instructor pilots on base who'd flown the two-seater, and even if we did, I'm pretty sure they wouldn't have flown in it again. So we found ourselves flying this piece of garbage solo from the back seat just to fulfill the regulation. Not only was our vision all but obstructed, but the plane was downright unstable. The stick felt like it was mired in a barrel of mud. This was the only time I flew the two-seater version of the P-39 and it undoubtedly ranks as the worst airplane I ever flew.

For months the rumor mill had it that we were going to be getting Bell P-63 Kingcobras, but in those days the smart money believed nothing until it happened. Then one afternoon while flying I heard a throaty female voice come up on the radio asking for landing instructions. Whoa, what's this all about? I wondered. After landing, I spotted a factory-fresh, shiny P-63 sitting on the ramp. A WASP (Women's Army Service Pilot) had ferried it in. We later had five WASPs stationed at Laredo, and these women were always groomed to perfection. They wore bright smiles and we soon came to appreciate the fact that they were pretty damn good pilots as well. And the guys all agreed: these gals added a long-needed and welcome touch of class to the base.

Shortly after their arrival we hit the jackpot when we received thirty new Kingcobras. This was a special treat since our P-40s and P-39s had seen better days and were constantly in need of more and more maintenance.

The P-63 was a neat airplane. It virtually leaped into the sky, and although it looked like its cousin the P-39, it was a larger, more powerful, and a far more stable craft. Its performance was similar to a P-51 Mustang, and at low altitude it could probably have out-turned a P-51 (of course, with me flying the P-63), but its range was nowhere near comparable. Bell built thousands of these P-63s, but none saw combat with our air forces. We gave the bulk of them to the Russians under the Lend Lease Act.

In early 1945, as part of the gunnery-training syllabus, the school would send out regular formations of B-17s to simulate bombing runs on Houston. We, in our fighters, would make a number of passes at them on the way to the target, land at Foster Field for a quick refueling, then repeat the exercise on the homeward leg until the student gunners ran out of camera film. With the mission over, the bomber pilots would ask us to put on a show for the boys. We happily obliged by doing rolls and aerobatics around their airplanes while they snapped scores of pictures with their personal cameras. Talk about fun!

Later, Bell produced a P-63 with armor plating on the front of the fuselage and on the leading edges of the wings, and replaced the front of the canopy with one made of heavy Plexiglas. When we flew this model, the gunners would actually fire at us with thirty-caliber frangible bullets. We called these P-63s "pinballs" because the nose lit up when a hit was registered on the airplane. There was also a machine in the cockpit that counted the hits, but we could also tally the strikes manually once we were back on the ground because those frangible bullets left chalk marks on the aircraft.

Everything worked fine as long as the gunners only fired at you from a front angle. But if they nailed you from either the side or the rear, they could actually shoot you down! On one occasion a pilot took some hits by an overzealous gunner which blew out his engine. Luckily, he was able to make a dead-stick landing on one of the several emergency strips near the gunnery range, and the errant gunner was summarily washed out for being reckless. I must admit, I was always extra cautious when flying those pinballs!

By 1945 I had been made a flight leader, and one night while having drinks at the officers' club, a group of us got into a bragging-rights conversation with a transient pilot on a two-day layover. He was ferrying a new Douglas B-26 out to the West Coast and was proudly telling us how fast his plane was. Of course we countered with tales about our hot P-63s. I decided we would find out the next day which plane was the fastest.

A group of us took off early, one B-26 and four P-63s with me flying lead. After climbing up to about eight thousand feet we all pushed our throttles to full forward and flew neck to neck for about five minutes until the B-26's starboard engine started billowing smoke. I immediately declared it a dead heat and we all eased off the throttles. My guys flew back to the field, landed, waved at the B-26 pilot and never saw him again. The next day I saw the B-26 still parked on the ramp. Unusual, because the pilot had mentioned that night in the club how he would be leaving early this morning. I asked my crew chief why the bird was still there.

"You didn't hear, Lieutenant?"

"Hear what?"

"The pilot burned out both her engines the day before yesterday. So I ask you, how in the hell do you do that? Anyway, it'll be a couple of weeks at the earliest before they can get the replacements flown in here. Guess he's going to have some fancy explaining to do, Lieutenant."

I walked away whistling and grinning. And I rescinded my dead heat decision. Because upon reflection it didn't sound like a draw to me now. We all still had our noisemakers humming nicely. None of our engines had turned into big, fused blocks of metal.

Near the end of the war, the Lockheed P-80 Shooting Star, America's first jet fighter, became operational. A short time later, in the summer of 1945, the base received a quota for two pilots to go to P-80 school, then off to combat in the Pacific. I volunteered, and a few days later was placed on orders to go. But before I could leave, we dropped two atomic bombs on Japan, Emperor Hirohito surrendered, and my orders were rescinded.

I sure would have enjoyed flying jets against those Japanese prop-driven planes.

6

The Big Bang

After Japan surrendered, time stood still, and like everyone else in uniform, I had no idea what was going to happen next. I had applied for a regular army commission several months earlier, but hadn't heard anything more about it.

In early 1946 I was transferred to Las Vegas Army Airfield along with Captain "Red" Fuqua, my boss and good friend. We were being transferred because Vegas had a gunnery school and the powers-that-be were betting that flexible gunnery training would continue in some fashion or another.

Dorie and I sold our car and rode with Red and his wife, Clara. This was my first trip out west (I don't count that flight to Phoenix) and I thoroughly enjoyed it. As a boy I had been thrilled and awed by cowboys and all things to do with the Wild West. I had admired the on-screen antics of Buck Jones, Tom Mix and Bob Steele, and that kid in me was still alive and well. We stopped at the Grand Canyon, and while admiring the breathtaking view at Lookout Point, we saw three B-25s thunder into the gorge a couple of hundred feet below us. They turned and headed directly toward us, zooming overhead at a distance no greater than twenty-five feet. We were buffeted by their propwash and the four of us screamed in delight. I was thrilled beyond words, covered with goose bumps, and imbued with an overpowering feeling of pride in my country. And what a singularly great country the U.S. of A was in those early months of 1946.

Not a lot was happening when we arrived at the base; in fact, Red and I fast began to wonder why we were even there. The pilots assembled each morning only to be dismissed and told to hang loose. There was jack for us to do, and we were only being allowed four hours of flying each month. We found ourselves mired in a glorified pilots' pool some two-hundred-men strong. Morale was in the dumpster.

Las Vegas was a backwater town in 1946. There were only two hotels on the strip: the Last Frontier and the El Rancho Vegas. I could have bought up all the surrounding land if I wanted for a dollar an acre. This was wide-open country, and the towns were few and far between. I quickly came to the conclusion I needed wheels, so Dorie and I bought a 1941 Ford coupe for $1300.00. That car was definitely used, but not used up, so we began to explore.

One Sunday we stood on a deck on the second floor of the Last Frontier and watched navy planes putting on a firepower demonstration across the street over a field where the Sahara Hotel would stand years later. I distinctly remember seeing an experimental plane that had a prop up front and a jet in the rear. It was both novel and weird, but I can understand why it was never produced in numbers. It simply had no idea what it was!

Another time, while walking down Main Street, a P-63 came whizzing out of nowhere a mere fifty feet above the buildings (which weren't very tall at the time), rolled upside down and flew the length of the street inverted. Turned out it was the pilot's last flight before leaving the service and he wanted it to be a memorable one. We later learned that he was out of an auxiliary field at Indian Springs, and got away with his little stunt only because the base brass insisted it couldn't have been him. Their reasoning: he got back there too quickly and landed before the word reached them.

✈ ✈ ✈

Late in the fall I received orders transferring me to Columbus, Mississippi, another base with an uncertain future. So we loaded our stuff and headed east: first stop, Gallup, New Mexico. Somewhere between Vegas and Flagstaff, Arizona, we joined up with Route 66, a road I'd driven several times. And believe me, it wasn't nearly as romantic as the song implied. Back then, traveling through the desert with no air conditioning was not something folks stood in line to do.

We found ourselves in Gallup, a town with only one motel and it was full. Seems there had been a train wreck that afternoon and all the passengers were there. Dorie and I lolled around in the lounge until closing time then tried to catch a few hours of shuteye in a booth. Not a good experience. At the crack of a chilly dawn we headed east again and had only gone a few miles when the car started steaming. How the hell could that be, I wondered aloud. I had filled the radiator with enough antifreeze to protect to it to 10 degrees below, yet here it was, obviously still frozen.

I pulled into an ancient Indian trading post and asked for some warm water to thaw it out. The owner laughed at my request, said all his water was frozen also, but he'd be happy to give us however much we wanted after the sun did its work. He then hustled us inside for breakfast where the three of us began sipping on Old Granddad. Some breakfast!

Five days later we pulled into Columbus, Mississippi, tired, hungry and damn glad to be getting out of that car.

✈ ✈ ✈

Columbus was another Vegas. There were tons of pilots, all scrambling for four hours a month flying time. The primary airplane was the AT-6 and since I had lots of time in it I was made an instructor. My job was to check out mostly former bomber pilots who hadn't flown singles for a long time, a real hairy assignment because the AT-6 was easy to ground loop if you weren't on your toes. And some of these guys were not just mildly rusty, but very rusty. I was supposed to have them do spins, but mostly I just demonstrated the spin and all we agreed that they caught the hang of it real quick.

About this time the base maintenance squadron got a few P-47s assigned for some much-needed engine work. After a bit of snooping around I discovered they needed test hops when the maintenance was finished, so I went to the officer in charge (OIC) and asked him if I could get in on this flying. He agreed and had me report to a captain on the flight line. This guy had already flight-tested several of the planes and didn't see me as someone horning in on his turf, so he gladly checked me out, and I started flying.

This was great until another captain showed up and told me he had been assigned to work for the major in charge of maintenance. He then informed me that some of his ex-combat buddies were going to test fly the rest of the P-47s. This pissed me off royally, but I was a lieutenant and he was a captain. No contest. I often hoped to return the favor in later years, but never ran across him again. But at least I managed to get in 14 hours flying before the good times ended.

✈ ✈ ✈

I was assigned to the supply squadron to perform additional duties, and found myself working for a ground-pounder first lieutenant who immediately transferred his biggest account, the one for base housing, to me. As it turned out, housing was being shut down, and all the furniture had to be turned in. And since there were no enlisted troops to do the work he shanghaied men from the civilian fire department to move the furniture from the houses into a huge warehouse.

By the time I got down to the last fifteen units, it was obvious the account was going to be miserably short and I started to panic. But not for long. Those good ol' Mississippi boys figured out my plight and came riding to my rescue. They began moving furniture in through the front door of the warehouse where it was counted, then trundled the load out the back only to be brought around to the front again and checked in as a new shipment. At the end of the job the account was less than fifteen dollars short, an amount easily written off. I later realized that the slick weenie lieutenant knew the base was going to close, knew that the housing account was woefully short when he had me sign for it, and had in essence set it up for me to take the fall. Fooled him, the rotten little weasel.

✈ ✈ ✈

Before Dorie and I could plant our feet firmly on the ground in Columbus, the army sent me off TDY to Walnut Ridge, Arkansas, home to a mammoth aircraft storage facility. Walnut Ridge housed at least 7,500 airplanes parked wingtip to wingtip in rows too many to count. There were all kinds of planes; P-51s, P-47s, B-17s, B-25s, and on, and on, and on.

General Jimmy Doolittle showed up looking for a B-25 similar to the one he'd flown to Tokyo. The men found such a plane, but had to move a helluva lot of other planes around to get it out. The armaments factories were still ferrying brand-new airplanes into Walnut Ridge. It didn't matter that the war was over; the government was honoring its commitment to take possession of the materiel it had already contracted for.

There was a crew on base of one hundred soldiers whose only job was to take the instruments out of the planes, place fifty at a time into gunnysacks then pound them to rubble with sledgehammers. It seems the government had an agreement with the manufacturers to destroy them all rather than putting them on the market for sale as excess government property.

But while such airplane parts were sacrosanct, the planes themselves were not, and could be bought by anyone with the cash to do so. And a lot of folks had the money. The going price for a P-51 was twenty-five hundred dollars. The guys would get them into flying condition, charge the batteries, start up the engines, then the rest was up to the buyer.

When I left for my next assignment one month later, the army was still ferrying brand-new airplanes into Walnut Ridge.

✈ ✈ ✈

Dorie and I went home to Louisville for a week's leave, then it was off to San Bernardino, California, where I had orders to report as a supply liaison officer for Williams Field, in Chandler, Arizona. My job was to expedite the shipment of critical aircraft parts back to Willy, as that desert base was affectionately called. We spent six months in California then I separated from the service. I had decided not to stay in unless granted a regular commission, a prospect which now seemed to be going nowhere.

Upon discharge I was promoted to captain. I guess that was the army's goodbye present, and it sure did impress the folks back home.

✈ ✈ ✈

I was a civilian again with no idea what I wanted to do with the rest of my life, so I went back to the university and got another night job. This time I sat in the front row in class and began hanging out in the library instead of the Cardinal Inn. My grades shot from C's and D's to A's and B's. I had grown up.

Our first son, Ted, was born on July 24, 1947. Dorie's labor was not short. I stayed in the hospital waiting room with my in-laws, where I pretended to read dozens of outdated magazines in order to avoid protracted conversations with Ruth. The whole event seemed like it lasted a year. I returned alone three days later to take my family home, firmly letting Ruth know I had no intention of having Dorie stay with her for the next few weeks, or "at least until you find your family a more suitable home," as she disdainfully put it.

Night and day, I peeked in on that sleeping baby every chance I got, awed by his small size, scared to pick him up lest I drop him. Dorie got a kick out of that, but didn't press for me to hold him for any extended periods. But I was oh, so proud of that next generation of the Johnson clan.

✈ ✈ ✈

A month to the day after Ted's arrival, I received a wire from the Army Air Corps informing me I had been awarded a Regular Army commission as a first lieutenant. The news was totally unexpected and certainly couldn't have come at a better time. Dorie and I still hadn't managed to find a decent place to live, and besides, I had liked the military and found that I wanted to get back into flying again. I was told I would be on probation for the first year, which meant the government could rescind my commission with the stroke of a bureaucratic pen. But what did I care? Here I was, a high school graduate, somehow leaping over a very competitive pack of college-educated combat pilots all vying for one of a very limited number of slots in the permanent Air Corps. Many of these men had awards and decorations I could only envy, yet somehow I had been chosen and not them to become a part of this select fraternity of officers and gentlemen. It was a life-defining moment.

Going to school and working nights had strained my eyes to the point I was worried about passing the strenuous physical exam. And my hearing wasn't so hot either. But with some rest, my eyes turned out okay and I was able to fudge my way through the hearing test. If they had audiometers as sophisticated as those in use today I would never have made it. When I first entered the Army Air Corps, the hearing test consisted of the doctor standing in the corner and whispering, "Do you hear me?"

I'd been told what to expect so naturally I said, "Yes, Doctor."

Things hadn't changed much in the intervening years.

In September I received a wire ordering me to duty at Warner Robbins Army Airfield at Macon, Georgia. When I reported in, I was made a PX (Post Exchange) officer. This caused a serious blow to my ego, but I was happy just to be back in the service, so I coped. My immediate boss was a man named Lieutenant Colonel Short, the nattiest dresser in the entire State of Georgia, and he wore observers' wings on his perfectly tailored uniform. I had heard all about officers sporting this rating while at Laredo. It was a trumped-up aeronautical badge for a select few ground-pounders to get flight pay as long as they met the monthly minimums. And Short made sure he logged those four hours every month, come rain or come shine. But the colonel in charge of the airfield was another matter. This guy actually wore balloon pilot's wings, for God's sake. Balloons! Seems he had actually pinned on one star for a while in 1945, but had been demoted back to his permanent rank of colonel once the war was over. He was a pompous old fool but thoroughly harmless, and he still referred to himself as the Commanding General of the Warner Robbins Air Material Area.

The base had a couple of new P-51s which I managed to get checked-out in. I had about a dozen hours under my belt when Colonel Short decided to send me to a ten-week PX school at Fort Monmouth, NJ. The whole experience was humiliating, and like the proverbial bad penny, came back to haunt me many, many times over the years.

Before I left for New Jersey I met a pilot who had just returned from F-80 school, and remembering how I had almost gone to the same school just before the end of the war I asked him how it was.

"It was rough, Scrappy, real rough. That plane just flat wears you out. Flying jets is for the young guys."

I found this assessment rather amusing since he was all of twenty-nine. I would have given my right arm and one you-know-what to have been sent to jet school with a follow-on to a fighter squadron.

My dad became terminally ill while I was stationed at Warner Robbins. I was able to make it home a couple of days prior to his passing and was with him in the hospital the evening he died. Lying there he spoke to me only once and that was to ask me to take care of my mother. That was it. No words of endearment or of love for his wife and no whispered words of affection for me. So typical of him, right to the end.

A month later mother came to Georgia to visit but didn't stay long. She arrived under a false flag; her purpose was to test the waters to see if she could move in with us but quickly realized that was not going to happen. She cornered Dorie one day and told her that she did not raise me to drink liquor like we did, suggesting in a righteous manner that we were flying down the road of perdition. She packed and went to visit her sister, Stella, in Jacksonville, then returned to Knoxville to live with her brother, my favorite uncle, Bud.

Then I faithfully sent her money every month until her death.

In the late summer of 1948 I volunteered for an overseas assignment and it was approved in record time. I was going to Japan. Since it was not known where I would end up, or even if dependent housing would be available once I got there, I had to leave Dorie and Ted behind knowing there was at least a one-year wait for them to come live with me.

I flew to San Francisco and waited to board my ship for Japan. In those days, Air Corps personnel heading for the Far East stayed at Hamilton Field, in Marin County.

I spent two weeks with very little to do. The base gave me some make-work assignments such as taking inventory in the supply squadron, or checking the enlisted men's mess to see that the food was edible, or that they had enough knives and forks. Boring! Most nights I went into San Francisco and ended up in one particular downtown bar tended by a man named Bill Montgomery.

Bill was a professional who really knew how to run a bar and dispense generous libations. He would introduce the newcomers to his regulars, and once he'd met someone, he made it a point to remember the name. For that particular sliver of time I became one of his regulars, and that's where I spent my last night. By closing time I had become somewhat chummy with one of the ladies, and as she pulled her lightweight coat tightly around herself she murmured in my ear that she would wait for me on the corner. I squared away my tab, left a generous tip, and as I headed for the door I waved a goodbye to Bill. He hailed me from the far end of the bar and asked me to hold on for a farewell drink. He shooed out the stragglers, locked the door, poured us each a generous helping of Wild Turkey, and we retired to a booth and talked about everything and nothing. All thoughts of the lady and a possible tryst were long gone.

Toward sunup I told Bill I really needed to be shoving off, suggesting that my ship wouldn't wait. He saluted, unlocked the door and made me promise to come see him next time I was in town. "I'll own the place by then, Lieutenant Scrappy, I promise you that."

I told Dorie about Bill, and years later when we happened to be in San Francisco, we decided on a whim to hunt down that bar. Sure enough, Bill was still there, and true to his word, was now the owner. But the years had taken their toll. He had lost his fire, and the bar was certainly no longer the magical place I'd remembered.

The next day I sailed out the Golden Gate on board a small World War II troop carrier. This was one slow boat that rocked and rolled, and it took three, long, boring, seasick-filled weeks for me to make that journey to Japan. When I arrived at the port, I was handed my assignment orders by a military police major who insisted I sign for them in triplicate and show my military ID to prove I was who I claimed to be. I tore open the package and emptied its contents. My eyes bulged. I was heading for the 41st Fighter Squadron of the 35th Fighter Group based at Johnson Field, north of Tokyo! Hot damn, I couldn't have been happier. Although I had lots of time in fighters, this was my first assignment to an operational, honest to God, fighter squadron. To this day I cannot describe the feeling of utter joy and accomplishment. I was now a real fighter pilot in a real fighter squadron. Great balls of fire!

Japan was still very much a war-ravaged country, a fact that became all the more obvious to me on the ride to Johnson Field. Battered buildings still littered the landscape, especially in and around Tokyo where huge sections of the city had literally been leveled by our heavy bombers. It was one sobering sight.

At the 41st Fighter Squadron I was met by Captain Harry H. Moreland, known as "Mo" to everyone from new lieutenant to the lone lieutenant colonel, commanding. He quickly became one of my best all-time friends, ranking right up there alongside Eddie Wilson and Jack Pruitt. Mo had flown P-47s in Europe during the war, and again during a follow-on assignment back in the States. But the 41st Squadron was equipped with P-51s, a plane neither of us had much time in, but we were determined to become fast learners. This was the reason I had wanted to stay in the Air Corps. From here on out life was going to be good!

One day, less than a month later and completely out of the blue, I was informed by the first sergeant that permanent change-of-station orders had come down sending me to 5th Air Force Headquarters at Nagoya, for a PX assignment. My morale was shattered. Tell me this shit can't be happening! But it was. Mo accompanied me to Tokyo where we said our good-byes and I boarded a train for Nagoya. I arrived early on a Saturday only to be told in the orderly room not to bother trying to sign in or report to work until Monday morning.

That night while commiserating my misfortune in the officers' club, the airfield had an earthquake. I remember looking around nervously, wondering what the hell I should do, but noticed that my fellow patrons didn't seem to be too concerned. None had chosen to abandon their stools, and the bartenders had remained steadfast at their posts. Drink on, mates, seemed to be the order of the day, so that's what I did, toasting the gods with several rounds of bourbon. Turned out the damage to the base was minimal.

Sunday morning I decided to play a round of golf, and since I was a stranger and didn't know a soul, I set off on the course alone. I caught up with five Australian fighter pilots from Iwakuni on the fourth tee, and they insisted I join them for the rest of the round. They were without a doubt the world's worst golfers, but we had a great time, and when finished we went back to the club where we all ordered beers. After downing seconds, an Aussie stuck his head into the room, spotted his buddies and yelled as loud as he could, "Let's go, you bloody cobbers, the weather's cleared." They all rushed to the flight line and flew their P-51s back to their base at Iwakuni. Since then I have run across many Australians during my long military career, and I can truthfully report I never met one I didn't instantly take a shine to.

Monday morning I reported to headquarters and was directed to see a certain lieutenant colonel. The man seemed genuinely glad to see me, and was visibly impressed as he read in my folder that I was a graduate of that damn PX school back in New Jersey.

"This job will require a lot of traveling to all of the bases in 5th Air Force," he said, looking up from his notes. "You married, son?"

"Yes, sir."

He frowned at that. "Ah, well, that could be a problem. You won't be able to get your family over here because you'll be too busy traveling all the time." He put my folder down. "This won't do. I'm relieving you of the assignment right now, Lieutenant. Go over to personnel and have them cut orders sending you back to your old squadron. Any problem, tell the OIC to call me. You're dismissed."

I saluted, and hightailed it out of there. Mo was shocked but delighted to see me back at the squadron bright and early Tuesday morning. Turned out that colonel was an ordained minister and he felt it would be morally wrong to separate me from my family. Of course, he had no idea my family was still tucked away Stateside, with no hope of joining me for at least another year.

Two weeks later, the squadron flew over to Niagato for three days of gunnery practice. The group had a dumb-ass regulation which did not allow Mo or me to fire on any aerial gunnery missions because we didn't have enough training. This was undoubtedly the stupidest regulation I'd ever run into. Fer chrissakes, Mo had flown two combat tours in Europe and I'd flown hundreds of hours of aerial gunnery training missions at Laredo. In spite of this idiocy I had a great time. We slept in old, bombed-out Japanese barracks and the flying was absolutely the best.

The squadron commanding officer hosted an impromptu picnic just prior to our returning to Johnson Field. One of his flight leaders, a Captain Joe Powers, took a never-used P-51 drop tank, ran a rod through the center, attached some paddles, then where the rod protruded out from the front of the tank he added a propeller. He hung this contraption under a P-51, filled it with a mixture of milk, eggs, and other goodies, and took off. He climbed to 25,000 feet, flew around until the prop he'd attached to the tank stopped turning, then made a record-breaking descent and landed with a ton of fresh ice cream for dessert. Who could ever top that for sheer ingenuity?

The next morning we flew our P-51s back to Johnson Field. We were one contented bunch of pilots.

✈ ✈ ✈

On Friday of that week I was part of a four-ship flight ordered by 5th Air Force Headquarters to escort a Russian plane leaving Japan bound for a base in Siberia. Our instructions were to keep the plane in a corridor that would deny it exposure to our military installations. We were told to park two fighters on either side of the Russian then charge our fifty-caliber machine guns in his presence so that he could see we meant business. I had noticed the Russian pilot in base operations and wasn't impressed. He was about 45 years old, wore ugly glasses, and his uniform was a mess. Boy was I wrong about judging that particular book by its cover. He turned out to be one sly old fox.

His airplane was one of hundreds of PBY flying boats America had given the Ruskies during the heydays of the Lend Lease Program. The flight started out uneventfully. Even at top speed the PBY was notoriously slow, but this old codger was flying it at a crawl. We were only able to stay with him by flying our fighters in a weaving pattern along his flight path, which worked out okay until we started encountering clouds. I was in a steep bank when, whoosh, suddenly we all were in the clouds. I looked at my instruments and found that my gyro (Flight Indicator) was caged.

This was the Corpus Christi fog bank all over again and, like before, I found myself left with only the needle-ball-airspeed to save my ass. But this time it was worse, much worse; I was in an unusual attitude to start with, which meant I had probably gained and lost a ton of altitude. This nasty situation lasted several minutes, but to me it seemed like hours. Luckily, I broke into the clear before completely losing it. My first task was to scan the sky from horizon to horizon, then up and down as best I could. Nothing. No PBY and no P-51s. I was all alone. Time to make a decision. I exercised the only smart option I had left in my bag of tricks—I contacted ground radar, told them my problem which they resolved by giving me a steer to the strip at Niagato. I wasn't the only screwup; the rest of the flight staggered in behind me, and after refueling, we flew in formation back across the island to Johnson

Field. We were particularly quiet going home, embarrassed at how easily we had been snookered by the Russian.

I remember him with a lot of admiration now, and oftentimes visualize what a good time he must have had back home telling his comrades about the dumb bunch of American fighter jocks he had gotten the best of while flying in Japan.

7

The Philippines

While stationed at Johnson Field, I had been given an additional duty as base housing supply officer (surprise, surprise!) and now, Captain Dave Cherry, the OIC, was pressing me to sign for this monster account. Naturally, I was dragging my feet, because I knew from experience it had to be royally screwed up. I finally sucked it in and told him I wouldn't sign unless we had a complete inventory, to include the contents of every single house—no mean request that, from the base's newest supply officer. He agreed and we set a date for the audit, but before we had a chance to start counting dining room tables and nightstands, I received orders transferring me to the 18th Fighter Group, at Clark Field in the Philippines. Hallelujah! But my good fortune came about as the result of a major disaster.

A sizeable number of pilots from the 18th had been tasked to ferry a squadron of P-47s to the Chinese Nationalists on Taiwan when the weather had suddenly turned nasty. Because of a lack of navigation aids on the island, most of the P-47s got lost and crashed. Ten pilots were killed, and there were planes now strewn all over the mountains. So ten of us were culled from among several groups in Japan and sent to Taiwan to replace them. I left Johnson Field on a Saturday, along with Mo Moreland and Bob Hinck, and I remember the day only because all the base company grade officers were busy inventorying the housing supply lists on this, their one day off, and only because I had demanded an audit.

Scrappy had lucked out again!

Accompanied by Mo and Bob, I reported to Tachikawa Field, home to the big MATS transports where I was told by an unsavory looking, orange-haired sergeant that the next flight for Clark Field would be leaving in three days. "Do what you want until then," he said, around a huge wad of chewing gum, "just make sure you're back at least two hours before departure."

What to do for three whole days? Well, Mo, Bob and I decided that instead of hanging around Tachikawa critiquing takeoffs and landings, we'd spend the time loafing in one of the resort hotels nestled in the hills. We settled on the Gora and grabbed the first train.

The Gora turned out to be an inspired choice. The setting was idyllic, reason enough why our military was using it to house newly arrived officers' families until they could be accommodated on the various bases and posts around Japan.

On our second evening there, and while sitting on the open-air veranda enjoying our après-doing-nothing-all-afternoon martinis, we struck up a conversation with several ladies (translate to mean military wives) at a nearby table. Soon we joined forces and things began to get cozy.

About 10:00 P.M., Martha, a willowy redhead with a plummy voice motioned me aside where she looped her arm in mine and proceeded to melt my heart with her fast-fluttering eyelashes and the coyest of looks.

"In a minute I'm going upstairs," she cooed in a whisky voice. "Room 305." She then flashed her key under my nose for me to read the numbers stamped into the polished brass. "So, Scrappy, my love, why don't you give me ten minutes then come join me for a nightcap, hmm?" To these ears the voice was akin to the purring of the world's most contented cat.

When my ten minutes was up I said my goodnights and beat a retreat. I headed straight for room 305, but only because I was mildly curious to see what Martha wanted. Indeed, if my memory serves me correctly, I can report that nightcaps were served by hostess Martha *two* nights in a row in Room 305! Anyway, that's my story and I'm sticking to it.

✈ ✈ ✈

The Philippines was a fighter pilot's heaven. The weather was good, and seen from the air, the countryside was breathtakingly beautiful. Although the wheels had issued a ton of "be no's" to be observed while flying, they were never in the air to find out whether the rest of us were complying or not. We had a ball—buzzing, rat racing and generally chasing each other like a gang of deranged school kids from one end of the island of Luzon to the other. And for the first time in a long time I had no additional duties outside the squadron! All I had to do was fly. This was life at its best!

Clark Field was located in a lush, green valley dotted with simple bamboo-topped huts, and the only mar on the idyllic landscape in our tabletop valley was a volcano called Arriat, which blossomed forth from the earth, dead center. The first day I landed at Clark there was a battle underway between the Philippine Constabulary and the local communist guerrillas, a group known as the Hukbalahap Insurrectionists, or to the locals, simply the Huks. These two factions were still going at it when I left three years later, but the battle this day was being waged on and around Arriat, and very much within sight of Clark Field. Even before I landed I could see bursts of artillery shells on the side of the mountain. The Constabulary had it surrounded, and were lobbing their shells from the valley.

Two days later they closed the trap but drew a zero. The Huks had filtered through their lines and melted away. These guys were night fighters who posed as ordinary citizens by day. I would soon learn this fighting was very much the norm and it occurred almost every night.

In the 12th Fighter Squadron I was assigned to a flight led by Captain "Pappy" Hood. Pappy was a real straight shooter from Georgia and he was only a couple of years older than the rest of us. But his name fit him like a glove. Pappy had a cotton top of hair, an easy sense of humor, and he sure knew how to fly.

One day he led us north to Lingayen Gulf where we started circling the beach General MacArthur had led his army ashore in the re-taking of the Philippines during World War II. We had a real yank and banker in the flight, a guy named Lieutenant Sherman, who thought he was hot stuff. He'd rack his P-51 around real well but was not blessed with too much gray matter between the ears. Pappy was about to cool this turkey.

We were circling at 10,000 feet when Pappy ordered my element to climb to 12,000 feet and orbit while he and Sherman practiced some air-to-air. Pappy then instructed Sherman to fly eastward, following the coastline, while he did the same, only he'd be flying west. Then on his radio call they were to make 180-degree turns and come back head on for a simulated dogfight.

When Pappy radioed his command to start, Sherman racked his aircraft into a steep bank and headed east. Pappy, instead of turning west as promised, slid in tight behind hot stuff and stayed there. After a minute Pappy piped up, "OK, Red Two, turn back towards me and let's have at it."

As they approached the proposed meeting point Sherman frantically searched the clear sky for Pappy. Nothing! Pappy stayed tucked in right behind him while we all laughed at the show. After a minute of this tomfoolery Pappy pulled up on Sherman's wing and said, "OK, Red Two, I waxed you that time. Join up and we'll do it again." They did, and of course, the result was the same.

Red Four and I watched this entire occurrence with a sense of total disbelief, but we never told Sherman what happened. A few weeks later I beat Sherman in a practice dogfight, which thoroughly pissed him off. When we got back on the ground he only muttered something about not having flown much lately as he marched away.

In those days the wheels (brass) frowned on what was later called air-to-air practice. Luckily, we fighter pilots recognized the need for it—and we loved the thrill of it—so we did it anyway! This non-sanctioned training served many of us well, first in Korea, later in Vietnam.

One Sunday, while a group of us were relaxing around the Officers' Club pool, Pappy and three others were playing bridge. The squadron adjutant's wife was sitting behind Pappy where she had a view of his cards, and when Pappy and his partner contracted for a hand, she shook her head and said, "You'll never make that." Pappy didn't like this lady to begin with, and he responded with a tart "If I don't make this hand I'll do a swan dive off the high board." He didn't make it. True to his promise, he dove off the high board fully dressed. His wife stormed off into the parking lot and drove herself home, miffed at her husband because he was wearing a new pair of slacks and a sport shirt she had bought him the day before for his birthday.

One particular incident brings back fond memories of many fun-filled days playing golf at Clark. This took place during our yearly group golf tournament. Pappy, a two-time champion, was by any standard a good golfer, but it was well-known that a newcomer, Lieutenant Harry Duncan in the 44th Squadron was a longer hitter and the word on the street was that he just might be able to beat Pappy. This was not to be confused with the showdown at the OK Corral, but it was close. Pappy hustled the pilots in the 12th Squadron and collected five hundred bucks to bet on himself, then ventured into enemy territory, the 44th, and told Duncan, "My buddies are betting five hundred dollars that I'll take you in the group tournament." Duncan was convinced by his mates to accept the bet, and that was his downfall. All the guys in the 12th Squadron turned out to watch the event, yelling and carrying on in a most unsportsmanlike fashion. With the weight of having his friends' five hundred on the line, Duncan crumpled under the pressure and Pappy was once more crowned group golf champion. He proudly admitted to me later that he had won with his wits and not his brawn. "One-on-one and with just the two of us playing, that kid would thrash me every day of the week."

The Air Corps built new bachelor officers' quarters (BOQs) in the hills west of the field, and I moved into one with our squadron operations officer, Captain Don Scherer, as my roommate. Don was a great guy: slightly chubby, always smiling, and at times capable of displaying a really weird sense of humor.

Being the squadron ops officer's roommate was a good deal for me. Sometimes on a Saturday or Sunday we would go to the flight line, check the forms, find a couple of "in commission" P-51s, kick the chocks out of the way and go fly for an hour or two. There's no way you could do that in later years without reams of paperwork and a slug of maintenance personnel wanting to know what you were up to. And just try it once in today's air force. You'd shake up three higher headquarters then get your ass court-martialed.

One Saturday, as number two in a four-ship, I was flying a loose formation on Don's left wing with the sun beating down on us and the emerald islands of the Southern Philippines shimmering below. Don looked over, smiled and gave me a thumbs up. The weather was great, the scenery was beautiful and we were flying south to the island of Cebu. Numbers three and four were spread out on Don's right. We were on a cross-country mission, a rare event in the 18th Fighter Group.

As we neared Cebu I slid under Don, and three and four closed in to create a right echelon formation. Don flew an initial pattern down the lone coral strip at Cebu City airport then landed. I delayed my pitch, as Don had briefed us to spread out our landings because of the exceptionally narrow runway. He wanted only one plane on the runway at a time. A wise decision. I turned on a short final just as he was heading onto the taxiway at the far end of the runway, and when I leveled the little bird for a three-point landing, the narrowness of the runway came into full play on rollout. With the tail wheel on the ground and the long nose of my Mustang pointing skyward, my forward vision was all but non-existent. And being able to see only thirty or forty feet ahead, made me damn glad I didn't have to worry about another plane. It was difficult enough to keep my airplane straight, but with skill and cunning I managed to slow her down and taxi safely off the runway, thus making room for number three to land.

We parked our planes, held a brief discussion about the perils of flying onto such a shitty little runway, then found a taxi and headed into Cebu. We checked into a shabby, two-story wooden hotel, supposedly the town's best, and after what passed for a shower and a change into some civvies, we met in the lobby to figure out the plan for our Saturday night.

By now it was five o'clock so we agreed on finding a place where the beer was cold and the atmosphere hot. We hailed a cab and instructed the driver to take us someplace nice: a spot where the women were all gorgeous and outnumbered the men ten-to-one. His idea of such an idyllic spot turned out to differ wildly from ours. After a nail-biting drive that made flying my P-51 feel like sitting home in a rocking chair, he pulled up in front of an ancient wooden house. His instructions were for us to go around back, climb the stairs, knock on the door, then voilà, paradise!

Paradise turned out to be a dimly lit room with a grungy, pre–World War I linoleum floor, four scarred and bare tables, each with four chairs. That was the extent of the decor.

We settled on the closest, figuring on a quick getaway if the situation suddenly turned south.

Once seated, a woman sauntered over, took our order and returned shortly with our beers. She then dragged over a chair and plopped herself down uninvited.

"So, where are you fellas from?" Our hostess wore a shapeless dress, her hair was adorned with a wilted purple flower, and she stared at us through almond-shaped eyes—one brown, the other the color of spoiled milk.

"Clark Field. Came in some P-51s," I said, then took a long draw on my San Miguel beer.

Her face lit up on that piece of news. "You boys created quite the uproar this afternoon. The last time folks around here saw P-51s was during the war, and they were strafing and bombing anything that moved because the Japs were everywhere. Some actually thought we were under attack again."

"You from Cebu?" Don asked, wanting to get her mind off our scaring the shit out of the locals.

She shook her head. "Mindanao." Then she said something that broke us up. "Other women come over here to get money, then they go back home and tell their families they've landed jobs as secretaries." She grinned at the very thought of it, displaying a surprising mouthful of dazzling white teeth. "Not me," she said proudly. "No, sir, I tell my family and friends that I work in a fuck house." With that tidbit out of the way, she got up and pushed her chair back. "If you boys want to party later, just tell me, and I'll round up some of those secretaries." She left laughing at her own wicked humor.

We had already decided this wasn't where we intended to spend the night so we downed our beers, said our goodbyes, and got the hell out of there. Our driver was still out front, and after raising hell with him on his idea of what a good spot was, we told him again we wanted to go someplace nice to drink, to eat and dance with a lot of beautiful girls.

He drove us back to the main part of town and a nightclub where we indeed had a great dinner, wonderful drinks, and danced with a roomful of pretty women. This was more like it! When it was time to go, we each tried to talk a girl into making it an evening back at the hotel. Nothing doing! These girls really were secretaries!

Being close to our inn, we decided to walk, and on the way came upon a member of the local constabulary sound asleep on the curb, his carbine draped across his knees. Don decided it would be a swell idea to wake him with a firecracker. I wasn't too keen on this; I could visualize the guy coming awake and starting to shoot wildly. Well, the firecracker woke him all right, but instead of shooting us, he reached into his pocket, pulled out some firecrackers of his own, lit them, and began heaving them in our direction. We took off laughing. That was the high point of our trip to Cebu.

✈ ✈ ✈

In order to get in extra flying time I often volunteered to slow-fly P-51s when they'd had an engine overhaul. After this maintenance they needed to be flown at a low throttle setting for ten hours.

Now, any P-51 flying slow over Luzon and near Clark Field was always a sitting duck for many over-eager fighter pilots. It attracted them like honey would flies. After having several jokers make passes at me on different occasions, I devised a plan to prevent these hotshots from having too much fun at my expense. Let me explain.

When someone initiates a pass at you, the proper reaction is to push the throttle to the stop and turn up into the aggressor. But since I was not supposed to use a lot of throttle, I was prevented from doing this. So when I observed someone diving at my plane from the rear, I'd do the opposite of what was expected. I'd wait until just the right moment, then retard the throttle and dive into his attack, and since he had already built up a lot of speed, this tactic often worked. He would overshoot me and go whistling by.

On another day and while in a mock dogfight, I found myself turning the P-51 as tight as I could, yet not improving on my position. The "enemy" would gain on me slightly, or we'd stay even with each other in the turn, and no matter how tight my turn, he was always right there. Having now run out of ideas, I started diving the plane within the turn and pulling up towards my opponent, getting above his turning plane then diving back at him. Doing this I was able to slowly gain position and finally ended up on his tail. Years later the folks running the fighter school at Nellis AFB started calling this maneuver the yo-yo. Hell, I'd been yo-yoing for years; I just didn't know what it was called!

All the pilots in the 18th Fighter Group had been in the business of flying fighters since World War II, and like everything else in life, some were good, some not so good, and some barely above mediocre. This latter group had long ago lost their touch and they knew it. They would say things like, "My tight turns have really deteriorated since getting married," or, "I used to be able to do this shit!"

I would just nod and cluck in sympathy.

During these years the field had no mechanized equipment capable of clearing weeds and brush, so twice a year a special Saturday was dedicated to this task with all the company grade officers and enlisted men expected to participate.

The evening prior to this D-Day, Don brought home a bunch of machetes to sharpen, but not before stopping off at the club for beer call. It was 10:00

P.M. when he started putting blades to an electric emery wheel, and within seconds all the occupants of the BOQ were up in arms. The noise was unbearable. Didn't phase Don in the least. He simply locked our door and continued to work. For the better part of an hour I was worried that I might lose my roommate to the frenzied mob outside.

Don also liked to build model airplanes, and he had spent four months building one in particular. This beauty had a three-foot wingspan and had been painstakingly put together from hundreds of pieces of balsa wood and lacquer-coated paper. One evening his pride and joy was finally finished and he invited me to go with him to the golf course to fly it. After all the preflight preparations were complete, Don started up the engine, tinkered with a knob for a moment or two then launched it. The plane took off without a mishap and started climbing in a lazy circular pattern until it reached a couple of thousand feet. There the prevailing winds took charge and the last we saw of it, it was still climbing, heading out over the mountains to the west. Too late Don realized he had put too much gasoline into the tank. We stood helplessly watching all of those months of tedious work fly off into the setting sun.

✈ ✈ ✈

I had a superb relationship with my crew chief, Alan Shea. Alan was a staff sergeant and we both took a lot of pride in our P-51. When he'd pull an inspection, I would roll up my sleeves and pitch in to help. About the only thing he asked for in return for a job well done was an occasional loan to tide him over till payday.

When going to fly, I would always ask if the airplane was ready, and he'd always reply, "Yes, sir." Upon hearing those words I wouldn't dare pull a detailed inspection for fear of hurting his feelings.

But one day he screwed up. I had taken off on a pre-dawn training flight with Don leading, and when it came time for us to head back to Clark the sun was already up. Just prior to landing, I asked Don if I could land on his wing. He grinned, then eased his ship down to where he could eyeball under my wing.

I pressed to transmit. "Yeah, it's still there," I said, embarrassed and ticked, meaning I didn't have any airspeed indication because the pitot cover was still attached to the pitot tube. My landing was uneventful and when I taxied up to the hardstand, Sergeant Shea immediately spotted the pitot cover. He looked up at me and I could actually see tears welling in his eyes. I never said a word, because I didn't need to.

Mo Moreland was flying along one day and, with nothing better to do, decided to clean out his cockpit. He rolled the canopy back and proceeded to flip the airplane over on its back, the idea being to dump any debris that may have accumulated on the bottom of the cockpit. He did indeed rid his P-51 of a lot of dust and other bits of crud, but he also got drenched with a putrid smelling liquid. Seems someone had used the relief tube then forgot to write it up!

The rules for getting one's family into the theater were the same for the Philippines as for Japan. Men who had served a prior unaccompanied tour got to send for their families first, so, after a year's wait, Dorie and Ted finally joined me. They arrived in Manila by boat from San Francisco and I met them at the dock. We moved into a newly constructed cottage located in the hills east of the base. Dorie quickly hired a fulltime Filipino maid, and in no time at all slipped into a happy and contented life at Clark Field. Ted was now a thriving two-year-old, and a true joy for me to be around. I had missed my family.

Colonel Marion Malcom was the 18th Fighter Group Commander. The man had something wrong with his nose, which made it impossible for him to wear an oxygen mask. Since this was a required piece of equipment to fly the P-51, he didn't. And because his nose was somewhat large, the pilots took to calling him "Hose Nose."

A fighter pilot's get-together was scheduled to be held at Johnson Field in Japan and Colonel Malcom decided that he would like to attend, and to also take some pilots along with him. One cloudless autumn morning, a group of us departed the Philippines in a formation of 18 P-51s with Malcom in the lead flying a Douglas B-26.

We flew from Clark to Naha, Okinawa, fueled, and pressed on to Japan. The leg to Naha was uneventful, but the next one taking us to Itazuki, Japan, turned out to be a real thriller. According to the weather forecast at our briefing, we were told to expect clear skies, but when we approached the southern coast of the Japanese Islands, we hit a solid wall of clouds from sea level up to tops too high for us to climb over. What now?

Hose Nose radioed back to Naha for a weather update only to be told we couldn't return because of severe thunderstorms over the field. And since we didn't have any radio aids in our P-51s, we found ourselves forced into flying in close formation with, and totally dependent upon, Colonel Malcom's B-26. After circling for what seemed like an hour, we all got lined up, and headed directly into the wall of clouds. There were two P-51s on either wing of the B-26, each with flights of four following in trail, and then me. I was leading the last element which consisted of two spares. I could only see the flight directly in front of me, and found myself praying that they could hang onto the rest of the formation. We flew in this manner for an hour and twenty minutes. It seemed like two days. We were damn lucky we didn't hit any turbulence because that could have easily scattered our P-51s all over Southern Japan.

Near Itazuki, ground radar picked us up and directed us out over the water, then to a safe letdown and landing. On the ground Hose Nose was visibly elated that we all had made it, because that meant he wouldn't get fired for pulling off such a stupid stunt. I'm sure that during the latter part of the flight Malcom kept thinking about all of those P-47s that had crashed on Taiwan, costing the previous group commander his job.

It was about this time that the Air Force—which had come in existence on July 26, 1947—started renaming places like Clark Field, to Clark Air Force Base. The officer in charge became the squadron commander, and the flight leader became the flight commander.

✈ ✈ ✈

We had leaders at Clark during my tour that left a lot to be desired as COs. When Vic Walton left for the States, a Major Mack McGowan replaced him, but McGowan got himself fired after several months for not flying the airplane.

I remember one night being called out for an alert at 2:00 A.M. Ground radar had picked up something that looked like a dozen ships off the East Coast of Luzon, so we were ordered to arm our planes, hang bombs on them, and be ready to go if given the word. About this time Colonel Malcom blew into our operations room. It was obvious he'd had a few drinks. He walked over to Don Scherer who was busy assigning pilots to aircraft.

"Scherer, if my troops are going to fly, by God, I'm going to fly, too. The hell with the regs on oxygen masks, just get me into a plane."

"Yes, sir!" Don slapped Malcom's nametag up with the number of a P-51. After hanging around for a while and making a further nuisance out of himself, he disappeared, not to be seen for the rest of the night. Hose Nose never knew that the P-51 Scherer tagged for him was parked in the hangar without a propeller!

Lieutenant Colonel Hank Norman replaced Hose Nose. Norman was a West Pointer, and not a bad guy, except he soon got carried away with all the paperwork associated with running the group, and as a result he didn't get to fly much. It seemed most of our leaders flew as little as possible, unless it was to lead the group once a month in a big formation which we called a group gaggle. Unfortunately, these deskbound colonels didn't realize what effect a rusty leader had on "Ass End Charlie."

One day Colonel Norman decided he'd lead the gaggle. Three squadrons lined up, each with sixteen ships. When we were cleared for takeoff, Colonel Norman shoved his throttle full forward. Of course the torque caught him completely off guard and he ran off the runway, blowing up a huge cloud of dust. Somehow he managed to recover and continued his takeoff.

Mo was leading our squadron and had one helluva hard time joining up, because Colonel Norman, leading the lead squadron, kept making head on passes at us and railing at Mo over the radio because we weren't joining up with him!

We didn't spend all our time in the skies. On Friday nights we had beer call, an almost mandatory formation, and anyway it was always a hoot. Beer call took place at the officers' club, and all the pilots in the 12th, 44th and 67th squadrons would set up long tables, each with one end butted up to the bar. This made life easier for the harried bartenders, enabling them to pass us pitchers of free beer directly from the bar. We would spend all week deciding on which songs we'd sing, usually selecting those overtly slanderous toward the pilots in the other squadrons. Every Friday I took it upon myself to place a big sign on the blackboard.

TODAY IS FREE BEER NIGHT!

Fighter pilots love to sing, and usually bellow songs concocted by some long-dead guys from World War II, who, I'm sure, were also gassed to the gills at the time. Our repertoire would include the following:

A Poor Aviator Lay Dying

(Second World War version, traditional.
To the tune: My Bonnie Lies Over the Ocean)

◆ ◆ ◆

Take the cylinders out of my kidneys
The connecting rod out of my brain, my brain
From the small of my back get the crankshaft
And assemble the engine again.

Then there was this ever-popular little gem:

I Started Down the Runway

I started down the runway, headed for a ditch.
I looked down at my prop; My God it's in high pitch.
I pulled back on the stick; I rose into the air.
Glory, Glory, Hallelujah, how did I get there?
Oh Hallelujah, Oh Hallelujah.
Throw a nickel on the grass
Save a fighter pilot's ass.
Oh Hallelujah! Oh Hallelujah!
Throw a nickel on the grass, and you'll be saved.

◆ ◆ ◆

I flew my traffic pattern; to me it looked all right.
I made my final turn; My God I racked it tight.
The engine coughed and sputtered, the ship began to weave.
Mayday! Mayday! Colonel Malcom, spin instructions-please.
Oh Hallelujah! Oh Hallelujah!
Throw a nickel on the grass,
Save a fighter pilot's ass,
Oh Hallelujah! Oh Hallelujah!
Throw a nickel on the grass and you'll be saved.

I had the world by the tail. I was enjoying myself immensely, but I should have known that this was too good to last. And that's when the PX black cloud struck again. Clark Field needed a PX officer, so the folks in personnel screened the records and guess whose name came up? This was one of the lowest points of my career. The group was scheduled to transition into P-80s in a few months, and here I was, stuck in this miserable job. I had that damned observer and the pompous old balloon pilot back at Warner Robbins to thank for it.

I was still allowed to fly with the squadron, and one month I actually flew the P-51 more than any other pilot. The worst part of my new duty assignment was the guys all knew how I felt and kidded me unmercifully. I'd been on the job for about three months when, one night at a party, I was able to convince Colonel Norman to come to my rescue. He gave them a lieutenant who had been grounded to serve in my place and I got to go back to the squadron. In gratitude, I spread it around that Colonel Norman was a good guy in my book, and only grudgingly agreed when pressed that he maybe wasn't the best stick on the base.

Shortly after my return to the squadron, I made captain and was promoted to a flight commander's slot. My first flight was made up of eight second lieutenants, all fresh out of flying school. My immediate problem was that they'd been sent to us because we were going to be getting P-80s, and of course they'd all been trained to fly jets. But now I had to check them out in the P-51. I've long been rather proud of the fact that I accomplished this without losing any of them, or even having one of them involved in a bad incident. I shepherded this flight of brown bars around and taught them how to fly in an operational fighter squadron. And we got along great. They took to calling me "Coach" and spent huge chunks of their off-duty time at my house.

Our P-80s finally arrived by ship in late 1949, and after four long years I got my chance to fly one after they were assembled at our depot. Maintenance painted big blue lightning strips down the sides and emblazoned our names below the canopies. God, those planes sure looked great even when they were sitting idly on the ramp.

We flew our P-51s down to Manila and turned them over to the Philippine Air Force. I didn't know it at the time, but the P-51 and I would cross paths again, and in the not too distant future.

The transition to P-80s did not go as smoothly as when checking out the kids in the P-51. One day Lieutenant Lyle augered in. He'd stalled out turning final. I was the airdrome officer that day and was already on-scene as the pumper arrived to tackle the raging inferno. The firemen began spraying foam onto the tail section until I angrily directed them to "concentrate your efforts on the cockpit area, dammit!" It wouldn't have mattered though. He was already dead.

There was an ironic, but sad aftermath. The following day his wife arrived on base. Seems they had met in a bar in San Francisco and had gotten married the day his ship sailed. They had known each other all of two days. Second lieutenants do strange things at times.

Shortly before this period President Truman signed an executive order integrating blacks into the services. One day I came into operations to hear a group of pilots talking about a tall black man who was a new pilot in the squadron. Seems he had scored 30 points for us in a basketball game the previous night. This star of the hardwood turned out to be First Lieutenant Daniel "Chappie" James, an extremely personable guy who was accepted by his squadron mates with open arms. However, I later heard that his son and daughter did not fare as well. Some of the kids were giving them a hard time at the school bus stop. Captain Claude "Spud" Taylor, one of our pilots and a friend of Chappie's heard about this, and for several mornings took it upon himself to escort Chappie's children to the bus stop where he finally convinced the other kids to cool it.

✈ ✈ ✈

Even though Mo was only a captain, Colonel Norman made him our squadron commander. The brass at higher headquarters had become tired of squadron commanders who were reluctant flyers. All the guys heartily approved of Mo's new position.

Once a month it was customary to hold a parade—a carryover from our old army days. The parade ground at Clark was a large, manicured, grass field nestled between the whitewashed buildings that housed the 13th Air Force Headquarters and the 18th Fighter Wing Headquarters. A stately line of large Cape Cod houses replete with wrap-around screen porches bordered the north side. These were the homes of the base's higher-ranking officers, and it was not difficult to conjure up images of famous men such as MacArthur and Eisenhower who had lived in those homes and had marched on this very field.

For these parades we wore steel helmets, carried carbines, and actually donned web belts and canteens. For a while we had bayonets fixed to our carbines, but after one of the troops passed out from the heat and almost stabbed his buddy on his way to the ground, that accouterment quickly became a discontinued item.

This particular month, Mo was leading our squadron, and I found myself in the adjutant's position. We had to march from the squadron area—which was on the flight line up—to the headquarters area, and then onto the parade ground. We arrived early, and were standing at parade rest just prior to passing in revue when suddenly, Mo's eyes rolled upward, his knees gave way and he passed out, flopping to the ground as if he'd been shot!

Oh, shit! Don't do this to me, Lord! I looked around wildly for someone to take over. Guys behind me began to titter.

I wanted to rush to Mo's side. "You can't do this to me! I'm your buddy, remember? I don't know how to get the frigging squadron off this bloody field. Ah, Jeez, Mo!"

To my dismay a couple of burly guys with red-cross armbands came and lugged Mo off the parade ground. Passing out in the heat was such a common occurrence that the medics were well prepared for it, even to having an ambulance on standby. Well, they might have been well prepared, but I sure as shooting was not!

Then the officer in charge bellowed out, "Squadrons, ten hut!" And a couple of beats later followed-up with the command, "Pass in revue."

We started forward, huge blocks of men, all lined up by squadron, all moving together and in step, just as soldiers had done for centuries.

Now what? During training I had always been way to the rear during drills and parades, simply because I stood 5'8"; not ever being confused with one of the giants up front. And, remember, I had skipped preflight where most of this kind of military training was given, so I knew squat about leading a bunch of pilots off a parade field.

I called out, hoping someone close by would hear my plea. "What the hell do I do now?" For a millisecond I even entertained the idea of pretending to faint, but knew that would cause instant havoc on the parade ground that sunshiny day!

Then out of the blue, an answered prayer. "Just repeat after me. Say, 'right turn, now.'" It was the first sergeant riding to my rescue.

"Right turn, now!" When we arrived at the correct spot he said, "Left turn, now" and I confidently shouted out loud enough for folks in Texas to hear, "Left turn, now!"

In this manner I was able to get the squadron off the parade ground, avoiding a complete disaster. And you can believe this to be gospel when I say I thanked the top sergeant over and over from the bottom of my heart for saving me from a very embarrassing situation.

He just saluted and grinned, his face saying it all. "Think nothing of it, kid!"

✈ ✈ ✈

One day we were told the wing was going to participate in a full-blown war game exercise where C-54s from Guam would serve as attacking bombers. Our job was to defend the Philippines. Sectors were established, and we were ordered to patrol in designated areas. On the second day of the exercise, I was leading a two-ship element on a patrol near Manila Bay when I received orders to fly between two specific points for one hour. I whizzed us down to our patrol area and about twenty minutes into our mission a C-54 appeared at 12,000 feet heading right for Clark Field. With my wingman behind me, I immediately made two quick passes at the intruder, firing gun camera film on both passes. As we were preparing to make a third pass, a voice boomed over the radio on guard channel, calling Clark Field, "Clark tower, this is the captain of Pan American Airlines Flight 240. Two fighter jets are making passes at my ship and I have a team of FAA inspectors on board. Call them off."

It turned out to be a DC-4 and not a C-54! Both were similar planes, except for the markings. I'd been so engrossed in my work that I hadn't noticed this was a civilian airliner. Damn!

I didn't wait for Clark to respond. I flew out of there like a hound dog that had had turpentine rubbed on his nuts. I returned to base and landed with my heart in my mouth.

The upshot was the commander had the Wing Inspector General (IG) investigate the incident. A lieutenant colonel took the camera film from my airplane. I told him the complete truth about what had happened and began sweating out the court marshal I just knew was about to be convened.

Time passed and nothing happened. I finally concluded that the wing staff decided that since it had not been a deliberate act, and since I had told the investigating officer the complete truth, a decision was made on high to squash the whole affair. No one had been hurt and no property had been damaged. But it scared the hell out of me for a very long time.

While at Clark, I both managed our softball team and played third base. Mo was shortstop, and Chappie covered first. There was another lieutenant— a man named Stark, who was far better at first base, but Chappie's overwhelming personality helped the team's spirit so much, that I kept him in the lineup. We also had an airman in center field who was a real thumper with the bat, so we were undefeated at season's end and would have been the base champs.

Then life changed. In the pre-dawn hours of June 25, 1950, North Korean artillery and mortars opened fire on Republic of Korea army outposts just south of the 38th Parallel. The Korean War had officially begun, and we soon found ourselves in an all-together new ball game where the rules were different and we played for keeps.

8

The Police Action

Two days later Mo gave us the word we were expecting: we were going to Korea. He also said we were supposed to be volunteers, so that prompted some shuffling and scuffling among the guys in the 12th, 44th and 67th Squadrons. Technically, I suppose, we were volunteers because any of us could have gotten out of it if we had really wanted to.

There's an old saying in the military: "Never volunteer for anything." But in this instance I was eager to go. As I mentioned earlier, I hadn't served in combat in World War II so I sure didn't want to miss out on this one. And let's not kid ourselves. I wasn't elbowing my way to be first in line because I was a super patriot. Hell no, it was more about being around when my buddies would be telling war stories and my being able to belly up to the bar next to the best of them and spin a few tales of my own. And I felt that since I was being paid to be a fighter pilot, then I ought to do some fighting.

We coined a name, the Foxy Few, for ourselves so naturally, original thinkers that we were, our logo's mascot had to be a Reynard. We dressed our good-luck vulpine up as a baseball pitcher and irreverently had him tossing a whiskey bottle. We were indeed a jubilant bunch and more than a tad cocky. Slapping each other on the shoulders we pronounced that this skirmish would be over in less than two weeks! Hot damn! Were we ever in for a surprise.

The plan called for us to fly P-51s again because the brass considered them better suited than jets for operating in the hilly terrain of Korea. Wisdom held that the mustang boasted more range at lower altitude, which also translated to mean longer loiter time over the target, but more important we were able to fly off of dirt strips.

I could not have been more prepared. I had beaucoup hours in the plane and I knew I was damn good at dive-bombing, rocket firing and strafing.

In high school my most ardent desire had been to play football and I would have given anything to be the star halfback, but alas, due to my size, or lack thereof, it was not to be. But now I had finally found something I could do well: something where size didn't matter.

We boarded a C-54 and headed out for Ashya, Japan. Upon arrival, we found ourselves without planes. Earlier, the squadron had sent an advance party to K-2 (Taegu) to join forces with a small group of Americans who had been training South Korean pilots, so we now joined up with them. Although the South Korean pilots had flown Japanese Zeros during World War II, they had been away from the flying game way too long, and certainly no one could compare a high-performance P-51 to a Zero. This meant the entire experiment had turned out to be a world-class loser. Several of the Korean pilots had crashed; the Americans had given up on them and were now flying the missions themselves.

The advanced detachment at K-2 was first referred to as "Dallas," for reasons known only to the headquarters guys, but upon our arrival the name was changed to the 51st Provisional Squadron and Mo was still our commander. We launched 426 combat sorties from K-2 in July of 1950, and many times we found ourselves pulled off a hot target to stand orbit duty, circling and waiting for a flight of F-80s to make a couple of fast strafing passes then beat it back to Itazuke because they were low on fuel.

At that time there were no navigational aids in Korea: no homers, no DFs, no radar, no instrument procedures, no nothing! Standard procedure—when the weather turned bad, which was often—was to fly to Japan where ground radar could give us a steer. The only alternative left in our bag of tricks was to fly out over the water, let down, and hope to break out of the clouds before hitting something.

✈ ✈ ✈

As I mentioned, we were certain the skirmish would end quickly, but it wasn't long before we learned the real facts of life. The communists proved to be a sneaky lot; they moved and fought at night then hid themselves and their equipment come daylight, making it damn difficult for us to search, find, and then destroy them.

As soon as I came to the conclusion that this war was not going to fizzle out as I had originally thought, I reluctantly decided it would be best if Dorie and Ted returned to the States. The tactical situation on the Korean peninsula had fast turned extremely unstable and, frankly, no one knew what was going to happen next. My fear now was that the war could quickly spread to the Philippines, and my family could fall into enemy hands. I wrote Dorie and told her to pack up and head home. She didn't argue, and left a couple of weeks later, along with most of the other wives and children. I didn't know it at the time, but like MacArthur, I, too, would eventually return to the Philippines.

Clustered around the dirt strip at K-2 there were the remnants of World War II buildings: all battle damaged, all uninhabitable. Twelve-man squad tents were used to shelter our operations, maintenance, billeting, and messing, and we erected most of them ourselves. One night during a violent storm the tent next to ours blew down onto its startled occupants, proving that good fighter pilots ain't necessarily good tent erectors!

Mo had divided the squadron's pilots into two sections. Captain Jerome "Jerry" Mau headed one and I headed the other. We rotated the flying assignments with one section flying mornings, the other in the afternoons.

One morning I hustled over to operations about an hour after sunrise just as the Frag Order (fragmentation operations order spelling out the mission for the day) came in over an ancient crank-operated telephone from the command post in Taegu. I was taken aback to read how a short time earlier the North Koreans had attacked and surrounded the 24th Army Division, just south of Taejon. The message went on to say that thirteen carloads of arms and ammunition had been abandoned in the railway yard and ended with the cryptic command: "Destroy at all cost."

With Mo leading, we took off as a two-ship flight and headed for Taejon, following the railroad tracks. The weather went from lousy, to lousier, to downright nasty, and still the scud kept forcing us lower and lower. By the time we were down to hugging the deck Mo concluded this was not the answer and that the only way we were going to make it to the target was to get on top of the mess. With me tucked in tight on his wing, we headed upstairs and broke into the clear at about 8,000 feet. Mo then flew a basic time and distance run, and we made our letdown into the Kum-Gang Valley.

We had no idea what we could expect to find but luck was with us because we broke out over the target at 2,000 feet, and there they were: thirteen railroad cars in the marshalling yard just as described in the frag order. We proceeded to methodically strafe and firebomb all thirteen. I was chary, worried about getting my butt blown out of the sky due to the force of some wicked explosion, but we got some good fierce fires started and only lingered long enough to confirm the beginning of a series of detonations before heading out for home.

Now we had to get back to K-2. Mo re-worked the time-distance problem again and upon our arrival over Taegu we found a small hole which we dove through and landed. Mission accomplished. I felt great!

On another occasion the squadron got a call to fly a night patrol mission over the bridge at Seoul which had been knocked out earlier, but one which the commies had rigged up a pontoon bridge beside and were now moving supplies across the river. 7th Air Force Headquarters wanted us on hand to harass them the moment they turned on their lights to start bringing their stuff across, which meant keeping a P-51 over the area during the entire period of darkness. Mo immediately scheduled himself for one of the flights and asked for volunteers to fill the other five slots. I remember William "Bill" Slater volunteered for one, and four of the squadron pilots quickly filled the others. I was dog-tired and bowed out. Later, I felt bad about it. Mo and I were good friends, and tired or not, I should have backed him by example. It was a hard lesson well learned.

When the North Korean Army finally got to within seven miles of Taegu we could easily hear the crump of their exploding artillery. I felt like an actor in a war movie—it was weird, and when I'd fly missions late in the evening I could see hordes of refugees, dressed mostly in white, crossing the Naktong River.

I was flying one evening just before dusk when the FAC (Forward Air Controller) ordered me to strafe a column.

I peered down and got on the radio. "Negative, negative. Those are civilians down there. They're dressed in white."

The FAC replied immediately. "Listen up, pal, the order is to strafe them. There's a ton of North Korean troops mixed in with that lot and they'll pulverize the hell out of our guys tonight if you don't."

Knowing that our troops were greatly outnumbered yet valiantly trying to hold back the North Koreans, I obeyed.

That was the night I was introduced to the very ugly side of war.

We were flying so many sorties and flying them so fast that the maintenance and armament crews were having a problem turning our planes around. One afternoon when my section was on duty, I devised a plan whereby my pilots would remain in their planes, taxi from the refueling point to where they were to be armed then they'd move down the line as various types of armaments were attached to their ships. The guys in the squadron began referring to the procedure as production line armament, and it worked so well that other flights from Itazuki and Ashya began landing at Taegu to refuel, re-arm and fly another mission on the way back to their bases. Moe told me later that the wheels gave the armament officer a Bronze Star for implementing such an ingenious setup.

I felt a little pissed at not being singled out for the credit, but I quickly got over it. What the hell, sometimes, that's just the way the ball bounces.

The rest of the squadron joined us in the last week of July when we reclaimed our official identity as the 12th Fighter-Bomber Squadron. Major Robert "Bob" Dow took over command from Mo, which in my book was a giant step backward. Mo was a much better combat leader. However, his talents did not go unrecognized because he was rewarded with a spot promotion to major a short time later.

Along with the squadron came the camp followers: the group's desk jockeys and the wing's-ground pounding weenies, which included the wing commander who thought it was a wonderful idea to blow reveille by opening up on the anti-aircraft guns, instead of sounding off on a frigging bugle! I kid you not. And trust me when I write this: you'll roll out of bed in one hell of a hurry when two quad-forty millimeters start firing ten yards from your tent!

Major General Earle Partridge was the 5th Air Force commander, and had his executive B-17 parked near us on the ramp. The guys often joked among themselves, "When that B-17 leaves, we're jumping into our P-51s and hauling ass for Itazuke."

Well, when the enemy's bombing line got to within seven miles of K-2 we were ordered into our planes and sent packing to Ashya, Japan. We later found out Partridge had bugged out several days earlier but had purposely left his B-17 tied down at K-2 for "morale purposes."

The commies never took K-2, but they came damn close.

At Ashya I met Daniel "Danny" Farr and Ted "Mother" Baader, who both became friends. They were bunking in the BOQ room next to mine, and that first afternoon, at about four (close enough to bar time) I was with them having a drink when Danny decided he needed something from his footlocker, but try as he might, he couldn't find the key. He went into the hall and began pounding on several nearby doors, yelling out that he needed a screwdriver or something to pry off a lock. No one offered to help, so he came back, dragged the footlocker out onto the porch, cocked his .45 pistol and blasted the offending lock. Moments later a second lieutenant rushed in yelling, "Christ Almighty, are you frigging mad? Here's a screwdriver!" This little caper all happened within the first few hours of my meeting Danny Farr, and I soon came to understand that this was not particularly unusual behavior. The man not only acted wild, he looked the part, too.

Danny stood six-foot-three and weighed in at two hundred-twenty pounds. He sported a headful of flaming red hair, lots of freckles, and a raspy voice that came at you from deep within his chest. He was undoubtedly the most colorful character I met during my entire career. Danny had graduated from West Point yet all that discipline stuff had zero effect on his way of doing things. And he wore a Bancroft Flighter with his flying suit. (A Bancroft Flighter was an officer's hat with a flexible bill, a popular item with World War II pilots because it could be folded up for storage, or crushed down so that earphones could sit snuggly over it.) But Danny was different. He wore his Flighter with its flexible bill turned up like a baseball catcher's.

I led Danny on his first combat mission, an uneventful two-ship flight. Afterwards, walking back to ops he asked, "So, Scrappy, how did I do?"

I answered truthfully. "You did fine except your formation flying is a little sloppy."

He wore a momentary hurt look then said, "I didn't think it was all that bad considering the amount of time I have in the P-51."

I stopped on the tarmac mid-stride. "What are you telling me, Danny? I thought all you guys who came over on the Boxer had lots of P-51 time. Could I be wrong about such an inconsequential, petty detail?"

He grinned. "Well, Sport, I didn't, I just told them I did! Remember when you saw me ferry that airplane over here from Japan last week? That was the first time I ever flew a P-51. One of my buddies had to show me how to start it."

I began walking again. "You're crazier than I thought," I said, then began to laugh at the sheer balls of it all.

✈ ✈ ✈

That same month I reconstituted my flight which now included Mother Baader, Spud Taylor, Chappie James and me. We named ourselves "The Ferocious Four." I was lead—not just by dint of rank—but because of my experience and all those sneaky tricks I'd learned from Pappy Hood back in the Philippines.

We four flew over 60 missions together. Ours was a flight of nicknames: Scrappy, Chappie, Mother, and Spud. Baader got the name Mother because whenever he'd have more than one drink he'd love to say in a most disapproving way, "Mother wouldn't like this." I suspected the name was pinned on him by Danny Farr.

"The Ferocious Four" and some friends around a P-51 at Pusan AFB in Korea, 1950. (L to R) Cpt. Mickelwaite, Cpt. Denmam, Cpt. Daniel "Chappie" James, Scrappy, Ted "Mother" Baader, Unknown officer. (Seated) Cpt. Claude "Spud" Taylor (courtesy of USAF).

✈ ✈ ✈

The North Koreans had very little by way of an air force—mainly a few Russian Yaks, a plane kind of similar to our P-51. But when one compared both countries' pilots, similarities ended. Hell, it wasn't even close. Any Yak sighted by an American was shot down. Period. And if you were lucky enough to spot one you had better not announce it on the radio or you'd have thirty U.S. planes racing to beat you to it. My flight was not lucky enough to ever sight one, but I guarantee you that if we had, we'd have quickly downed the SOB.

No North Korean aircraft ever dared to attack K-2, but just in case someone might decide to venture south on such a suicide mission, we always had a two-ship flight take-off at dawn then proceed to fly cover over the base.

One morning it was Mother and I taking our turn. After we had patrolled for the required one hour after sunup, I instructed Mother to fly east while I flew west. About a minute later I told him to turn back and meet me head on for a little air-to-air. Mother had come to us from flying jets in the States and had a pretty cocky attitude, exactly what's wanted in a fighter pilot. After I waxed him two out of two, the man grew more respectful for his flight commander.

I had trained the Ferocious Four never to follow in trail when strafing a target. And we always made our passes from different points of the compass. It was a good tactic. One day we were strafing a target near Pohang (K-3) in this fashion and I was on my last pass when a P-51 flashed in front of me at about a 90 degree angle. I didn't think much of it until I was joining up the flight and discovered that Red Four (Chappie) was missing. Christ, say it isn't so! I thought, my mind conjuring up the worst. We headed for K-2 to refuel before returning to base, and all the way there I had a sinking feeling that I had shot Chappie down.

After landing, and during the after-mission de-briefing, we were told that Four had landed ahead of us.

"Where is he?" I wanted to know.

"Sacked out in a tent in area two," the de-briefing officer replied.

With huge sighs of relief the three of us raced over there, rousted Chappie out of bed and gave him holy, bloody hell!

Seems our buddy had in fact used his head and had flown home ahead of us because his radio had gone out and he had no way of letting the rest of us know about his problem.

✈ ✈ ✈

One day we were bombing and strafing near Taejon when an enemy tank came out of a bomb-damaged building and sped off northward in a cloud of dust toward Suwan. We'd already dropped all our bombs so we took turns strafing it, but after several passes the crew must have grown weary of all those .50 caliber rounds bouncing off their tank so they pulled up under a small railway trestle, popped the hatch and abandoned ship. We continued to strafe and soon started a fire. Moments later its fuel started to burn, then its ammo ignited and exploded, sending huge chunks of tank flying in every direction and bringing down the trestle in the process.

Another favorite tactic of the commies was to drive their tanks inside buildings, then park. (Hell, the buildings weren't theirs so what did they care?) And they would drive right through a wall if that's what it took to hide from us. I saw several instances of this when I was flying as a FAC, and once I watched as a crew blindly backed their tank out of a building. Why they decided to do so at that particular moment, I couldn't even guess. They were perfectly hidden and would have been safe if they had stayed put. I had our guys hose them. Scratch one more Russian tank!

On another mission, in a town on the eastern side of South Korea (enemy-occupied then), I spotted several camouflaged vehicles parked behind a large building which looked like it could have been the city hall. Four large columns stood in front, and strung high up was a huge banner with Joe

Stalin's mug painted on it. I decided it was probably now being used as a military command post or a headquarters of some sort, so after making several strafing passes at the vehicles, I made one last run and killed old Uncle Joe Stalin with my fifties! God, let me tell you, waxing that son of a bitch sure felt good!

One morning while flying a recce mission, I had us up at 3000 feet and east of the perimeter when I spotted a commie artillery unit in a shallow river directly below. They had managed to place themselves high and dry on a sandbar and had their six artillery pieces all lined up in perfect formation from which they were pouring accurate fire onto our troops.

I was lead in the four-ship with each of us carrying two napalm bombs. We came around fast, and swhoooooosh, we dropped our napalm from tree-top level. But, as happened lots of times in those early days, the damn fuses didn't work. Oh sure, our drops were all bull's-eyes and all the gun crews were soaked in napalm but the stuff didn't ignite. Those soldiers must have been heaving great sighs of relief at finding themselves still alive, but their reprieve was sure short lived because on the next pass we strafed the area and the incendiaries in our API (armor piercing/incendiary) ammunition set off the jellied mess. The entire vicinity burst into flames, swallowing everything and everyone into a huge orange and yellow fireball.

For the most part, our pilots flew and, sadly, in some cases, died with honor. A solid example of what I speak was one Major "Lou" Sebille of the 67th Squadron in our 18th Group. Lou was killed by deliberately flying his crippled plane into an enemy gun emplacement, and in the process saving countless American lives. For this selfless act of heroism Major Sebille was awarded the Medal of Honor.

However, there's another incident which still remains fresh in my mind these many decades later. One day while on the way home from a mission, a pilot from another group was hit bigtime in a ferocious, and totally unexpected burst of ground fire. The guy lost it, and began screaming into his radio, "I'm hit, oh Jesus, I'm going down, I'm hit, I'm going to crash and I can't get out!"

Another pilot got on the radio and said in a disgusted voice, "Shut up, fella, and die like a man."

When I first began flying in Korea I was under the impression that there just wasn't much ground fire. My attitude changed real fast late one evening when suddenly, for the first time, I could really see it. It was slowly getting dark. We were strafing a position in a small town north of Taegu when I spotted withering machine gun fire pouring out of the window of a chewed-up stone house, and the son of a bitch's tracer rounds told me he was firing at Mother! As fate would have it, I was in a perfect position and all I had to do was lower my nose and let him have it right down the chute with all six of my .50 calibers. Not only did I wipe the bastard out, but several explosions erupted from the house telling me that he had a fair-sized arsenal stashed away in there with him. Had it not been near dark, I would never have seen the gunfire. And I've often wondered: what would have happened to good old Mother if I hadn't?

By now I'd flown 60 missions, and had been at it daily from dawn to oftentimes well after dusk. The tempo was getting to me and I was constantly tired. I was also becoming snappish. Mo noticed, and made a command decision.

"Scrappy, I want you to take a few days R&R and that's an order."

I didn't argue with the boss. Bill Slater and I had flown about the same number of missions, so Mo told him to go with me. Good deal! I told Bill about the Gora Hotel in the mountains in Japan, and filled him in on what a super time I had spent there. Bill didn't need much persuading, so off we went.

The Gora was a world-class hotel and home to a beautifully manicured rooftop garden—a true work of living art sculpted from exotic plants and shrubs which were surrounded by intricate, patterned pebbled areas, and several small, gurgling fountains. Benches were strategically placed about for hotel guests to sit and contemplate undisturbed in this little corner of paradise. We found ourselves up there nosing around when two ladies about our age got off the elevator and began oohing and aahing in hushed tones at the beauty of the place. Both were way above average in looks, so we worked our way over in their direction. The short version of what followed is they agreed to rendezvous with us in the bar for drinks at 5:30 P.M.

We met on time, and after two rounds of martinis the newly acquainted and happy foursome dined under candlelight and in the hands of attentive, white-gloved waiters. Things went smashingly, and at midnight I found myself upstairs sharing a room with a woman named Wanda and not a pilot named Bill. Wanda was a Texan: a slender brunette beauty with legs that seemed to go up and up forever. And to paraphrase Yogi Berra: this was déjà vu all over again, except this was not room 305.

But things did not go well between the sheets that night and not for a lack of my giving it my all.

The next morning at breakfast I gulped down two cups of coffee before leaning toward the middle of the table and asking Bill how his night went.

"Great!" He waggled his eyebrows and grinned like a frat boy back from his first foray into Tijuana.

But when I recounted my tale of woe he came back with the strangest remark. "Then consider yourself damn lucky."

"What the hell do you mean?" I sure didn't feel lucky.

"Scrappy, Sheila told me the reason they're here at the Gora. Seems Wanda's husband had been screwing around with their Japanese house girl and got a real bad case of the clap. Well, guess what?" Bill leaned way back in his chair, stared at me, then shot forward until he was leaning inches from my nose. "Yeah, I can tell by the look on your face that you've already figured it out. He gave it to Wanda. End of story. She's now waiting for a sailing date back to the States, but meantime, she and Sheila came up here to get away from it all. Of course Wanda told her husband the marriage is over, but the woman obviously was not about to pass on to you his little gift which we both know tends to keep on giving and giving until it's cleared with penicillin. So, yeah, you are indeed damn lucky. That Wanda did right by you, pal."

It was a long, sobering trip for me back to K-9.

✈ ✈ ✈

After being chased from K-2, we flew out of Ashya for about a month, then the whole group, along with the 12th and 67th squadrons, moved over to K-9, near Pusan where we stayed put for two months. The United Nations had built a hospital about a mile down the road, and it boasted having a small social club attached for staff and guests to unwind. Most nights it was possible to catch sight of an American nurse or two, so the place was usually packed with horny pilots on the prowl.

One night, with none of Miss Nightingale's protégées in sight and the prospects of meeting any turning dimmer by the minute, Mother Baader started slugging down his drinks and soon began looking around the room, spoiling for a fight. He zeroed in on a likely target, then proceeded to get into a heated argument with a marine major who was loudly declaiming that Air Force jet jockeys didn't know jack-shit about flying close air support. This crap did not sit well with any of us since we had been fighting the war from the start, and to our way of thinking the marines were a bunch of Johnny-come-latelys. Mother Baader was ready to pound some sense into, and shit out of, Major Loudmouth, but our cooler heads prevailed and we hustled him out of the club before things turned ugly and the MPs were called to arrest us all. When he told us a couple of minutes later in the parking lot that the major was not a pilot and not even an infantryman but a public relations puke, we almost let Mother loose to go back in and hammer the guy into the dirt!

As we drove back to our base, the subject turned to the merits of the Colt single action .45 that I had in a shoulder holster. I had carried this piece every waking moment since the start of the war, and I wore it in a quick-draw, spring-loaded holster that Mother's brother had sent him from Chicago, and that he in turn had given to me. As we bounced along, Chappie threw down a giant-sized gauntlet from the driver's seat.

"Hey, Scrappy, you've been carrying that hunk of iron all this time and I'll bet anyone here a bottle of Jack Daniel's Old No. 7 that the sucker won't even shoot!"

That was all the goading the others needed. They began razzing me, daring me to prove Chappie wrong while pretending to place their bets, fast and furious. Since we were riding in an open weapon's carrier and were passing through an unpopulated area, I decided, what the hell. I drew my Colt, pointed it skyward and squeezed off three fast rounds. Bam! Bam! Bam! It sounded like a frigging cannon going off next to my ear!

The laughter that followed quickly subsided when we realized we had just passed in front of 5th Air Force Headquarters. Oooh shit! Chappie floored the accelerator and we rocketed forward. Luckily, no one came out to see if this was the start of some big commie offensive!

And that obnoxious, piss-ant major may well have been the literary genius behind the front page story that appeared in the Stars and Stripes only hours later trumpeting the First Marine Division's landing at Pusan. The million-point headline screamed for all the world to see: "Marines Land At Pusan: Drive 25 Miles Into The Enemy's Lines." I'm told President Truman read this back in Washington and was heard to remark that the marines seemed to have a better propaganda minister than had his nemesis, the late, not so great, Herr Hitler. That statement was bang-on the mark, but I heard he later retracted it. And the next day the jarheads were pushed back most of those 25 miles so fast that they had to abandon much of their equipment and all of their vehicles in the process. No follow-on headlines ever appeared about that little embarrassment in the Stars and Stripes.

Now don't get the idea that I want to piss off any marines at this point in my life; I sure as hell don't, but I can still vividly remember those brave army kids in Korea. Though badly outnumbered from day one, they had all fought like hell and had held the Pusan Perimeter when it really counted. So this crap about the marines from their PR machine did not sit well with any of us flyers.

One day I found myself leading an element with Lieutenant Harlan Ball on my wing. We were ordered to hightail it to a road northeast of K-2 where we were told to destroy nine trucks that some of our boys had been forced to abandon. We were able to get eight of them burning almost immediately, but the last one refused to ignite. We strafed it again and again, but still no luck. I took stock of our situation. We each still had two five-inch rockets, so as a last resort I got into a good position and launched one. That missile flew right into the cab through an open side window and blew the hell out of it. My William Tell accuracy demonstration impressed young Harlan no end, but I never confessed to him that it was a one-in-a-million lucky shot. Let the man think I was shit-hot. Do him good to have a little respect for his elders!

At K-9 we found ourselves reduced to sleeping in squad tents again, but at least these ones had wooden floors and reinforced sides. Good thing, because it was now well into fall, and getting colder by the night. We used oil-burning stoves to heat these tents, but the downside was the fuel tanks were stored outside and held only enough juice to last until about three in the morning. Definitely not good, because this meant someone had to get up, get dressed, go outside and fill them. Many a night we would all lie in our cots and have a twelve-man debate about which one of us was going to freeze his butt off outside to get the heater going again. We'd carry on like a bunch of spoiled brats at some snooty summer camp, except we had no adult counselor to force one of us outside to perform the dirty deed. So most nights we suffered together, each holding his ground, all counting the hours until sunup. What a bunch of hardheaded idiots we were!

Crazy as it sounds to the uninitiated, I never knew what my target was going to be on any given day. Sometimes I would patrol the railroad which ran down the western side of South Korea, each time hoping to luck out and come across a train to either bomb or strafe. I well remember some of those recce missions where if I couldn't find a train, I would strafe the water towers out of frustration, or go down real low and blow off some rounds just to mess up the tracks. One day I hit the tracks with two five-inch rockets, did a fair amount of damage, then flew off northward for an hour looking for any and all targets of opportunity. Zip. Nada. When I flew back, the North Koreans had already repaired the tracks and were nowhere to be seen. This left me with an almost overwhelming feeling of futility, but after thinking about it as I cruised on home, I concluded that I at least had made them work their scrawny commie asses off for an hour.

On another day, with Mother on my wing, I spotted smoke billowing out of a tunnel. It was pretty obvious there was a train hiding in there—standard operating procedure for the enemy when our planes were spotted in the area. The crews thought they were safe, and they usually were, but this day we fooled them. I positioned us so that I could skip a napalm tank right into one end of the tunnel while Mother slammed one into the other. Both drops actually ignited, hallelujah! And you just know the conflagration we created sucked all of the oxygen out of that tunnel in no time flat. I imagine that also made breathing more than just a little difficult for any occupants inside.

✈ ✈ ✈

The bosses made sure we always kept a two-ship flight on alert so that if something "hot" came up, we could react in a hurry. One morning Mother and I were pulling the duty when we were told to take-off and fly to the assistance of an army division that had been stopped by a roadblock about 50 miles to the northwest. Our only problem was the shitty weather: the ceiling was less than 1000 feet and the visibility worse than bad.

After take-off we flew west in a riverbed for about 20 miles, then the weather began to improve slightly. We found the division and made contact with their air controller. They had about forty trucks lined bumper-to-bumper with the lead stopped just around a bend in the road. A small village lay less than half a mile away and already there were machine gunners firing from a couple of the houses on its outskirts. Those unlucky bastards were about to meet their maker.

Mother and I flew in, made several strafing passes and silenced their guns. We then flew back and made a couple of victory rolls over the column of trucks, got a big thank you from the controller and plenty of waves from the troops. We headed home, feeling good, knowing we had made a difference that day. Luckily, the fog had lifted minutes earlier and we made an uneventful touchdown. I was not eager to test the alternative, which would have called for us to fly out over the water, let down, and pray we could find our way back to Pusan. On nasty-weather days like that one, we sure did earn our flight pay.

✈ ✈ ✈

The week before General MacArthur's famous landing at Inchon, an intelligence officer told me all about the upcoming big show at an early morning flight briefing. This moron included the date, the time, the place; I mean he laid out the whole frigging plan for me! I flew several missions with this potentially compromising knowledge strapped under my helmet, and I'm here to write that I was not a happy pilot until after MacArthur did his thing. I never did learn how this dumbass intel officer had gained access to such information, or more importantly, how he had managed to get a security clearance in the first place!

Anyway, the landing was a huge success and the troops coming ashore cut off the commies around the Pusan Perimeter, forcing them to make a mad dash north and the sanctuary of the Yalu River which separated Korea from China. The ensuing rout provided us with lots of daytime targets, and for the first time in the war the enemy did not have the prerogative of only moving at night. The Ferocious Four got its licks in bigtime. Now, it would have suited me fine to have kept on flying all day, every day during this target-rich period, but instead, I was ordered to forward air controller duty with a South Korean mechanized division. I was steamed!

Our operations officer was a wimp who couldn't make the hard decisions, so he had selected me for the tour by holding a make-believe lottery. Cards with all the squadron's pilots' names on them were placed in a hat and he drew mine, making me the "winner." Mo would never have allowed this shit. He would have felt that drawing cards for an assignment such as this was passing the buck, or, said differently, a classic example of shirking one's responsibility.

By this time I had already flown 83 missions, and since the squadron was only tasked to supply one FAC per month, had I not been chosen that particular time, I would have flown a hundred missions before our next quota came down. Not an important milestone at the time, but it would prove to be a very defining one a little later.

I was issued a jeep and drove out of Taegu, arriving at the ROK (Republic of Korea) Corps headquarters the next day. On the way I saw two smoldering commie tanks lying on their sides in a ravine by a turn in the road, their crewmembers in shredded pieces among the wreckage. I found out later that on the previous night the South Koreans had set a trap. They knew these particular tanks had been by-passed in the big push north, so they placed a 75-MM gun at a curve in the road and when the commies trundled into view, they fired point-blank at them from about 50 meters. Back home we would have called it a Kentucky Turkey Shoot!

My particular ROK Division did not enjoy a high priority with the folks at 5th Air Force when it came to air strikes so I didn't do a hell of a lot of controlling during my tour. But, to be honest, as we pushed our way north we had little need for air strikes because enemy opposition was extremely light. We were moving at a fast clip—better than twenty miles a day—and the South Koreans were being led by a no-nonsense U.S. Army lieutenant colonel and not their nominal commander, a ROK two-star with no battlefield experience.

There must have been a God in his heaven looking out for me because I was replaced as FAC just before the Chinese entered the war. My replacement bought the farm when this ROK division, and several others, collapsed under a ferocious Chinese onslaught. The date was November 25, 1950.

And I came home to hear of some really devastating news. While I was away Spud had gotten shot down leading the flight on a mission. Chappie took over command and set up an immediate rescap by orbiting overhead along with his remaining two ships, then got on the horn for a rescue chopper. Hoping to lead the rescue team in, Chappie peeled off and made a dash for the chopper base in the interest of saving precious minutes, but while en route his request for help was denied. Chappie couldn't believe his ears! "Repeat," he had angrily demanded, only to be told all choppers were being held on ground-alert because General MacArthur was making a flying inspection over the battlefield. Seems that if he should be shot down, they all would be scrambled to save Dugout Doug's ass!

Chappie was not about to take that as a final answer. He went so far as to land at the base and plead with the brass to get Spud out. Couldn't and wouldn't, they said, their orders were to stay on the ground until released by higher headquarters, and that's what they intended to do. Obey their orders.

Time and fuel finally ran out and the two-ship element had to break-off and fly home in the gathering darkness, in essence, abandoning Spud to a certain fate.

Spud was found dead the next day less than a quarter of a mile where he had landed, his bullet-ridden body retrieved by one of those grounded helicopter crews. We all knew the North Koreans did not take pilots as prisoners. And I really doubt that MacArthur knew anything about the order to keep the choppers on the ground while he was in the area. A good man was lost that day, and Chappie was beyond devastated. Mother told me how a couple of nights later he had sung an emotional, heart-rending version of "My Buddy" to a packed house in the Officers Club. Many an eye turned to water that night in tribute to a fallen friend.

I quickly flew five more missions. Meanwhile, Chappie was transferred to K-2 (Taegu) to fly a combat cameraman around the war zone in a T-33. It was the commander's way of giving him a break from flying combat missions for a while; the man had lost a big slug of his confidence after seeing Spud shot down and, wrongly, Chappie was blaming himself for not having done enough for his friend. It would take Chappie a long time to get over his grief.

With Spud and Chappie now gone, Mother and I were the only ones left of the Ferocious Four. Life was just not the same.

The group had established an informal rotation system among the pilots in Korea and the guys back at Clark Field, so when my number came up and I was offered the opportunity to rotate, I readily accepted. At that time no official combat duty tour had been announced for pilots, the weather was getting to be miserably cold, those squad tents were less than insulated and I had lost a fair-sized chunk of my enthusiasm for this frustrating war. But my accepting that rotation offer turned out to be a bad decision because I was rotated with 87 missions under my belt. Shortly thereafter, the 100-mission tour was announced. I could have finished that magic number in a just couple more weeks and gone home, for good, but what the hell, it wasn't in the cards—at least in the hand that I'd been dealt!

I quickly flew five more missions. Meanwhile, Chappie was transferred to K-2 (Taegu) to fly a combat cameraman around the war zone in a T-33. It

Many caustic—but often warranted—remarks were made about those crewmembers who didn't pull their weight or know their jobs and, unfortunately, my squadron had its share of these Artful Dodgers. I ran into one such turkey on my last mission.

It was a pre-dawn take-off, and Captain Charles "Chuck" Hauver was running this particular show. He had been tagged to take over my flight, so I had transferred all the responsibility onto his shoulders and had spent a relaxing evening at the Officers' Club—two squad tents cobbled together by the engineers—and had downed more than just a few bourbons and soda. I can say it now. I was shit-faced when I finally stumbled into my bed shortly before midnight.

Ours was a five-hour mission with a pre-dawn takeoff, and the plan called for us to go all the way north to the Yalu River. And because we were carrying external fuel tanks to give us extra-long legs for the trip, it called for a guns-only armament package. I was really hungover, causing me to fumble-fart around with clumsy hands on the various switches during taxing out. Somehow I managed to pop my liquid engine coolant. Ah, shit! What else could I screw up? Embarrassed, I called Chuck who was already airborne and told him to go on ahead without me.

He didn't know just how bad I was. "That's okay, Scrappy, get another plane, we'll wait for you." After all it was to be a five hour mission so what did another ten minutes matter?

It turned out to be one very long, very agonizing flight. And it got longer as the previous night's festivities wore off. I wanted to curl up and die. I was flying the number three position; the number two slot was being manned by a first lieutenant airhead who couldn't fly worth a tinker's damn.

When the flight finally arrived in the reconnaissance area, we found it hazy as hell, making it impossible to find any targets. Then the visibility managed to go from bad to worse, so much so that I found myself tucking in closer and closer to number two. Big, stupid mistake on my part because within moments the idiot lost the leader. Now Chuck was alone, and definitely not a happy warrior, while his number two is now leading me and his number four to God knows where. I'm pissed, I'm nauseous and I'm fighting a losing battle with a force-ten hangover. Why me? Why now? After a few minutes of aimless circling, I had had enough of this foolishness so I took the lead from two, found Chuck, who quickly formed us up again into a proper flight. But by now he was so thoroughly disgusted at his number two that he scrubbed the mission and led us home.

That was my swan song in Korea. Good thing or I'd have throttled that air headed idiot right on the tarmac as soon as he'd gotten out of his plane!

9

Back to the Philippines

Two days after that screwed-up mission, I returned to the Philippines and joined the 44th Squadron which had been left behind. Chuck's orders were inexplicably changed and he came back, too, so we scoured the base together looking for a place to call home. We settled on one particular BOQ, which in reality was just one half of a Quonset Hut, but strategically located mere steps from the officers' club and mess. Chappie showed up a week later and moved into the apartment in the other end.

At Clark we were treated like returning heroes, so, of course we played it for all it was worth. It was impossible to buy our own drinks; everyone wanted to hear our tall tales of combat and derring-do. Life became an around-the-clock blur consisting of flying, partying, more flying and more partying. It was definitely a young man's game.

One night Chappie and his roommate, a smooth operator named Jim Arnaut, decided to host a party in their apartment. Chuck had left that morning for a TDY assignment to Japan, so after dinner I grabbed a bottle of bourbon and headed next door. Lots of folks were already jammed in the little space, including several Filipinos from Spud's old band. It was a grand, noisy, smoky, whiskey-filled affair that eventually spilled over to the outside. I counted myself down and out around eleven and crawled home to bed. Chappie tired of the festivities around midnight and came over to sack out in Chuck's bunk. A little later there were only three left at the shindig: Jim Arnaut, a sultry young Filipino movie star, and the airhead lieutenant from my last mission in Korea, now also stationed at Clark. Smooth Operator was trying to make out with the movie queen but first he had to get rid of the airhead. I could hear the conversation clearly because the partition between our apartments did not go all the way to the top of the rounded roof.

Jim finally managed to get the lieutenant to leave. The lieutenant came over to my side, woke Chappie and started telling him his sad story about how everyone was picking on him.

"Come on, man," Chappie growled. "It's late, and no one's picking on you. Just go home and go to bed, okay?"

At Clark AFB we were treated like returning heroes. Colonel Davies presents a DFC to Captain Scrappy Johnson, 1950 (courtesy of USAF).

Airhead went around to the other end of the hut and began banging on the door. He was a persistent clown; I'll give him that much.

But Jim wasn't about to let him back in. "Beat it," I heard him call out, his voice downright hostile.

Back to our side shit-for-brains came, rousing Chappie once more.

Now Chappie was really pissed. "Look, it's late, man, I told you before: go on home to bed."

And that's when the airhead made his fatal mistake. "What are you doing, Chappie," he whined, "you taking the white guy's side against a fellow black?"

Chappie came out of his bed like a rocket and grabbed a fistful of airhead's shirtfront. "You stupid little turd. If I take anybody's side, it'll be Jim's every time and never yours. He's my roommate, he's my pal, and you're an overbearing ass! Now get your scrawny butt out of here before I decide to do some real damage to your head." With that Chappie backpedaled the fool to the door and tossed him out. I feigned sleep, pretending to snore so Chappie had no idea I had heard the whole damn thing. The next morning at breakfast he said something about it, so I felt free to recount my last mission in Korea with the guy. We both agreed that the lieutenant was an asshole of the first order.

As I said earlier, we were treated like conquering heroes back at Clark, and we certainly enjoyed being back to flying the F-80. Mornings, when the air was smooth, we would shoot ground or aerial gunnery, and in the afternoons we would either fly again or play golf. The Huks and the Filipino Constabulary were still fighting each other—nothing had changed on that front—but we Americans stayed out of the fray and didn't interfere unless the action either came too close to our base, or was about to. We had some local allies (a band of indigenous pygmies called Negritoes) who kept us informed of the guerrillas' movements. The pygmies were extremely shy, they had their own language and they lived in very primitive conditions in the jungle just outside the base. One day a Negrito emissary came onto the base and told of the wheels of a Huk camp being built two miles away—up in the mountains and west of Clark. He also mentioned that the Negritos had further learned that the Huks were planning an attack on Clark with the possibility of taking someone prisoner for ransom. Bad move on their part. The commander made an instant decision. Let's send a flight of four F-80s to destroy the camp.

I was selected to lead the flight against the Huks. Armed with WP (White Phosphorus) firebombs and fifty caliber machine guns, we came in at treetop level, dropped the firebombs and strafed the campsite until our ammo ran out. I felt pretty good as I led the flight back to base.

The next day I tagged along with a ground party composed of twenty military police officers and two Negrito guides to assess the damage. Big surprise. We could hardly tell where our bombs had hit. The jungle had completely absorbed their effect. And any fires that had blossomed apparently had been quickly extinguished. But it was also apparent that the Huks had fled. We reported our findings to the commander who immediately declared the mission a resounding success. He had only intended to send a message to the guerrillas to stay the hell away from Clark. And they did.

Because we had just returned from combat in Korea we were cut a whole bunch of slack and could do just about anything we wanted—as long as it wasn't outright illegal, or against Air Force regs. So we formed an aerobatics team. Chuck was the leader, I flew right wing and Bill Slater was left wing. We didn't fly a slot position because no one was readily available that we could trust without a lot of practice. We only did loops, rolls, Emmelman turns and spins. (Oops, just kidding, we didn't do spins!) We put on several demonstrations with only a couple of rehearsals, and our efforts were lauded by some very appreciative audiences.

A Royal Air Force squadron stopped over at Clark on their way to the British base at Hong Kong. They were flying Vampires, the replacement for a squadron of very outdated Spitfires, and they had flown those little airplanes all the way from England. Why the Brits hadn't crated them up and sent them by sea, I'll never know. Those pilots must have made at least a hundred refueling stops. And then the Spitfire pilots flew their planes all the way back to England. Now that took balls!

While at Clark, the Vampire squadron leader put on a show, which turned out to be a challenge. Bill and I were away from base, up in Baguio playing golf, so Chuck had to rise to the occasion alone. He tried to duplicate everything in the F-80 that the Brit had done in the Vampire. The result was disastrous, and fortunately for Chuck, not fatally so.

As a finale, the squadron leader did an outside turn at low altitude and stayed within the boundaries of the airfield. Chuck repeated the maneuver in his F-80—after a fashion—but he so over-stressed the airplane and popped so many rivets that the bird had to be totaled by the maintenance folks!

✈ ✈ ✈

Major William Gibson was the commander of the 44th Squadron; he was a good pilot and a hellava great guy. His experience in fighters was limited, but he was eager to learn.

I had mentioned earlier that we had given our P-51s to the Filipinos. Their base, Florida Blanca, was only 15 miles south of Clark and oftentimes for kicks we would fly our F-80s down there and buzz them. They would scramble off six or eight P-51s in a hurry and a big dogfight would then ensue right over the base. Major Gibson loved joining us on these flights.

Clark Field had one really crappy ground radar system, so one day the commanders decided to add something of a safety margin in case of an attack. That something was putting us on a rotating runway alert. Four F-80s were parked at the end of the runway and a squad tent erected for us to stay in while on alert. We also had an ancient crank telephone to announce the scramble. This was the pits, so rather than sit in that hot tent for hours on end, we would call up headquarters and get practice scrambles so as to get airborne and out of the heat.

One particular morning I called up for such a scramble and took off with Chappie on my wing. We flew around aimlessly for a while and even after failing to get a rise out of the P-51s at Florida Blanca, we came back and buzzed Clark. I figured this would be a no sweat move, because it was a Sunday and all the wheels were far away from the main base, up in the housing area nestled in the hills.

With Chappie in string formation, I flew over the squad tent as low as I could get, then rolled my F-80 and flew down the runway inverted. In those days we didn't spend a lot of time reading tech manuals, but even I knew that if you flew the F-80 inverted for too long the engine could be permanently damaged from loss of oil. I'd also heard that it could be flown inverted for just about eight seconds without harm. At the end of the runway I rolled upright and pulled up into an Emmelman turn. Chappie then joined up on my wing; we came around, pitched out and landed.

We were back in the tent filling out our forms when a jeep roared up and slid to a stop in the gravel. A very pissed-off Major William Gibson jumped out and yelled, "Who the hell was leading that flight?"

I stepped out, came to attention, saluted, and said, "I was, sir."

"Be in my office the first thing Monday morning, Johnson." Then he got back in his jeep and roared away. Bad omen, that, calling me Johnson and not Scrappy like he always did. Christ Almighty! It now dawned on me the day wasn't Sunday like I'd thought, but Saturday, and Gibson was in his office near the flight line taking care of squadron paper work. Holy shit!

After he left, Chappie and Harlan Ball began speculating in very loud voices about what sort of punishment would fit the crime. Words like court marshal, Leavenworth, reprimand, and letter of admonishment flew back and forth, then they would laugh themselves silly while waving taunting fingers at the soon-to-be-damned aviator. I failed to see the humor.

That evening there was a dance at the club and I showed up and sat at the squadron table. Major Gibson was there but refused to even acknowledge my presence. I was a non-person in his eyes and I knew my flying career was over.

I reported to the commander's office at 7:55 Monday morning. The first sergeant invited me to sit, saying that Major Gibson would see me soon. But soon did not come very soon, because I remember waiting for what seemed like two or three years. Finally, the first shirt announced the major would see me now. I went in, saluted, and waited at attention for him to lower the boom.

He looked up from behind a desk crammed with papers and said in a most conversational tone, "Damn it, Scrappy, you know better than to pull something like that. Now get your ass out of here and don't ever let me catch you doing anything like that again!"

His psychological ploy worked its intended effect and his was a lesson I never forgot. No yelling, no threats, no theatrics. And I felt like a pipsqueak in his presence. I later used similar tactics after I had piled on a lot more rank and had young hotshot pilots working for me.

But we were allowed to do a little legal buzzing from time to time—strange but true—but with somewhat of a different twist. Because the war in Korea now involved the Chinese Communists, Chiang Kai-Chek and his Chinese Nationalists on Taiwan were justifiably edgy. The Commies had acquired some MiGs and had them stationed on the coast, very near to Taiwan. So in order to instill some confidence into the Nationalists, the U.S. commanders decided to send up a flight of F-80s from Clark every Friday with instructions to buzz the hell out of their southernmost air base. We would do so until our fuel was low, then we'd land, refuel and fly low level up to their base at Taipei, buzzing everything and everyone along the way. Then we'd land, refuel, and repeat the same thing on the way back. And we could perform any aerobatic maneuver we damn well felt like with no commanders waiting on the ramp to chew us out. I can't tell you how much fun we had—and it was all completely legal!

While life in the air was fun, it wasn't that way on the ground after Chuck and I discovered we had rats in our hut. And I mean big, mean, fire-breathing, man-eating rats. Because of the Quonset Hut's peculiar rounded roof, the partitions inside did not extend completely up to the ceiling, so a whole series of exposed 2 × 4s lay on top of the partitions which made great walkways for the rats.

One night while Chuck and I were lying in our bunks reading, a humongous rat with flaming red eyes boldly crawled along the partition, then stopped and stared down malevolently at us. Chuck grabbed one of his shoes and took a full swing at the monster, hitting its tail, and hitting it hard. The animal reared up, screamed, then took off in the direction of Chappie's apartment.

We didn't sleep a wink after that, and the next morning Chuck went to the base engineering office and checked out a rat trap. And guess where he put it? Yep. Right on top of the partition, smack dab over our heads!

Shortly after midnight a huge rat sprung the trap and fell off the walkway thrashing wildly. He landed square on my chest still pinned in the trap. I flew out of my bed too terrified to utter a sound, and ran outside to the safety of the night. It took me the better part of an hour to calm down.

I was none too friendly towards Chuck for days afterward and I turned two mighty deaf ears to his many repeated apologies. I still shudder at the memory of that beast flopping about on my chest in the dark all those years ago.

I wasn't the only pilot affected by the new 100-mission regulation. About ten of us had left Korea with between seventy to ninety-five missions, and to add to the confusion, a crazy addendum had been tacked onto the 100-mission-tour reg which said no pilot could leave the theater without those 100 missions completed. Finally, after about six months, the powers-that-be decided anyone with over 85 missions could go back to the States, and anyone with less would return to Korea and finish their one hundred. I had 87 missions so, in June of 1951, I was allowed to go home. I had volunteered for three bases: Otis AFB, Massachusetts; Selfridge AFB, Michigan; and Hamilton AFB, California. I'd picked these bases because their squadrons were equipped with the new F-86 Sabre. F-86 pilots were shooting down a lot of MiGs in Korea at the time, and I wanted to fly that hot, hot plane.

My assignment came down for Otis AFB, located on Cape Cod—but not to fly the F-86. Unbeknownst to me, the wing had already converted to the F-94B Starfire, an all-weather fighter.

10

Cape Cod

At Otis I was assigned to the 59th Fighter Interceptor Squadron to fly the F-94, a plane similar to a two-seater F-80 except it sported an afterburner, radar, and a guy called a radar operator (RO) strapped into the back seat.

I'd always flown single-seat, single-engine fighters, so this was a new twist. Like most fighter pilots, I was not particularly thrilled about having someone in the back seat, nor could I imagine why anyone would want to ride back there during all the wild gyrations. When I asked one of these guys at the bar one evening whatever possessed him to become a radar observer, he tossed back his shot of whiskey à la John Wayne, then replied in a deep-voiced drawl, "Everyone has to be some place, pardner."

I couldn't tell if he was pulling my joystick or not, so I just shrugged, upended my beer and changed the subject.

These guys fell into two distinct groups. Some were in their thirties—holdover night-fighters from World War II—while the others were all new kids in their twenties looking for adventure.

One of these older fellows was a first lieutenant named Joe Tuck, a good old back home boy. Now Joe was driving down a rural road one Saturday evening when a farmer unexpectedly pulled out from a field and Tuck hit him—nothing serious, mind you, just a fender bender. But the farmer refused to admit guilt, and because he was the hometown dude, he decided to foist the blame on Tuck, saying he must have been drinking because he sure had slurred his words.

Another RO in the squadron who had a couple years of law school under his belt volunteered to help Tuck, so he spent a few hours before the court date telling Tuck just what he should do once in front of the judge.

On the appointed day, the farmer told his story to the judge first and repeated his accusation about Tuck being drunk because he had slurred his words. When it was Tuck's turn to speak, he rose and said, "Sure, Your Honor, I sometimes slur my words but that's only because I have false teeth." With a flourish he took out his lower bridge and held it up high for the judge to see. Bam! Down came the gavel and the farmer was found guilty. That evening, Tuck and his Perry Mason wannabe celebrated their victory at the O' Club by hosting a round for the entire house.

✈ ✈ ✈

The 59th Squadron was sent to Eglin AFB, in the Florida Panhandle for a month of gunnery training and the squadron flew down as a group. I didn't go because the commander wanted me to wait for an airplane that was being repaired. The night my ship was ready, the weather around the eastern United States was marginal, but I was still able to get a clearance for Shaw AFB, South Carolina. When I arrived over Shaw, I was told that the base was below minimums and that I would have to go to my alternate. In those days a pilot with a green instrument card could decide to land no matter what the weather. Approach control told me that the visibility was 1/8th of a mile, but passing over the base I could look down and see lights. It didn't look all that bad so I decided to press on. Everything went fine until I was on final and encountered the 1/8th mile visibility. The runway was totally obscured. At this point I sincerely wished I had heeded their advice and had pressed on to my alternate. I lucked out, however, because suddenly I saw the runway lights and was able to land safely. Hard, but safely.

✈ ✈ ✈

Colonel Harry Thyng was our wing commander for several months but then he went to Korea to head up an F-86 wing and shoot down some MiGs. Colonel Leon Gray was his replacement. The day Gray arrived at Otis the base was shrouded in thick fog. You couldn't see past two airplanes on the ramp. Someone hollered that the new wing commander was in the GCA (ground controlled approach) pattern, so we all trooped out of squadron operations and onto the ramp.

Out of the fog a T-33 taxied up with a colonel in the front seat and a two-star in the back. Surprise, surprise! It was Colonel Gray and the general was commander of the Eastern Air Defense Command. We all popped to attention and saluted en masse, holding our salutes until both men disappeared inside base ops.

Several days later Colonel Gray made his first official appearance at a group flying safety meeting. Oh, man, did he ever! He walked in and sat down in the front row while the wing flying safety officer was droning on from a published report detailing a C-47 accident from about a hundred years ago. I could see Gray was getting really steamed, and finally he stood up and lowered the boom on the flying safety officer.

"What the hell are you doing reading these guys a bunch of dull, useless shit like this?"

And that was the moment Lieutenant Bassett, a very junior pilot in our squadron, chose to saunter in with a big, shit-eating grin on his face. His timing couldn't have been worse and Gray had him for lunch right on the spot! It sure wasn't pretty, and I made up my mind then and there to never, ever, be late for any meeting Gray might show up at. And I kind of suspect all the other pilots present fine-tuned themselves to that same frequency.

All-weather flying was new to most fighter pilots at this time in the early fifties, and soon after taking command, Colonel Gray lay down the law that the flight pulling alert would go airborne and check the weather each morning. Weather flying was old hat to him, and I had heard that he had been an airline pilot in his previous creation. Soon after his new rule went into effect, my flight was on duty, and since it was my turn, I took off at about 6:00 A.M. to go upstairs for a look-see.

There was a ceiling at about 1000 feet and the tops were unknown. My mission was to find out how high those tops were. After entering the clouds, I started a large, climbing turn. We didn't have stringent instrument procedures at the time, so I climbed through 10,000, 15,000, and 20,000 feet without breaking out into the clear. At 30,000 I began to wonder if I was ever going to pop out of those damn clouds. Then it dawned to me. Say it ain't so! I reached up with a gloved forefinger and wiped off a small section of the canopy instantly allowing bright moonlight to burst into my cockpit! Ah, shit! After turning on the defroster I found that I had broken out of the clouds at about ten thousand feet! A soft white blanket spread out below me from horizon to horizon. Stupid me. This was one day I was double glad not to have an R O along for the ride. The guy would have laughed himself silly the entire way home.

The fact of the matter was that Colonel Gray didn't really give a rat's ass what the weather was each morning. He just wanted to get those of us who had been daytime fighter pilots acclimated to flying in some serious weather.

One day soon after that incident I was again flying in the soup where the ceiling was pretty low. I had been sent out to fly a round-robin cross-country. (A round-robin is where you fly to a distant location but land back at your original takeoff point.) When I returned to Otis, the weather hadn't improved. In fact, the wind was now from the northeast which meant I had to land in the opposite direction from the normal GCA pattern. Which also meant I would not have a glide path to fly: azimuth only (left or right; no up and down).

Everything went fine until I turned onto final and the GCA operator informed me that the top of the base's water tower was in the clouds and that he would have to steer me slightly right of course for safety reasons. I gave him a curt "Roger" and proceeded down final. When I broke out I was too far right of the runway to land; in fact I was lined up with the parallel taxiway. I sure wasn't about to land on that, but if I had gone around and flown a second GCA I realized I would have found myself right back where I was now. No frigging way. So with gear and flaps down I made a 360-degree turn at 100 feet and manhandled my way back onto a new final approach. Ironically the same water tower that had caused the problem with my first approach was now my ally on this one. This time, using it as my aiming point, I lined up perfectly with the runway and landed.

A month later, returning from a night flight, the tower informed me that it was snowing and advised there were already a couple of inches accumulated on the runway. This news bothered me more than just being a nuisance because I had never landed on snow. I proceeded down final and made up my mind to land as short as I possibly could. I mean, really short! I lowered the plane gently onto the concrete and immediately discovered the snow not only made for a soft landing, but it also helped slow down the aircraft which meant my landing roll was way shorter than normal. Neat!

And since I was the only one flying I asked for, and received, permission from the tower to taxi back up the runway to see just how short I had landed. Holy cow! I found that my tire tracks had started less than 50 feet from the threshold! Man, are you good, or what, Scrappy Johnson? I crowed aloud to myself. This was one proud dude who taxied back to the ramp that picture-perfect winter night.

That fall I purchased a Remington 12-gauge shotgun and drove up to the north shore of the cape to try my hand at duck hunting. I noted there were some flats and sand dunes lying short of the beach and as I wandered onto the flats I crossed several man-made canals which were dug to be three to four feet deeper than the rest of the flats. After wandering around out there and losing all track of time, I noticed the water was rising. Then it dawned on me—holy shit, the tide was coming in, and coming in fast! I looked back toward the shore and saw that I was way far out on the flats. It was time for me to get the hell out of there, and pronto, because if the tide got high enough I would not be able to distinguish the canals from the rest of the field and that would become the start of one really hairy situation. After several minutes of well-deserved panic, I was able to make my way to safety with only some wet clothing. But I had sure learned a valuable lesson that afternoon. Don't ever wander out onto any flats, anywhere, without first knowing the local tide schedule.

个 个 个

There's a saying that the Air Force takes care of its own. And it does. When someone has a problem, we all rise to the occasion. Let me give you a "for example."

When the mother of one of the majors assigned to the wing died, he was granted an immediate emergency leave to go home to Texas. I was assigned to fly him to San Antonio. We flew in a T-33 and landed at Kelly Air Force Base, where he thanked me and departed on his somber mission. My task completed, I grabbed a ride into town and checked into the Gunter Hotel. No visiting officers' quarters for me this trip. The Gunter had been a popular hangout with flying cadets during World War II for their weekend escapades. It was always filled to capacity on Saturday nights, and this Saturday night proved no exception.

I visited several nearby clubs and was back in the hotel coffee shop shortly after midnight enjoying a snack when I noticed three fairly attractive young ladies sitting nearby. As they got up to leave, one paused by my table, winked and said, "Hi, I'm Hilda, would you like to join me and my friends at a party?"

"Is the Pope Catholic?' I asked, jumping up from my half-finished meal. I paid my bill in record time and joined them. Her friends quickly disappeared leaving Hilda and me to walk arm in arm to her nearby apartment. She had a European accent, so I asked where she was from.

"Germany," she replied. Seems she had married a GI but the marriage hadn't worked out. We sure got to do a great deal of communicating that evening and as a result I got very little sleep.

The next morning I went out to Kelly, climbed into my T-33 and headed off for Maxwell AFB, at Montgomery, Alabama, where I landed, and parked on the ramp. While they serviced the plane, I went to a nearby coffee shop and grabbed a bite. All I'd had before leaving San Antonio was a "fighter pilot's breakfast"—a coke and a cigarette. Except in my case it was a coke and a cigar since I didn't smoke cigarettes.

When I returned to the ramp with my clearance, I walked up to the T-33, stared at it for a couple of seconds and nearly peed in my flightsuit. Holy shit, this wasn't my T-Bird! How could I have been so stupid? Of course it looked the same, hell, they all did, but the serial number sure was different! I began to sweat like a drunk in a sauna; I could already see the many flying safety reports being written about this numbskull who called himself a pilot.

"Not only did the pilot fail to properly preflight the airplane, but he further compounded his negligence by taking the wrong plane and flying it away!"

Now wouldn't that be a humdinger of a headline? My pals would laugh me off the planet.

I quickly asked myself, "Scrappy, you think you could fly this T-33 back to Kelly and get the right one without anyone knowing?"

As this thought was rolling about in my head the line chief strolled up and told me they'd refueled my T-33. He then mentioned that he had had it towed it to another spot on the ramp. Seems a second T-33 had landed and the maintenance folks needed my place to work on the newcomer. Man, was I one happy fellow when he told me this. Thank God! So this bird parked in front of me wasn't mine, and I hadn't taken the wrong plane at Kelly after all. Still hungover but, oh, so relieved, I jumped into my T-Bird and made a hasty flight back to Otis, swearing all the way home never to drink another drop of alcohol ever again. Alas, I must confess it was a promise not kept.

✈ ✈ ✈

Bob Dow, our squadron commander from the 12th Squadron in Korea, arrived at Otis as a newly minted lieutenant colonel and with orders to take over as squadron commander of the 59th. This news was cheered by the guys in the squadron, plus they all agreed: our last commander had been a world-class jerk.

Major Ben Atwood was our ops officer and in many ways reminded me of Don Scherer, my old roommate and ops officer from the squadron in the Philippines. Both men had similar personalities.

Ben's car had been a big black hearse until he bought a new Cadillac Coupe Deville convertible. Now this was some fancy set of wheels, and shortly after buying it he insisted on driving three of us to the officers' club for lunch one day. On the way back to the squadron, Ben dropped the cigarette that he was smoking and lost it under the seat. Although the four of us frantically searched, we couldn't find it. The consensus reached finally was that the cigarette had to be out and thus posed no threat to the car, so we all went inside.

When everyone was settled back at work in the squadron, I snuck out, got back into the car, lay down on the front floorboards and began puffing away on my cigar, making lots of smoke which was soon visible for all to see.

One of the pilots finally spotted this and yelled, "Hey, Ben, your new car's on fire! Move, move, move!"

Ben came running out, threw open the driver's door and saw me all spread out, puffing away around a silly grin on my face. And that's when my little joke backfired. Ben had brought along a fire extinguisher and he let me have it. We all enjoyed a good laugh at my expense at the bar in the O Club later.

✈ ✈ ✈

A week passed and lo and behold, Chappie showed up at Otis. He had been assigned to another fighter group, but unfortunately was not received with the same open arms as he had been with the pilots in the 12th Fighter Squadron. Some of the men had even tried to have him grounded. I wanted to get Chappie to come and join me, but his orders were to the 58th and he said he preferred to leave it that way. Turned out to be a good decision. He was soon promoted to captain and the squadron commander made him a flight commander. Chappie later made major, then operations officer, and finally the squadron commander.

One evening Chappie and Ben Atwood got into a heated discussion at the club as to who was the best fighter pilot. This argument is not an unusual one. It plays out thousands of times a day in O Club bars inhabited by fighter pilots all over the world, and such an argument has actually been known to lead to fisticuffs. Naturally, both Ben and Chappie kept claiming to be the best, so at one point Ben offered to bet Chappie a thousand dollars he could beat him in a dogfight any place, any time.

Chappie sneered and said, "Hell, man, you've got somebody in your own squadron who can beat you, hands down. You don't need me to show you up."

"And just who in the hell would that be?"

"Scrappy Johnson, and I'll bet you a thousand dollars he can beat you head-on, three out of three."

Now those were fighting words!

I was down at operations sitting alert when I received a phone call from the bar. It was Ben who explained the situation and asked me if I would fly the next morning.

"Sure," I replied. It wasn't my thousand on the line. Chappie had seen what I could do in the Philippines so he was pretty confident I could pull it off. All I had to lose was my reputation, but one thing I knew for sure. Since I was going to spend the night on alert, I would be in far better shape than Ben come morning.

Well, Ben went home to bed, the whiskey wore off, and that was the last I ever heard of the thousand-dollar bet.

✦ ✦ ✦

One day I happened to wander into the 58th Squadron's operations room shortly after Chappie had become a flight commander and I saw he had his flight off in a corner briefing them, so I moved closer and listened in without appearing to do so. I heard him end his spiel by saying, "And if they want us to shut the door, then we're going to shut the door better than anybody else."

I walked away impressed. I think he meant that no matter how menial the task, he and his troops would do it better than anyone else. And that truly summed up Chappie's attitude toward life.

One day Chappie mentioned he was going to be interviewed for a radio talk show so I made it a point of listening in the day the program aired. He started off by singing a couple of flying songs—did a pretty darn good job, too, if memory serves me right—then the announcer formally introduced him to the audience as a jet ace from Korea.

That was when they lost me. I couldn't believe my ears. What? Chappie James a jet ace? Sure, Chappie had flown over sixty missions with Mother, Spud and me, but we had all been flying prop-driven P-51s, not jets. And we never saw a single frigging enemy aircraft all that time, let alone did any of us wax any! Heck, after Spud had been shot down and murdered by those North Korean bastards, Chappie had transferred to Taegu and had flown a camera-man around in the back seat of a T-33 for the remainder of his tour. Nope, Chappie James sure as hell had not shot down any enemy planes in his T-33! And besides, it takes five downed enemy airplanes to make any pilot an ace.

How could Chappie allow the announcer to introduce him in that manner without immediately correcting him? But he did. Later I would come to learn that Chappie would often take credit for something, whether deserved or not. I admit it was a minor little nothing in the greater scheme of things, but for some reason Chappie's silence really rubbed me the wrong way at the time. But later when I calmed down I realized: What the hell, that was just Chappie.

These were the days when it was the norm for pilots to fly as much as possible. The time was available and there for the asking. And I had asked the wing scheduling officer to keep me in mind if and when, any and all, cross-country missions came up. He said he would.

Sure enough, soon after that request he sent me out to Lockheed Aircraft Corporation at Burbank, California, to pick up a new T-33. The day I was scheduled to leave I was told that Colonel Gray wanted to see me. As I walked to his office, I kept thinking he was going to hand me a load of crap about "don't do this and don't do that." I should have known better. All he wanted was to ask me if I'd stop off at Williams AFB at Chandler, Arizona, on the way home and pick up a case of Johnny Walker Scotch at a bar just outside the base. He went out of his way to say that he owned a half interest in the place so no money would be changing hands. I smiled as I left his office. And to think I'd felt sure that he was going to give me a flying safety lecture. I didn't know much about Colonel Gray then, but I would soon learn a whole lot more about the guy later.

This trip was made before the advent of jet airliners, and my journey west was one long haul. I flew in a DC-3 from Hyannis to New York, then from New York to Chicago to Los Angeles on a DC-4. There were two stewardesses on board for the last leg, one named Jean Cook, the other Dawn Kelly, and I vaguely remembered Jean from the PX school I had attended at Ft. Monmouth. She was a pretty blonde and had been married to a lieutenant. During the long flight I came to discover that she had since gotten a divorce and had landed this job as a stewardess. As we neared LA, she and I graduated to some friendlier talk, so I finally said, "Play your cards right, I'll take you to dinner in Los Angeles."

Even I knew a corny line when I heard one, but it was out of my mouth before I could stop it.

Jean just smiled, nodded her pretty blonde head and sashayed her way down the aisle.

After landing, she told me the crew had reservations at a hotel in Long Beach. I took a cab to the hotel only to find they were full. Luckily, there was another hotel next door that still had rooms available. Since we'd already had dinner on the plane, Jean joined me thirty minutes later in the bar of my hotel, and after getting our drink order filled we went out on the beach to enjoy them. We immediately spotted a big boat anchored about a hundred yards offshore with one helluva party in progress. We laughingly joked about what a good time the people were having, and after finishing our drinks I walked Jean back over to her hotel and told her I'd phone tomorrow before noon to plan dinner for that night.

Mid-morning Saturday I made a huge mistake. I called Lockheed's flight office to let them I know was in LA and would fly the T-33 out first thing Monday morning. Boy, was I ever wrong! A frigging, shrieking shrew on the other end of the line yelled at me that the plane was long overdue for pickup and that I needed to shag my ass over there right now and fly it out this morning. What? I have a date tonight, you witch! I should have told her to shove it, but since she had threatened in her next breath to have several bad things happen to me if I didn't obey, I reluctantly called Jean, explained my problem, and after telling her how sorry I was, went out to Lockheed and took off for Williams AFB. I later thought I should have flown the damn thing over to LA International Airport, or better yet, told the old bag to fly it out herself!

I landed at Willie and spent the night in Phoenix. The next day I stopped at the bar, picked up the case of scotch and took off for Lake Charles, Louisiana. Passing over Texas I encountered a line of strong thunderstorms. I had previously mentioned that we were not big on reading regulations in those days, but somewhere I had been briefed that according to Air Force regs for ferrying aircraft, pilots were supposed to remain VFR. I did not know the exact wording of this particular dictate so I decided to interpret it my way.

When I neared the thunderstorms, I started climbing to remain VFR. I climbed and climbed, and by the time I reached the Dallas/Fort Worth area I eventually topped out at 53,000 feet. (There may be some smart-ass pilot reading this who will challenge me, but it's true.) This was a new T-33 and not one loaded down with electronics. All it had in it was a bird dog, a case of scotch and me. I stayed VFR, landed to refuel at Lake Charles, then flew on to Shaw AFB in South Carolina, where I spent the night.

The next morning I cleared for Otis. I had no problems staying VFR on this leg until I reached Long Island and came face-on with a low cloudbank that extended northeast as far as I could see. I had already heard some radio chatter indicating there was flying activity over Otis, and I had recognized one of the voices as belonging to one of my squadron mates, Fred Borman. I asked Fred what the weather was.

"Scrappy, we've got a one thousand feet ceiling and five miles visibility."

Hell, that was VFR weather, so I flew back to the edge of the cloudbank, dove down and headed for Otis underneath. Out over the water the overcast got lower and lower, until I found myself skimming the waves. This was getting downright hairy. As I neared the Cape it began to raise some, so I zeroed in on the Otis homer, entered the pattern, pitched out and landed. I'd skimmed the tops of the clouds at 53,000 feet and flew under the clouds at 10 feet above the water. Some flight. But by my rules I had stayed VFR.

The day I almost met my Maker I was scheduled to be on night alert starting at 5:00 P.M. There was a movie showing in Falmouth I had wanted to see, so I drove over and made the 2 o'clock feature. When the show let out it had started to snow so I headed back, and as I drove, the wind picked up and the snowfall intensified. Near the local landmark, The Coonamessett Inn, the road had been leveled through a natural hump, and just to the north was a small airstrip. Fifty-mile-per-hour winds were blowing off this airstrip and across this hump causing a snowdrift to form a couple of feet deep. I drove right into it I became stuck.

I was only wearing my uniform and no overcoat, and as I sat in my convertible pondering my next move, the wind picked up even more and the snow began to blow under the canvas top and into the car. Through the blizzard I could just make out the outline of another auto pointed in the opposite direction; it, too, bogged down. I was fast growing miserable with the snow blowing in on me, so I decided to get out and make my way to the other car, a hardtop sedan.

Inside were three people: a man and two women, all civilian workers at the base. The two in front introduced themselves as husband and wife—both about 50—then presented an attractive woman in her early thirties curled up in the back seat. They all welcomed me into their warm, dry car.

It was soon obvious the storm was going to get worse before it got better so we discussed my trying to walk across some fields to the inn to get help. We decided against it as the snow was now too deep and the wind too strong. We remained fairly comfortable until the snow started to cover the exhaust pipe. We recognized the inherent danger the moment we began smelling fumes inside the car. The wife reached over and turned off the engine, and before long it turned really cold. This hit me a whole lot more than it did the others only because they were wearing warm clothes and heavy overcoats. The situation was fast becoming untenable for me, so I decided to go dig the snow away from the exhaust, which would allow us to start the engine and get the heater pumping again.

Opening the door was difficult, but with considerable effort I was able to get out and make my way to the rear through knee-deep snow where I managed to dig a bunch away from the exhaust pipe. I knew this fix was not going to last long, and on my way back to the car door I had to dig more snow with my bare hands just to get it to open. I jumped back in, both hands numb, and without thinking, stuck them up the startled young lady's dress, the idea being to warm them. I swear, the action was spontaneous. I had read once of a man doing this after freezing his hands under similar circumstances. Sometime later I figured I must have been under the influence of those exhaust fumes or I would never have attempted such a thing. Of course, she quickly slapped my hands away, but she was a true lady and graciously said nothing more about it, then or later.

This misadventure began about 4:45 P.M., and continued to deteriorate further as the night wore on. Around ten o'clock, the older woman became worried for her husband. The guy was not faring well. The fumes had definitely affected him. Just when the situation seemed at its worst, lights from a snowplow appeared like some apparition out of nowhere about forty feet ahead of us. The driver stopped and made his way to our car, sized up the situation and told us his plan. He said he could only carry out two people at a time but would come back as quickly as possible for the other two. He took the older couple first, and because of the slow speed of the plow it was the better part of an hour before he returned. He took us to a nursing home where we spent the night sitting in chairs in the lobby.

The next day I was able to get a cab and go home. Dorie and Ted had been stranded at the base—she at the Officers' Club, Ted at the base nursery. But thank God they at least they had been safe and warm indoors.

When my car was finally dug out, I had it towed to a garage where it took some doing by the resident mechanic to get it running again. It had been buried under twenty feet of snow and the interior had been filled with the stuff. No doubt that snowplow driver saved four lives that night in the Bay State.

And for many years afterwards, my hands would start to tingle whenever I so much as thought about snow!

✈ ✈ ✈

Since the mission of the Air Defense Command (ADC) was to shoot down Soviet bombers if they attacked the United States, we were supposed to stay proficient in aerial gunnery. One Sunday I had a mission scheduled on our range out over the Atlantic. Once there I had managed to make two passes at the towed target before the weather deteriorated to the point where the pilot of the tow ship decided that the next pass would be my last. Okay by me, so I zoomed in real close, just barely missing the target as I squeezed off all my remaining ammunition.

Back on the ground I discovered that I had ripped the bejesus out of the target—it was riddled with enough red holes to add up to a 66 percent score. Hot damn, even I was impressed. Flushed with pride, I took the shredded target and draped it over the front door of the 58th Squadron along with a placard emblazoned with my name and squadron. Beat that, you weenies. Scrappy Johnson's a giant killer!

It was little things like that which sure made my life more than just passably interesting during my long Air Force career!

11

Way Up North

In the summer of 1952 I was ordered to report to Air Force Headquarters in The Pentagon. I was further told to bring the other seven members of my flight, and I was warned to keep everything hush-hush. This I found intriguing because no one had actually used the usual buzzwords like top secret or confidential.

The short version of what took place is that we were at The Pentagon for three days where we were briefed on the identification, performance characteristics and payloads of various Soviet aircraft, with special emphasis being placed on a particular make and model of a reconnaissance plane. It seems one of these bad boys had been photographed flying right over our base at Thule, Greenland, obviously on a spying mission. Anyway, the incident brought out a sense of paranoia in certain folks in The Pentagon who were now seeing Soviet bad guys everywhere. In fact, a nameless brigadier general went so far as to order us not to wear our wings while in Washington.

Now, I'll confess that I'm not always the sharpest guy in the crowd (and especially not after a long night of partying) so it took me a while to figure out the real purpose behind these briefings. Holy cow! The brass wanted us to shoot down that Russian spy plane! It had taken them three days to get this message across when all anyone had to do was just say so! Three days wasted on something which could have been over in ten minutes. A Colonel J. C. Meyer chaired most of the meetings, and he told us in a sort of oblique way that if we were successful, General Hoyt Vandenberg, Chief of Staff of the Air Force, would chastise us publicly (not by individual names, of course) but then after the heat had died down, would bring us back to Washington and pin medals on us. In secret. And we would not be authorized to wear the decoration's ribbon on our chests for years to come; maybe never. Got that? Yes, sir, got it!

One amusing incident happened while we were there. The eight of us were walking down an endless hallway after lunch on the second day when I turned to spot a group of high-ranking officers coming up behind us at a fast clip. I signaled the others to pull over and let them pass, which they did, the exception being Wally, my RO. Thinking we were still walking along beside him,

Wally continued on down the hall while keeping up the conversation. Finally a two-star said in a kind of loud voice, "Excuse us, son," and the generals hoofed their way around him. We kidded the hell out of him later for chatting so casually with his new-found buddy, five-star General Omar Bradley, Chief of Staff of the Army.

We returned to Otis to prepare for our flight north—further north than any other American jet fighters had ever flown before. Our departure was delayed at the last possible moment because some headquarters weenie suddenly came up with the bright idea we should take airplanes with de-icing boots on their wings. This proved to be an almost impossible requirement to fill. There were all sorts of problems just trying to find airplanes with that kind of equipment, and I suggested that de-icing boots would slow down the aircraft and hinted that we would rather have planes without them. Can it, Johnson, nothing doing. The staff weenie knew best.

On 16 August 1952 we at last departed Otis and flew to Bangor AFB, Maine, where we were met by none other than Lt. Gen. Charles T. Meyers, Commander of the North East Air Command (NEAC). The general had flown down from Pepperall AFB, Newfoundland, specifically to give us a final—and this time classified—top secret briefing. We assured him that if the Russian spy plane flew anywhere near Thule after we arrived, then we would shoot the son of a bitch down. I think he liked what he heard because he gave us a barely perceptible nod of his head and allowed a sly grin to crease his face.

Top secret, my ass! At all our refueling stops en route to Thule, every single ground crew member we encountered knew exactly where we were going and why. What a frigging joke, especially after all the hush-hush shit while we were at The Pentagon.

The second leg of our long trip took us from Bangor, Maine, to Goose Bay, Labrador. There, we were briefed about our getting to the next stop, Narsarsuak, Greenland, which was named "Bluie West One," the southernmost U.S. Air Force Base in Greenland. It seems Bluie was nestled up a fjord with really steep sides: 4,000 feet high in some spots. And we learned there were two homing beacons—one on the base, the other on the coast right at the entrance to the fjord. We were also briefed on several different scenarios, any one of which could come into play, and were finally warned not to get sucked up the wrong fjord because we would find it impossible to make a 180-degree turn in most of them. Now that last little nugget sure got our frigging attention!

We were delayed by weather at Goose Bay for ten days. Due to the distance involved and the fuel loads we needed, favorable winds were a must for

Scrappy's briefing prior to leading his flight from Goose Bay, Labrador, to Thule, Greenland (courtesy of USAF).

us to make it. The day we left Goose Bay we were briefed that the weather would be clear, the visibility unlimited. The flight went well until we neared the coast of Greenland.

We were aware there was a U.S. Navy ship stationed half way across the ocean with a radio beacon, and a rescue plane already in the air about three fourths of the way out in case we needed it.

About 150 miles from the coast my UHF radio receiver failed. No big deal, or so I thought as I signaled for my number-two man, Lieutenant Dick Hallenbach, to take over as lead. He did, and at the homer we descended to 6,000 feet and started to orbit. With my radio kaput I had no idea why in the hell we were orbiting, but I sure knew two things. This was not planned, and our planes were getting low on fuel.

We were now circling just under a deck of clouds which only added to my worry. There weren't supposed to be any clouds within a million miles! That frigging weatherman at Goose Bay hadn't mentioned any goddamn clouds. We'd waited ten days for good weather, and I could also make out that the cloud layer up the fjord looked even worse.

Shortly after beginning our orbit, a SA-16 Air/Sea Rescue medium-sized flying boat appeared. We joined formation with it: two on each wing, but continued to circle, and I didn't know why. Finally, with speed brakes deployed, full flaps, and our wheels down in order to stay on the wings of the much slower plane, we started up a fjord to the north of the one that I knew would lead us to the base. This really confused the hell out of me. This particular fjord was very narrow and we were flying in close formation with this SA-16 at a speed our jets were not designed for. The steep walls of the fjord were dangerously close and I could not help seeing them looming everywhere even though I was 100 percent focused on the wings of the flying boat. When we arrived at a point adjacent to the base, a small opening appeared between the two fjords—an opening with barely enough room for us to sneak through under the clouds.

We made it through that pass with less than 200 feet to spare, and suddenly, there was the base! I let loose a huge sigh of relief.

Calling it close was the understatement of the decade. In fact, Hollenbeck suffered a flameout on the taxiway en route to the parking area.

After landing, I learned that the mouth of the main fjord had been completely socked in by clouds and fog, and the discussion that had bounced back and forth when we were orbiting at the coast was whether or not we could make it up the adjacent fjord and through its pass to the base. And if that was not going to be possible, the decision was made for us to climb up and belly-in onto the ice cap. Holy shit, I would have certainly not looked forward to that!

Needless to say there was one hell of a party in the club later, and, no, those Air/Rescue guys didn't pay for a single drink.

We waited another week for suitable weather to fly to our next stop, BW-8, which was located halfway up the West Coast of Greenland. Regulations said we had to have an air/sea rescue ship—this time it was a converted B-17—in the air and on station. In order for it to take off and climb out of the fjord, the B-17's weather minimums were 2,500 feet whereas we could have easily climbed out using our afterburners. But then we would have had to wait for the rescue ship and that would have meant burning up precious fuel.

The bar in that Officers' Club had a sign hanging over it that read, "Our drinks are served with one thousand year-old ice."

A bunch of us were at the bar one evening and closing time came and went. The bartender, tired and grumpy, wanted to go home and was urging us to leave. We were not taking his hints too well since back at Otis, Colonel Gray had a rule that the bar would not close as long as a fighter pilot wanted a drink. Since NEAC ran the show here, this guy had never heard of such a rule, or Colonel Gray for that matter.

Finally he said, "If you guys don't leave, I'm calling Lieutenant Colonel Hennesey, he's the club president."

I laughed. "You wouldn't wake him up at this hour," to which he replied, "I wouldn't have to, he's in the back room playing poker."

My mumbled reply was, "Turn out the lights, the party's over."

Once we got going, the flight to BW-8 was uneventful and the scenery was spectacular. This base was also up a fjord, but the weather was perfect and we had no problems. The landing was a little different though. There was an 800-foot cliff just north of the runway, and as we came in and pitched out to the left, we completely lost sight of the runway. And it did not re-appear until we were turning final! Now that was spooky.

We spent two days on the ground waiting for suitable weather at Thule, our final destination, and on the morning of the third, the weatherman gave us the go to launch.

The B-17 took off, our cue to get into our cockpits. After sitting for half an hour we were told by the weather officer to forget it. Thule had just fogged in.

We took off the next day. We had all been kind of concerned about this last leg of our journey, after hearing tall tales about flying in that part of the world. Because Thule was situated close to the Arctic Circle, the meridians at that latitude were bunched together which could make for some very erratic compass readings. In spite of what we'd heard, the flight turned out to be a piece of cake. We were able to pick up the Thule homer during our climbout from BW-8, and our needles pointed unerringly toward the base the entire trip.

We descended into Thule, lined up with its runway, pitched up from the deck and made four scorching fighter plane approaches. We got by with this hot-dogging because the base commander, Colonel Charles Humphries, was a World War II ex-fighter pilot, and I had heard back at Goose Bay that he was a regular guy.

We went on alert status immediately, all of us hoping that the Russian spy plane would overfly us so that we could nail him.

✈ ✈ ✈

It wasn't long before I discovered it was not an easy thing getting to sleep in the arctic, especially at this time of year where it was daylight around the clock.

Our BOQ had a narrow hall down its center with small bedrooms off of each side. There was no laundry on the base so we did our own as best we could. And because there was no one around to impress, we only ironed the collars and cuffs of our shirts because that was all that showed with our blouses on.

That Russian plane never came near Thule again, probably because the word of our arrival had leaked out to the Commies.

We got in a lot of good flying, though. And the scenery was spectacular. One day Wally and I flew around at low level hoping to spot a polar bear. I had given him my camera before takeoff so that he could snap some pictures for the folks back home. We circled for almost two hours, but no bears, so before heading back upstairs for the run back to Thule, Wally began taking pictures of the landscape. It wasn't until we were back on the ground that he discovered he'd forgotten to remove the lens cover. He can sure thank God we hadn't spotted a bear or I'd have really done something bad to this Ansel Adams wannabe.

We later learned that we couldn't have found a polar bear that day, anyway. Someone who knew the arctic told us polar bears did not appear in Greenland until after the ice formed. And we also learned that it was not uncommon for these magnificent beasts to roam some 2,500 miles during the long winter season.

There was an Eskimo village just outside the main gate. No igloos mind you, but instead, scores of ramshackle huts made from scrap lumber, discarded bits of metal, cardboard boxes and other materials scrounged from the base. One day while airborne, I spotted a lone Eskimo far out on the ice, stalking a seal which was sitting patiently beside a hole in the ice. I could see the guy clearly, and thought this was one crafty fellow. He had a white shield lashed to the sled in front of him, and used it to conceal himself as he painstakingly closed in on his prey. I continued my orbit and continued to watch the drama unfold below, and just as he was about ready to fire, I swooped down and buzzed the startled animal which immediately took refuge by plunging into the hole.

That was the first and last time in my life an Eskimo ever gave me the finger!

Near the end of November my flight was replaced by another, one commanded by my good friend, Captain Bob Emberry. The day/night he took over the alert duty, it was officially dark for the full 24 hours. For my part, the luster of the mission had long ago worn off. I thought that the odds on our Russian ever returning had shrunk to near zero, and felt kind of sorry for Bob's flight knowing it was facing three months of bitter cold and total darkness. Brrrrr. Not my idea of fun!

General Meyers, the NEAC commander, just happened to be visiting Thule on an inspection tour when this rotation was taking place, so we were able to hitch a ride south in his C-54 to Newfoundland where his headquarters was located. The following day we hitched a ride in a C-47 to Goose Bay, and rejoined the rest of the squadron that had been deployed from Otis.

Three days later the general popped in at Goose for a surprise visit. It seems the guy hated hanging around his headquarters, and he truly enjoyed being out among his troops. The morning of his departure, Colonel Dow thought it would be a good gesture if we sent two F-94s to escort him part of the way back to Newfoundland, so he told me to pick a wingman and have at it. The weather wasn't great, but then again, it wasn't all that bad, either. There was a broken overcast at about 600 feet, so I asked who would like to go with me. Fred Borman immediately volunteered, so we took off behind the general's C-54 and joined up on top of the clouds. I flew a loose formation on the left wing of the general's bird and Fred did the same on his right. After a few minutes of cruising along, a voice came up on the radio.

"That as close as you guys can fly?"

Oh, yeah? Well, watch this. We maneuvered our fighters to within five feet of the C-54's wingtips, flew that way for about five minutes, then bid an adieu and returned home.

Several days later Colonel Dow got a phone call from some staff colonel in NEAC Headquarters raising hell about us flying too close to the general's airplane. Colonel Dow searched me out and told me about it. Dow was never one to raise hell with his people; it just wasn't his style. About the worst thing I ever heard him say was, "That doesn't show me very much." But when he told me about his phone call, I quickly replied, "Colonel, it wasn't our idea. Someone in the C-54 came on the radio and told us to close it up."

To which he responded, and not unkindly, "Scrappy, my instincts tell me that someone was probably the crewchief."

In December I took a 30-day leave to go back to Otis to visit my family. Because of my impeccable timing, I missed going to a scheduled arctic survival school, and in February I managed to miss going again. Now it's common knowledge that fighter pilots will do anything and everything to avoid certain Air Force-sponsored activities, like attending survival schools, going to the flight surgeon's office for shots, or serving in non-flying staff jobs. These are for starters.

For the record, I never did attend that survival school, and I also "forgot" to get my shots!

I flew back to the States on a Military Air Transport Service (MATS) flight and had a great thirty days. Shortly after returning to Otis, I made it a point to go out to the base and brief Colonel Gray on our trip to Thule. He seemed pleased with my report, then out of the blue invited me to go duck hunting with him the following Sunday.

I quickly agreed.

We left in his staff car and drove around several nearby lakes until deciding on what looked like a good spot. We could see there were quite a few birds already on the water, so we positioned ourselves in a nearby stand of trees, confident we would be right under the ducks' flight path once flushed. It wasn't long before a noise startled them, and sure enough, they flew right over our position. Colonel Gray graciously told me to take the shot, and I did. Well, I blew it. In my haste I had left the safety on my shotgun, and by the time I discovered my mistake, it was too late. The moment was gone. Turned out that was the only possible shot for the entire day. I felt like a fool.

On our way back to Otis, Colonel Gray laughed it off, said it was still a fun trip. Then he went on to muse about all of the civil laws and Air Force regulations we had either broken, or at the very least, we'd stretched that day. For starters, neither of us had duck stamps; we had requisitioned an Air Force staff car for personal use, and we had thumbed our noses at a Massachusetts State Law which specifically forbade hunting on Sundays.

But Colonel Gray was right. We sure did have fun.

The following Sunday I played golf with Chappie and two of his pilots. He had just been promoted to major and was now the commander of the 58th. His squadron had recently been equipped with the new F-94C and I mentioned how I'd really like to fly one.

"I can make it happen, Scrappy, my boy," he said. "As soon as we finish the game I'll set you up for a flight. We'll skip the nineteenth hole today."

After the game we returned to the base, and since it was Sunday the only pilots there were the guys on the "alert flight." Chappie told the flight commander to take me out to a ship, give me a cockpit check, show me how to start the bird then chase me around on a flight.

We flew for an hour while the rest of the pilots in the flight filled out a questionnaire for me.

There was an army post adjacent to Otis Air Force Base. One night Colonel Gray, Chappie and I were chatting at the O Club bar when an army major in full dress uniform came up and rudely shoved me out of his way.

I tapped him on the shoulder. "I was standing there first and I'm going to stand there again."

Chappie, thinking I was going to get in trouble with Colonel Gray, jumped in between us. "Whoa, take it easy, Scrappy."

Colonel Gray looked first at the major then to me, and all he said was, "Are you going to deck him Scrappy, or do I have to?"

The army major left, muttering something about juvenile Air Force guys. The three of us were dressed in civvies, but that son of a bitch sure as hell knew who Colonel Gray was!

✈ ✈ ✈

I wanted to take my springer spaniel, Gail, back with me to Goose Bay, but was told by the MATS folks that would rank as a major "be no." Okay, I thought, I'll go to plan B.

The squadron at Goose had a C-47, and after making a couple of phone calls discovered it was scheduled to fly to Montreal about the time my leave was up. Plan B was taking shape. The day before the plane was scheduled to arrive I hopped a train north to Canada.

I had to spend the night in Montreal, so after I got Gail fed, watered, and settled in my hotel room, I went out for dinner. After my meal I decided to stop in a nearby bar for a nightcap. The place was dark, smoky and loud, and while waiting for my drink I couldn't help but hear the two men next to me arguing. Whatever they had a disagreement about, it was getting worse.

Finally the shorter one yelled out in a pissed-off voice, "I know nine different ways to render you unconscious, you prick."

"Well, I only know one," the other yelled back, and landed one helluva haymaker, sending the smaller guy flying off his barstool. He landed at my feet and lay very still. Oh, boy. I picked up my drink, flipped a fifty-cent piece on the counter, upended the glass, stepped over the comatose pugilist and got the hell out of there.

Tough town, Montreal.

The next day Gail and I boarded the C-47 and flew to Goose Bay. That hound loved the place. The guys in the squadron spoiled her rotten, and she in turn treated each like her long lost buddy whenever one entered the room. She spent her days the center of attention in the operations room and slept under my bunk at night. Captain William P. "Doc" Dougherty was my roommate and he loved that dog as much as I did.

✈ ✈ ✈

I must admit, the squadron at Goose Bay was loosely run compared to most squadrons back in the States. We had our operations room inside the base ops building, and our maintenance shop was housed in a small hangar right next door. We kept a pair of F-94s on alert, parked just outside the door between our two buildings. And I can confess now, there were many days when we didn't go out and do a preflight check on those birds as we were supposed to.

I came on alert one evening with the weather clear, visibility unlimited, and a moon the size of Texas which lit the place up like it was daytime. The streets, the runways, and the taxiways were covered with snow, and the moonlight bouncing off all this whiteness was blinding—so much so that I had difficulty making out where the buildings were. Nights like that were few and far between at Goose.

I donned my flying suit and laid my helmet and parachute by the door, commandeered a comfortable chair and began to read. Gail was back in my room snoozing. At 9:00 P.M. I got scrambled, so I grabbed my gear, raced down the hall, threw open the outside door and jumped into the first airplane. The crew chief already had the start procedure in progress, and as the turbine began to wind up, I strapped myself in. When the engine was fully started I began to taxi out, and did so at a pretty fair clip.

As I approached the end of the runway the tower had already cleared me onto the active so I made a rolling takeoff, and as I lined myself up, I kicked in the afterburner. Caboom! Holy shit, there was one helluva roar. What in the hell was that? Definitely not the sound of any normal afterburner I'd ever heard lighting up!

For those of you not familiar with an afterburner, it's a gizmo found at the tail end of a jet turbine. It has metal eyelids (adjustable nozzles) that pop open the instant it's lit, thus releasing both a sudden burst of flame and some extra thrust that builds up inside the turbine when additional raw fuel is dumped in to mix with unused oxygen in the exhaust stream. Well, the eyelids on my F-94 had been wired closed by the maintenance folks—no doubt because of an already ordered, but not yet delivered, critical part. I was already rolling down the runway when all hell broke loose, so I immediately came out of afterburner and made a normal takeoff. The error was 100 percent mine. After landing I discovered that maintenance had written up the problem in detail and on the proper form but, yep, in my haste to get airborne I hadn't bothered to read it. That's what I should have done as soon as I came on alert. Preflight the aircraft and look for any write-ups.

✈ ✈ ✈

The squadron supply officer shipped my outboard motor to Goose Bay hidden among a whole lot of crates of squadron stuff, and I spent several hours over the course of the next week cleaning, fiddling, and fixing, until I had it running like new. Then I bought a small plywood boat from one of the airmen in the squadron who had built it during the long, boring winter.

In June, four of us checked out a canoe from the recreation department and took off for a few days of camping and fishing. I towed the canoe with two of the guys in it, that way we were able to make good time getting down river to what we thought was the perfect spot.

We didn't know it, but fish didn't migrate in from the ocean and up into the streams at that latitude until way later in the summer. That little fact didn't faze us. We had a super time, though near the end of our trip we found ourselves getting low on food. Because fish was not on the menu, I tried to shoot a duck with my .45, but missed. One of the others had a .22 caliber target pistol and bagged an arthritic porcupine, which was also missing most of its quills.

I honestly don't recommend dining on this species of rodent if you have any choice in the matter.

Later that summer, our ops officer, Major Bud Hultin, and Lt. Ted Louskes, one of the squadron ROs and I, had ourselves flown out to a remote lake in an L-20 Beaver floatplane for some serious fishing. We camped near a spot where the water spilled downhill from one lake and emptied into another. Holy cow, there were fish everywhere! Not only did we catch a ton of five-pound, 25-inch brook trout, we also caught a bunch of Northern Pike. Those guys are big ugly buggers, and about as delectable as porcupine.

✈ ✈ ✈

Toward the end of my tour at Goose I damn near got busted by none other than 4-star General Curtis LeMay, the SAC Commander. And here was one time I wasn't even the guilty party!

It was the spring of 1953, and Princess Elizabeth was about to be crowned Queen of England. LeMay was en route to London for the coronation, and scheduled to land at Goose Bay to refuel. Doc Dougherty learned the general's arrival time and for some weird reason decided it would be a great idea to intercept his plane. He made the necessary arrangements with the ground radar folks, executed a perfect intercept and pulled up real tight on LeMay's left wing. Only problem was that the intercept occurred in the soup (clouds). Now, LeMay had a reputation for being a hard-ass commander, a no-nonsense officer who fired people on the spot if they pissed him off. In this instance the man was beyond pissed; he was apoplectic. He radioed the tower and said he wanted the officer in charge of that fighter squadron to be on the tarmac when he landed. The base operations officer tore across the hall to our squadron ops room and relayed this piece of doomsday news to a group of us milling about. I quickly scanned the room. Shit! There was no one who outranked me. I was it. Double shit! And I'd only been in grade as a major less than a month.

I had been in the process of changing into a flying suit to go on alert when I learned of my imminent beheading, and as I zipped-up, the door flew open and in stormed LeMay followed by a whole gaggle of ashen-faced base wheels. Before General LeMay could open his mouth, in walked Doc with his helmet tucked under his arm and a huge grin plastered all over his face. LeMay immediately figured out who the guilty party was and tore into a terrified Doc. After a fearful chewing out, he turned to the rest of us and growled, "I'll have you all know that I have my family on board that airplane and if your radar had been out of calibration this pilot could have killed us all." He turned to Doc and poked him in the chest. "You can intercept my boys when they come through Goose Bay all you want, but don't you ever intercept me in the clouds again. You got that?" He turned to leave, and as he did he spotted Gail at his feet, her tail going a mile a minute. He reached down and patted her on the head. "You look like a good dog." She wagged her tail all the harder, causing LeMay to smile, albeit briefly.

For several weeks after that incident, all the wheels at our headquarters— as well as the SAC wing commander—lived in fear of getting fired. But from what I'd heard about LeMay I really didn't think so.

I figured if anyone was going to get fired then it would have already happened. And besides, I also had the feeling he was impressed by Doc's intercept.

One day while airborne I happened to overhear Bob Emberry call ground radar and suggest going to channel 22. Out of curiosity I switched to that channel and heard him ask for my position. I immediately knew what was in the wind. He wanted to sneak up and get on my tail. Oh, yeah? I flipped off my IFF (Identification, friend or foe), quickly put the plane in a dive and headed towards the GCI site. Bob and the radar guy were still discussing my position when I buzzed the building at less than fifty feet. The radar controller said to Bob, "Never mind, he just buzzed us." That sort of thing always made my day!

✈ ✈ ✈

Goose Bay was a refueling base for fighter planes being ferried to NATO countries in Europe. They were usually flown over in flights of eight or twelve aircraft to better utilize the Air/Sea rescue planes and their support people.

It was during the arrival of one of these flights that Dan Farr popped into my life again. Evidently some wheel had made him get rid of his Bancroft Flighter, because he wasn't wearing it. He was ferrying an F-86 to Europe and, as usual, they were held over for weather at BW-1. This gave us a few days to hash over old times. We would meet at the club each night, down a few drinks and talk for hours.

On the fourth day I ran into him walking down the street with a big CO-2 bottle on his shoulder. I knew from times past that he used this to cool his beer. He'd place his brew into a garbage can then spray it down with CO-2. I now asked him where he had gotten the carbon dioxide and he said in a nonchalant, matter-of-fact manner, "Scrappy, I got it at the fire department."

I asked what he had told the firemen, positive that he'd probably concocted some weird story. Instead, Dan replied, "I just told them I needed it to cool my beer."

No one but Dan Farr could have pulled that off.

The next morning I saw my friend off on his way to Greenland.

✈ ✈ ✈

After an event-packed year I left Goose Bay with orders for Hamilton AFB, California. And, again, MATS wouldn't fly Gail. And again, I dusted off my Plan B. I went through several different possibilities in rapid succession but none panned out. I began to worry. But a day later my problem was solved, and in a most unexpected way. One of my buddies, Chuck Bennett, was scheduled to fly an F-94 to the States for a major overhaul, so he came to me and said he'd take Gail back with him.

I was dubious. "You think it could be done? I mean, you could take Gail home in an F-94?"

He giggled like a kid, then turned as serious as a pastor at Sunday services. "Scrappy, there aren't any Air Force reg that I'm aware of that says a dog can't fly in a fighter jet. Nope, Gail's coming with me!"

I returned to Westover, the only passenger in the cargo bay of a huge, double-decker C-124. I was torqued. Those MATS weenies could have put a thousand springer spaniels in there with me, and still had room for a thousand more!

Gail rode home strapped into the back seat of a fighter. Because of headwinds, Chuck had to make a refueling stop at Logan Airport in Boston. He told me that when he was ready to re-board, Gail couldn't wait to get back into her cockpit. She apparently thought the whole thing was some kind of fabulous adventure. And to keep her our of mischief during the flight he had put her inside a barracks bag with her head sticking out the top and the drawstring loosely tied around her neck.

I'll bet that ground crew at Logan must have run around like crazy trying to find a camera that particular day. I know I would have! Gail was probably the only springer to ever ride in a jet fighter.

12

California

I departed Otis and the cape for Hamilton AFB, along with Dorie, Ted, and the latest addition to the Johnson clan, my daughter, Carol, who had come kicking and screaming into the world in April. Of course my pooch, Gail, was with us, too. We picked up a new Buick Super Convertible in Newburg, New York, and set out on a leisurely cross-country ride to California with pre-planned stops in Wyoming and Idaho for some world-class trout fishing.

Hamilton Air Force Base was located on the northern shore of San Francisco Bay in Marin County. It was in a truly beautiful setting, nestled in the greenest rolling hills imaginable—reminiscent of those found in Western Ireland—and the entire county is dotted with picture perfect small towns: San Rafael, Petaluma, Novato, to name a few. The temperature is mild year round, and a major attraction for airmen stationed at Hamilton is its proximity to San Francisco.

After signing in, I learned I was going to work for my old commander at the 18th Fighter Group, Colonel Ira "Ike" Wintermute. Oh, oh, not the dreaded headquarters job with the Western Air Defense Command. Like all fighter pilots, I had strong—no, make that word read rabid—feelings about a headquarters assignment and I let my opinion be known to the colonel. Bad move.

"That's too goddamned bad, Scrappy, because the assignment stands."

Well not if I had anything to say about it! That afternoon Ike left on a three-day TDY, and before the folks at personnel could cut my orders making it a done deal, I skipped over his head and went to bend the ear of his boss, Colonel Harry Thyng, my old wing commander at Otis.

"Colonel, I don't want to work in headquarters," I said. "I'm a fighter pilot and I belong in a fighter squadron."

Thyng saw right through me, but at least he didn't slam the door shut in my face. "Tell you what I'll do, Scrappy. I'll speak to Ike. He'll be back Monday morning, so I want you here in my office at noon."

Thyng and Ike were both there when I arrived, dressed in a freshly starched uniform and sporting brand new shoes. I saluted, stood at attention, and held my breath. This was do-or-die time.

The meeting lasted all of thirty seconds.

All Colonel Thyng said was, "Ike, get this guy in a fighter squadron." And that was that.

I ended up in the 84th, which was equipped with F-94Cs, the same model I'd flown compliments of Chappie, back at Otis, but rules were rules and I still had to go through all the bullshit training.

Major Marvin Miller was our squadron commander. Because the ops position was already filled—and because of my rank—Miller made me his executive officer. Truth be told I was a dismal failure at keeping the necessary squadron paperwork flowing, but thanks to the tireless efforts of a great first sergeant and an airman clerk-typist, I managed to muddle through.

In the 84th I met Captain Craig Keller, nicknamed "Steelie Eyes" and one helluva lot of fun to be around. Steelie was a flight commander, and as did most other interceptor squadrons, we worked on a rotating flight schedule. This guy loved to fly and scheduled his flight with so many hours they oftentimes flew the airplanes out of commission, which meant the flight on the rotation behind his was constantly complaining there were no planes to fly.

One weekend I joined in on a four-ship cross-country led by Steelie. After several fuel stops we arrived at our destination for the night, Spokane, Washington, but solely because Steelie had a girlfriend there. It was a civilian tower which meant it operated on a different radio frequency than military towers—a fact Steelie forgot in his haste to get on the ground. Unable to make radio contact, he nonetheless barged ahead and landed without permission, a major, super-duper, whopper of a no-no. And he did so as a T-33 was taking off, the two actually passing each other on the runway going in different directions!

The rest of us said our silent oh, shit's, executed fast go-arounds and landed in the right direction. Steelie was in deep doo-doo. We later discovered that the base ops officer—whose responsibility it was to file the violation report—was also dating the girl Steelie had come to visit.

I soon found out that Steelie had experienced prior such problems because of his erratic flying ways. A couple of years earlier he had gone through a court martial for buzzing his mother's home in Santa Maria, a suburb of San Francisco. He beat the rap only because a key witness—a lady in her eighties—insisted she saw his P-51 dive straight down from a height of two hundred feet! The presiding judge laughed out loud at that one and dismissed the charge.

He also got some help from the wing commander, Colonel Jack Hayes on the understanding that he agreed to play on the base football team. I didn't see how he would wangle his way out of this one, he was getting a little old to be playing football.

Hamilton AFB was also home to a reserve squadron of weekend warriors. Theirs was not a flying outfit, so we didn't interface much except maybe to nod at each other going to and from the O Club.

One Saturday a guy from the unit showed up in our squadron and very politely asked if he could get a ride in the back seat of an F-94. There was nothing in the regs against this so the commander gave his okay and told Steelie to give him a ride. After the flight he thanked Steelie profusely and inquired if maybe he could do it again the following Saturday.

Steelie shrugged. "Check with me Saturday. If we have an open seat, I don't see why not."

When he showed up the following Saturday the reservist asked, "Could we fly in a formation? I've never flown in a formation before."

Steelie said sure, and scheduled a flight of four. After they were airborne the guy said, "My hometown's about fifteen miles north of the base; any chance we could we fly over it? I've never seen it from the air." As they approached the town in the four-ship he asked, "Can we fly down the main street at about 1000 feet so I can take a picture?"

Seemed reasonable to Steelie, so he did.

Well, the shit hit the fan pronto. The press was already calling base ops wanting to know: since when was the Air Force in the advertising business?

Say, what? In a blinding flash of insight Steelie knew then and there that he'd been good and properly had.

Turned out this aw-shucks, homespun weekend warrior owned a television store and had taken out a full page ad in the paper that morning saying that a formation of Air Force jets would fly down Main Street to celebrate the opening of his new shop!

Talk about having a black cloud follow you around. The brass tore Steelie a new one. The poor guy couldn't ever seem to win for losing!

In our squadron, we had a navy exchange officer; a lieutenant named Jack Sickle. Jack was one cool guy, a terrific pilot, and he fit in well with everybody on the base.

One day while flying solo Jack had a flameout. Now the old saying about every cloud having a silver lining certainly proved prophetic in this instance because the tower passed along to Jack some good news and some bad news. The good news: He was close to the base and at 20,000 feet he had sufficient altitude and time to execute a dead-stick landing if he couldn't re-light the turbine with an air start. The bad news: There was a cloudbank over the base with tops about 8,000 and bottoms at about 4,000.

Jack acknowledged that he understood the situation, and with the help of the radio homer entered into a standard high key, circular, flameout pattern. He broke into the clear at 4,000 on a base leg approach and brought his plane in with a textbook perfect dead-stick landing.

To put this feat into its proper perspective, Jack's flying had to be flawless that day—and it was. The runway at Hamilton was only seven thousand feet long and he had the freezing waters of San Francisco Bay at both ends to contend with. Heck, his nickname should have been Steelie!

Two months later Major Roy Meeker, our squadron ops officer, was transferred upstairs to wing and I was given his job. It was a dream come true.

That weekend I checked out a T-33 for a cross-country to build up some hours. After landing at several airfields, my last stop that Saturday was Davis Monthan AFB, in Tucson. By pre-arrangement I had dinner with a lady I had met in Yuma some months earlier, and at noon on Sunday I was back in my plane having filed a clearance for Hamilton. As I taxied out to takeoff position, I found I was number two behind a C-47 Goony Bird. The pilot was taking forever doing his run-up and preparing for takeoff and I was fast falling into a foul mood as I sat cooking under a broiling sun and waiting for this clown to take off.

As the C-47 finally started to roll, I moved smartly into the number one position for takeoff. I watched as it lumbered some 1500 feet down the runway at which point it became airborne. A moment later it suddenly veered sharply to the left. Christ Almighty, I couldn't believe what I was seeing! The damn thing was heading straight for the ramp which was crammed full of B-47 bombers! The Goony Bird cleared the GCA shack literally by inches then slammed back down hard on the concrete. It bounced once then spun completely around before coming to a stop less than five feet from the nearest B-47. Out of the corner of my eye I spotted three terrified maintenance troops running as fast as their legs could carry them.

I just sat in my cockpit: heart pounding, eyes transfixed. Holy shit, this could easily have been one for the frigging record books. I couldn't think of anything to say except, "Tower, this is Air Force 8768 ready for take-off." After a long pause the tower operator came back in a ragged, out-of-breath, I don't believe what I just saw voice, "8768, clear for take-off."

I never found out what caused that C-47 pilot to lose control the way he did, but I suspect the silly bugger failed to remove one or more of his control locks during the walk around inspection he forgot to make. Not that I ever failed to do a proper walk around!

✈ ✈ ✈

After being declared proficient in the F-94C, I was made an instructor pilot, something I really enjoyed doing. I remember one particular young lieutenant newly assigned to the squadron who needed to fly some extra training missions in order to become combat ready, so I volunteered to help him. One particular mission I planned involved having him fly a series of aerobatics designed to give him confidence in the airplane. We briefed, then as planned, I flew chase to make sure he got through the mission in one piece.

Once in the aerobatics area I had him perform several rolls, Emmelman turns, and some loops. I was following him through a loop when suddenly I heard a loud thump that was followed by a cloud of dust which filled the cockpit. And I found myself sitting about 15 inches lower than normal. My frigging seat had bottomed out! Now this sure grabbed my undivided attention since seat bottoming was an integral part of the entire ejection process. As soon as I determined I was not about to be ejected into the wild blue I breathed a little easier, but knew I still had one whale of a problem on my hands. I was sitting so low in the cockpit that I could barely see out the side of the canopy, far less the front. No way could I land this bird as matters now stood!

After trying everything I could think of I decided that the only thing left was for me to unbuckle my parachute and place it on the seat sideways so that I could elevate myself high enough to see out the front to land. This would be dicey at best, and I didn't want to fool around too much and maybe get myself blown out without a chute. I was finally able to get it into a position where I could reach the pedals and also see out the front. Everything went okay until near the end of my landing roll. Without my parachute behind my back I couldn't get any leverage against the seat to use the foot brakes. Oh, man, I was really moving!

Thank God for the plane's drag chute. With its help I was able to slow down enough to turn off the runway before joining the zillions of fishes in San Francisco Bay.

Parties were a way of life in the Air Force. One night Dorie and I were invited to a flight party at the home of Captain Norm Lamb. Norm was the flight commander of A flight. Like most of these get togethers, it was a bring your own bottle affair.

We had noticed that in the past if you brought a bottle of good stuff it was gone before the evening was up, so we decided to use a little cunning. We bought two bottles that afternoon—one was Old Grand-Dad bonded bourbon, the other a bottle of something like Old Overshoes. We decanted the Old Overshoes into an empty milk bottle then poured the Old Grand-Dad into its bottle and filled the Old Grand-Dad bottle with tea. At the end of the evening's festivities the tea laden Old Grand-Dad bottle was empty. We took the Old Overshoes bottle home, two-thirds full of Old Grand-Dad.

There's got to be a lesson there someplace.

One day the commander of Air Defense Command, General Chidlow, paid the base a visit and I was assigned to give him a tour of our squadron. He, his staff, our wing commander, Colonel Anderson, and I, made the rounds of the squadron's buildings then drove to the end of the runway to inspect the alert hangar. This type of hangar was a newly built addition to all Air Defense Command bases and Colonel Anderson suggested that I show the general how well and how fast the huge door could be opened and closed.

That particular type of a door was a godsend in the more northerly climates, but in temperate Marin County we never had a need to close it. Consequently, when I hit the button to lower the door, a ton of leaves tumbled down and blew in on us. Chidlow seemed not amused as he brushed himself off.

One day the commander of Air Defense Command, General Chidlow, paid the base a visit and I was assigned to give him a tour of our squadron.

Even though Hamilton was a Western Air Defense Command base, it hosted the 28th Air Division as a tenant organization on the field. Their commander was a brigadier general named Monro MacCloskey, and he had his own T-33. MacCloskey was another of those commanders who had become addicted to headquarters' assignments early in his career and as a consequence never accumulated much stick time. To his credit he understood his flying limitations and wisely recruited an instructor pilot from our squadron, Captain Robert E. Schricker, to ride in the back seat during his infrequent ventures into the wild blue. Of course Schricker made all the landings from the back seat, but MacCloskey liked to make everyone believe he was flying the T-Bird. He never did find out that all four thousand people assigned to Hamilton were wise to his little secret.

It was customary for the commander, ops officer and any pilot not assigned to a flight to stand alert about once a month in order to give the guys in the flight a break and to see that things were going well at the alert hangar.

I was pulling this duty one night when the weather turned bad with a storm moving in off the Pacific. The 28th Air Division had a command post, and it was in charge of the alert flight. Some wienie on the division staff had come up with the idea that when the base went below its weather minimums, the alert function would be transferred to Castle AFB at Merced, California. The command post ordered us to move.

This was real dumb thinking. Here we were, taking off in near zero/zero weather (ceiling-zero/visibility-zero), with the wind blowing about a zillion miles per hour and moving to a base that had no alert facilities, which meant we would have had to sit up in base operations the rest of the night. Of course it would have made a lot more sense to just leave us at Hamilton, and if we got scrambled we could then recover at Castle where the storm hadn't yet reached. It was so bad that one of the pilots went out behind the alert hangar and threw up. He still took off with the rest of us when the guy in charge of the command post said we had to go.

I was in the clouds immediately after taking off to the southeast. I had to then make a 180 degree turn to fly back over the homer that was located on a hill about five miles northwest of the base, then begin a climbout towards the ocean. To my surprise, I broke out of the clouds at about 18,000 feet and turned to a heading for Castle AFB. This was going a whole lot better than expected, but just as I leveled out, a red light popped on in the cockpit and my flight indicator went out. I made it to Castle AFB because I was on top of the clouds and there was a moon, but had this happened during the climbout I would have been in deep, deep shit.

Marv Miller was transferred, and the 84th began switching to F-89s. The F-89 was a big, ugly, lumbering airplane and I had no desire to fly it. Most pilots felt honor-bound to stand up for the plane they flew, but when questioned, F-89 pilots could only come up with, "It'll really slow down in a hurry."

We had been having a "time war" with our sister squadron on the base, the 325th, which was led by Lt. Col. Vincent "Vince" Gordon. One month they would fly the most hours; the next month we would. Articles printed in the base paper only served to add fuel to this competition. I decided we would end the war, so I had someone call ADC headquarters operations and ask how much time any jet squadron anywhere had flown in a single month, thus setting the record. It turned out to be about 1,300 hours.

We set out to beat it, and duly announced our accomplishment at Marv's going away party. It turned out that he had been the commander of the squadron that had flown the most hours in one month. He knew that we were flying a lot but it was a complete surprise to him that we had broken the ADC record. When the news hit WADF Headquarters, it caused quite the commotion. They immediately wanted to know if we had used the flying time wisely, blah blah blah.

That was the end of the Hamilton AFB time war.

In early 1955 I was offered the chance to go to Castle AFB as the project officer for a new fighter squadron being activated there. I jumped at the opportunity. For the first month I worked out of the 28th Air Division Headquarters at Hamilton, then moved my operation over to Castle. It was a lot like Goose Bay, another SAC controlled base, and its mission was to train B-52 pilots.

The day I left Hamilton, General MacCloskey called me into his office to remind me that this new squadron would be under his command, and not the SAC wing commander at Castle. He ended by saying, "Scrappy, when you get to Castle, first thing I want you to do is pay a courtesy call on General White." A beat later he added, "And don't you be puffing on your cigar when you make that call. It's not polite to smoke in the presence of a general officer unless you ask permission first."

I came to attention and saluted. "Yes, sir."

Outside of his office, I took one last big draw on the cigar I'd been smoking, ground out the stub in a huge brass ashtray in the hallway then exhaled a humongous blue-gray cloud toward the ceiling. I sauntered away with a big shit-eating grin on my face and feeling like a million.

I recruited Steelie to come to Castle as my assistant. The squadron buildings were still under construction and a part of my job description called for me to work with the base civil engineer in solving any problems relating to their completion. Our fighters were to be F-86Ds, but since none had arrived yet, the division loaned us a C-45 to get in our flying time.

Once the buildings were finished and given certificates of occupancy, the rest of the squadron members began pouring in from all over the United States. I was hoping against hope to be made the new commander, but the honchos up at Air Force Headquarters had other ideas. A staff study had recently been adopted which had recommended that all fighter squadron commanders should hold the rank of lieutenant colonel. But because they didn't have enough fighter-qualified lieutenant colonels flying the line they brought a bunch out of desk jobs, retrained them, then slapped them into these jobs, ready or not. The program was code-named "Blue Flame" and we got one of its graduates as our commander, a guy named Lieutenant Colonel Lee Lambert.

Before Lambert arrived, Steelie and I flew the C-45 to Las Vegas for an evening on the town. We landed at McCarren Field, Las Vegas's municipal airport, only because it was closer to the strip than was Nellis. We parked the plane, grabbed a cab, and set off for the Dunes Hotel.

After checking in we headed for the casinos and hit several spots in rapid succession. Steelie quickly found himself on a losing streak. He began cashing checks which I knew he'd be hard-pressed to cover, but I kept my mouth shut. Finally, he found himself down to his last Morgan Silver Dollar. Steelie made his way to a roulette wheel, and after kissing it goodbye, plunked the coin down on number 34. Son of a bitch, it hit! With his newfound stake his luck turned, and within forty minutes he had won enough money to ransom all his hot checks and pay for our festivities the rest of the night. And what a night it was, and all from his last silver dollar!

That summer we found we were getting 28 lieutenants fresh out of flying school and follow-on F-86 training. Colonel Lambert tapped me to be his ops officer and Steelie was made my assistant. Besides Steelie, I had two other captains; the rest of the guys in the squadron were all brown bar lieutenants. Man, what a great situation this was. Those lieutenants would gladly do anything they were told (legal, of course), and because most were single there were few wives to nag them for showing up at home late for dinner.

One day, Lambert, Steelie, another squadron pilot and I were up flying when Steelie had a flameout. We were within gliding distance of the field, so Colonel Lambert called the tower to tell them to clear the runway. Steelie came in and greased her down on the first 500 feet of pavement. It was a damn fine landing and we all congratulated him on his coolheaded performance. But

Steelie wasn't having any of it. Pale and shaky, he took off for operations without a word, leaving us huddled on the ramp to puzzle over his bizarre behavior.

I should have recognized the symptoms, but I didn't. Two weeks later I had to go back to Hamilton for an ops officers' meeting, so I asked Steelie to come along. We took off early with Steelie in the left seat of the C-45, and when we arrived over Hamilton we found ourselves in instrument flying conditions, but nothing serious. Visibility was generally good. But Steelie was having none of it. He was the aircraft commander, he made the decision not to continue, so we aborted and flew back to Castle. Lambert was pissed, and rightfully so, because I had missed the meeting, but not wanting to shove the blame onto Steelie, I took the rap.

The following Saturday I was leading a twelve-ship formation, and on a pass over the field and while I was looking down at the shadows of all 12 ships racing across the ground, I saw one abruptly break out of formation and hastily land. And through it all, not a word of explanation on the radio from the breakout pilot. After the rest of us landed I discovered my bolter was Steelie and that he had gone directly to see the flight surgeon. Later he mumbled something to me about vertigo. Now vertigo is something a pilot gets while flying in clouds, or on a very dark night. This day the weather was clear and we had a one-hundred-mile visibility range. I should have recognized there was now a serious problem with Steelie, and that his future as a pilot was now in doubt.

✈ ✈ ✈

After all our new airplanes had been thoroughly checked by maintenance and flown through several shakedown hours of rough and tumble maneuvers, we held an open house to introduce the locals in the valley to our squadron members and to explain our mission. We got a great write-up in both the local newspapers and a ton of sightseers showed up on a clear Saturday morning. North American Aircraft Corporation—the manufacturer of our F-86s— sent several company reps up from Los Angeles to be on hand for the big event.

We had two superduper, highly polished F-86 SabreJets sitting on the ramp as static displays, their canopies opened and ladders in place for sightseers to climb up and look inside the cockpit. A couple of highly charged lieutenants were assigned to each of these ships to tell our visitors all about the planes we flew. I had told them in an early morning briefing not to be bashful about telling our story. Well, one of them really took me at my word. He grabbed a North American rep as he was walking by and started his canned spiel. The visitor put his hand on the lieutenant's shoulder and said, "I know all that stuff, fella. My name's Bob Hoover, and I flew all the tests on this airplane."

When spring rolled around I started a squadron softball team. I was now thirty-six years old—no longer a kid—and my legs were starting to get kinda wobbly. I realized my limitations, so once I got the team up and running, I traded my position on the field with that of the manager. After our third game a new first sergeant arrived in the squadron: a man who also had a whole bunch of experience under his pinstripes as a baseball manager. I gladly turned over my duties to him, and he showed his appreciation by leading us to the base championship. Then, after picking up a pitcher from one of the other teams on base, we went on to win the worldwide USAF softball title that year. Talk about a celebration, I still get hangover-headaches today just thinking about it!

One evening at 7:00 P.M. the 28th Air Division Headquarters Staff sprung an exercise on us. They had several T-33s with radar reflectors attached to make them look like hostile bombers show up unannounced as blips on our base radar screens. Our job was simple: scramble the fighters and intercept the hostiles, then shoot them down (simulated, of course). One item we were graded on was the time it took us to get all our in-commission airplanes on a five-minute alert. Sneaky me, I had discovered that I could beat the system by calling in and saying that all our aircraft were on five-minute status as soon as the first five or six pilots had gotten into their planes. I knew they would never be able to scramble that many aircraft all at the same time, if for no other reason than they didn't have the capability to control them all. So when they finally did scramble, I had all my birds raring to go.

On one such occasion I'd been on the hotline several times in just as many minutes, yakking at the officer in charge of the command post, when I got momentarily distracted by something needing my immediate attention in our ops room. I put the phone down, took care of a problem then came back on the line to hear a voice on the other end asking me a question in somewhat of an abrupt manner.

"Jesus Christ, Mac, if you'll just hold your frigging horses, I'll get you that info when I can find a spare minute."

Turned out General MacCloskey had requisitioned the phone from the ops officer and was now on the line with me.

Lambert was sure I was history, and voiced his very real surprise a couple of days later when nothing had been said about it by the general. I suspect MacCloskey got a good laugh over the incident every time he told the story to his general officer buddies.

Our unofficial squadron patch had on its shield an angry looking octopus with all eight tentacles pointing downward and firing tracers. I had no idea where this creation had come from, but my guess is it was the creation of some well-oiled fighter pilots in the South Pacific during World War II. Customarily, such service patches include an inspirational motto in Latin inscribed across a heraldic banner beneath the shield, so I had the resident squadron artist add the words: "Exertus Mostus, Fightus Bestus." Most of the guys thought this was real Latin, and many voiced actual wonder at my knowledge of this long-dead lingo.

And because our squadron patch featured an octopus, I went one step further and decided we needed a real one for a mascot. I sent a new lieutenant on a mission to the U.S. Marine Service office at Monterey Bay to learn all about octopuses, and strongly suggested (half in jest) that when he came back he should be accompanied by a real live animal. The kid delivered, and proceeded to tell us all about the correct water temperature, the right salt content, the right sunlight, the right this, the right that, blah, blah, blah—everything we had to do to make sure our mascot would live a long and fruitful life. And he did. For about a week.

Then someone suggested we needed one from the warmer Pacific waters further south. Good idea. One of our flight commanders was from San Diego, so he flew an F-86 down to visit his mother, and while there went to the zoo and sweet-talked them out of an octopus. The creature came back in a big plastic bowl perched on his lap while he flew the plane.

This ugly beast lasted a little longer than the first, but not by much. I think he died of exhaustion brought on by having to produce so much ink. The guys from maintenance would come over on their coffee breaks, or at lunchtime, and stand around staring at the tank. Poor guy was constantly squirting out batches of black ink like some navy destroyer laying down a smoke screen. Then he would dart across the tank and hide under some rocks.

We gave up on the idea of having a live octopus for a mascot one month later after we buried him in a grassy area behind the squadron.

✈ ✈ ✈

By the end of the year I had grown weary of working for my Blue Flame, paper-shuffling commander. I had heard that the 83rd Squadron back at Hamilton was scheduled to get the new Lockheed F-104 Starfighter; a Mach-2 screamer, and every fighter pilot's dream machine. The whisper on the street was that this plane was somewhat more than just a tad difficult to fly, and had been dubbed "The missile with a man in it." Colonel Lambert informed me that the 83rd Squadron commander was picking his pilots carefully, and had actually asked for me by name to become his ops officer. Hot diggity damn! What a vote of confidence in my flying skills and my operational leadership abilities. I rushed home to share the good news with Dorie.

But after several weeks had passed with no orders coming down for me to PCS over to the 83rd I got tired of waiting, and in a moment of frustration went to the squadron orderly room and signed a volunteer statement for an overseas assignment. Lambert had an instant shit-fit when he found out. He was well aware that I had a solid reputation with the wheels both at command and division headquarters, and he also knew that if I left his squadron under these circumstances it would adversely impact his chances for promotion.

So to keep me from forwarding the overseas request, he promised to expedite my transfer to the 83rd. Colonel Lambert was a man of his word. I got orders sending me back to Hamilton.

13

Starfighter

Life in the 83rd was grand, possibly because our commander, Lieutenant Colonel Ray Evans, was an experienced fighter pilot and a great guy to work for. All of us were eager to get our hands on the new F-104 but the actual delivery date was delayed for almost a year, due mainly to an inordinate number of engine failures during the test program phase. A number of these failures occurred at low altitude—an insurmountable problem because the aircraft had a downward ejection system. Several highly regarded pilots, including Lockheed's chief test pilot, lost their lives in such mishaps.

It was also during this time that I discovered Steelie was an out-of-control gambler and had finally gone off the deep end. In California, poker games could be set up in the backrooms of bars as long as the proprietor had the required state permit. Steelie, it seems, had been spending all his free time in such games, had managed to lose big, and now had to deal with the fact that he had some heavy-duty markers out and no earthly way to cover these losses. What in the hell was he going to do?

In a moment of panic and outright desperation Steelie robbed a supermarket. But then he turned himself in to the authorities less than twenty-four hours later. He knew he would have been caught because he'd left a trail of clues a blind man could have followed. First, he had checked out a .38-caliber revolver from the squadron. Next, he had worn an Air Force raincoat along with a straw cowboy hat that he had bought the last time he and I had played golf.

I was devastated when I heard the news and blamed myself for not recognizing the seriousness of his problems before he self-destructed. And as if all this weren't enough, I learned that his wife was a full-blown alcoholic, and had been for some time. Looking back, it's hard to say whether he drove her to drink or her drinking was the root cause of his problems, but just before his final slide into hell, she had taken off for Los Angeles with another man and left him with their four children to take care of. Of course Steelie's Air Force career was finished, but he was fortunate enough to find a really good lawyer, and the man managed to keep him out of prison.

✈ ✈ ✈

All of the pilots in the 83rd Squadron were handpicked. Some had been invited over from the 84th, the 456th, and some were retained in the 83rd. After what seemed like a lifetime, we finally got our planes. Colonel Evans sent Walt Irwin and me to Edwards Air Force Base to become the first line pilots to checkout in the Starfighter. My friend, Bob Titus, was our instructor. As part of his initial brief he told us to take off and fly to altitude in afterburner. We did, and what an indescribable gas that turned out to be! I swear to God my climb attitude was straight up. On debrief I asked Bob why he'd prescribed the afterburner climb. His response was simple. "Scrappy, I thought you should experience the same thrill I did on my first flight in this incredible bird."

Walt and I completed our five-flight syllabus without incident and returned to Hamilton to tell the rest of the guys what a thrill they had in store.

✈ ✈ ✈

The Lockheed Corporation commissioned an artist to paint a large F-104 for our squadron, and the finished product was absolutely top drawer. A similar sized picture of an F-89 belonging to the 84th graced the wall over the bar at the Officers' Club instead of their squadron ops room. Ray and I had taken note of that fact and decided some O Club redecorating was in order. We removed their F-89 and hung our new F-104 in its place. We then took the F-89 painting and found a new home for it over the line of urinals in the men's room.

It just so happened (yeah, right) that the wing was holding a dining in at the club that very night. Ray and I made sure we were in the men's room when Tom Gerbing, the 84th's squadron commander walked in and saw his prized F-89 Scorpion sitting alert over a bunch of urinals. Seeing the disbelieving look frozen on his face at that particular instant in time was worth the price of having to dress up in our formal monkey suits for the night's festivities. Tom took it like a gentleman. He, too, was one hell of a guy.

✈ ✈ ✈

There was considerable apprehension voiced by a number of the base brass about the difficult flying characteristics of this airplane and the fact that the 7,000-foot runway at Hamilton was considered somewhat short. But the line pilots had no such qualms, and after some of the early problems were solved, the F-104 turned out to be a truly magnificent plane.

Engine failures at low altitude—coupled with the downward ejection system—were the cause of most of the initial pilot fatalities. Later planes were converted to an upward ejection platform, and after the J-79 engine had the bugs ironed out, it became very reliable. But before the improved J-79 engine was deemed ready, the squadron was actually assigned a midget (I kid you not) whose only job was to climb into the intakes and painstakingly check each of the many rotor blades for tiny cracks. This unusual solution to a problem indeed saved lives, and our small friend stayed with us until the engine was performing as well as any other turbine in the inventory.

Another associated problem with the Starfighter was the ease in which it created a sonic boom. Hamilton was close to metropolitan San Francisco and the F-104 tended to go supersonic with only the slightest nudge. Colonel Evans decided to approach the problem head on with a demonstration of sonic booms, the intent being to show the public they were not all that bad.

The base advertised an open house and the next Saturday morning, Walt, Jim and I did our thing. Walt flew over the crowd at 20,000 feet, Jim whistled over at 10,000 feet, and I whizzed on by at 5,000 feet. Okay, I admit it: I cheated a little. It was really at 2,800 feet. After tearing across the base at better than Mach 1, I made a snappy right turn out over San Francisco Bay, but my trailing sonic boom followed me to Novato, a small town to the northwest, causing several store windows to smash into a thousand shards. The red-faced base wheels quickly agreed Evans' idea was not that great after all, but nothing was done about it other than to pay for the damage. Our little demonstration had been pre-approved by every headquarters all the way up to the commanding general of Air Defense Command, so there was no talk of any heads rolling. But so much for a public relations coup!

Walt Irwin and I were best friends, probably because we had two things in common: we both loved to fly, and we both loved to fish. And I freely admit with no sense of inferiority whatsoever that Walt Irwin was the best fisherman I ever met. And that covers some eight decades of every type of fishing imaginable by yours truly.

Now having said all that, there is one fishing story I've got to recount, and it deals with the one and only time my fishing skill/luck surpassed his.

The season for steelhead trout opened one Saturday, so Walt, Jim McGaw and I rose early and headed for the Russian River. We arrived just before dawn with two rental boats in tow and stopped at a nearby café for some obligatory coffee and donuts. As we were leaving, and on the spur of the moment, some inner voice convinced me to buy two large—expensive—Mepps spinners.

Walt took one boat for himself because he planned to fish with wet flies, so Mac and I joined forces in the other to fish with lures. I armed myself with a seven-and-one-half-foot fly rod and a spinning reel loaded with ten-pound test monofilament.

It was the perfect morning for fishing. A slight mist still hung in the air and the temperature on the water was probably 50 degrees. I started casting one of my new spinners into a deep hole close to where we had anchored, and in no time at all I had brought in six steelheads averaging 12 pounds apiece. Even with my light tackle I was able to land them all because every time I hooked one, Mac would row us over to the shore where I'd jump out, and with my legs planted on *terra firma*, played and landed those large trout just right. This little departure from the norm was quite necessary because in our haste to get to the river, we had forgotten to bring a net.

The limit on steelheads was two per fisherman and I had caught the limit for all three of us. On the way home Walt growled in a pretend pissed-off voice, "You can fish every day for the rest of your frigging life, Scrappy Johnson, and you will never, I repeat, never, do that again."

He was bang-on, but I told him he was full of shit, and that he knew I was the better fisherman!

✈ ✈ ✈

One month later disaster struck hard, fast and totally unexpected. During an early morning flight Lieutenant Colonel Ray Evans was on final approach in a GCA pattern when his engine quit. My friend never had a chance. At five hundred feet, low airspeed and that damned downward ejection seat, Ray's fate was sealed. He plunged into San Francisco Bay and sank. And as if that weren't bad enough, within days of this horrible accident the commander of a sister squadron at Wright Patterson AFB was also killed when his plane suffered a similar flameout shortly after take-off.

With Ray Evans' untimely death, I asked myself the same question I'd asked back at Castle when I was with the 456th. Would I be made the squadron commander? To borrow a phrase from Yogi Berra, it was déjà vu all over again. Again, the answer was no. They sent another Blue Flame lieutenant colonel desk jockey type to be our commander. His name was John Bennett, and at our very first meeting he told me he needed this assignment in order to be promoted to colonel. No shit, pal. Of course I had the good sense not to come back with a wiseass reply like that. Smart move, too, because a few days later the man helped change my life forever.

The date was early May 1958, and I was having dinner at home when the phone rang. It was Bennett. He told me in an excited voice that the Air Force had just sent an order down for the squadron to send a pilot to Palmdale, California, for the express purpose of breaking the existing world's altitude record for an airplane.

He rushed on. "Scrappy, Colonel Buckey (the wing commander) wants you in that cockpit, and I told him I concur. What do you say about that?"

I was dumbfounded. An eternity passed before I managed to blurt out, "Yes, sir, I'll do it," and hung up before I had a chance to say something really dumb and blow the whole deal. My legs went all rubbery. I had to sit. My thoughts harkened back to that first meeting I had with Bennett. What if I had popped off at him that day? Hell, I knew the answer to such a dimwitted question. I would never have gotten this call.

Dorie was alarmed. Her face turned ashen.

"What is it, Scrappy?" she whispered, her voice breaking. "You've got to tell me what's happening."

I stared at her. A couple of times I tried to speak but nothing came out. My tongue was stuck to the roof of my mouth. I grabbed up my tumbler and upended it, dribbling water and crushed ice down my chin and onto my shirt-front. And still I stared.

And Dorie stared back. Gail slunk out from under the table and parked herself at my feet, her little head cocked upward.

The spell finally broke and my face creased into the biggest grin possible. I began to laugh uncontrollably.

Dorie let loose a huge swoosh of air and giggled, a little nervously at first, but quickly allowed it to blossom into a full-throated laugh.

"The Air Force has chosen me to set a world altitude record in the One-oh-four," I blurted out, my voice a full octave higher than normal. "Me, Scrappy Johnson, Dorie. No sir, they want the best damn fighter pilot in the whole frigging world to do the job: the one guy they know will do it right." I was chock-ablock full of myself and jabbering like a fool. I hoisted Dorie out of her chair and began to waltz her around our small kitchen—a flat-footed Fred Astaire and his graceful, smiling Ginger Rogers. I planted a kiss on her pretty upturned face.

"Oh, Scrappy, I'm so proud of you I think I'm going to burst at the seams!" Halfway through a turning spin she broke free from my grasp. "I'm going to call mother right now with the news. She always said you wouldn't amount to anything. Well, let's see what she has to say for herself now!"

✈ ✈ ✈

The next day, Walt Irwin, Jim Low and I were flown in a C-123 Provider to the Lockheed Plant at Palmdale and given our assignments. I already knew mine. It was to break the world's altitude record. Walt and Jim's? Walt was supposed to break the world's speed record and Jim was to make history beating the time-to-climb records.

I expected to find an upbeat bunch of civilian test pilots at Lockheed, so I was rudely taken aback when I discovered morale was in the dumps. These guys were the best of the best, but several of their friends had been killed flying the F-104—including the chief pilot—and his replacement now refused to fly the plane.

Two of the pilots though, Jake Holloman and Bill Parks, had continued flying the Starfighter, including some high altitude missions in spite of their own lingering misgivings, so their knowledge of the plane's performance characteristics was very helpful to me.

The present world altitude record was held by a British Canberra jet whose pilot had taken her up to 77,000 feet. The Canberra pilot had set the record by simply putting the rocket-boosted plane into a climb then hanging on for all his worth. The engineers at Lockheed knew this Rube Goldfarb approach to setting the record would not be hard to beat, but Kelly Johnson, (no relation) the head of the design team, wanted to beat the Brits by a very convincing margin. I agreed.

Walt and Jim were not so lucky. A snafu in the bowels of The Pentagon prevented them from flying the officially sanctioned speed and time-to-climb flights that day. For some reason their clearances failed to arrive at Palmdale in time for them to break those records. Both men were sorely disappointed.

For setting the altitude record in a supersonic jet, Kelly Johnson had suggested building up as much speed as possible in level flight at the optimum altitude for the airplane, and at the best temperature, which for the Starfighter was around 40,000 feet. His thinking being that at this altitude I would simply zoom the aircraft and see just how high it would go. And as for the temperature—well, the colder the air at the best altitude the better.

The flight profile called for me to accelerate to top speed at my optimum altitude, then pull back on the stick and climb at a 52-degree angle as high as it would go. The Lockheed engineers had drawn the angle on the canopy with a grease pencil to show me exactly what 52 degrees looked like. Cripes, it looked straight up! Furthermore, the engineers had figured that during my climb the afterburner would blow out from a lack of oxygen at about 63,000 feet and that my engine would flameout somewhere near 67,000. The laws of physics said the airplane would fly the rest of the way without any additional thrust. That was the up side of the equation.

The down side was that when my engine quit, cockpit pressurization would be lost and my partial pressure suit would automatically inflate. Any armchair critic could sit back and say, so what? But the pressure suits of the era were damn uncomfortable to wear when inflated, and it was next to impossible to move around and function when they expanded.

Then there were other issues—like the restriction to the inlet guide vane temperature limiting the speed I would attain prior to the zoom. I knew I was going to exceed the engine's temperature redline—I just didn't know by how much. And therein lay the rub. Exceed it by too much, the engine would stall and sustain major—possibly fatal—damage. If that scenario played out, then the very best I could expect would be an aborted mission. That's it? Heck, I can handle that! Or can I? Try as I might, I couldn't get the engineers to commit themselves one way or another on this subject, so in the end I realized I would have to use my own judgment and call my own shots if I ran into trouble at altitude.

✈ ✈ ✈

May 7, 1958. Palmdale, California. For some inexplicable reason I was not anxious as I strapped myself into the regular production model F-104A and began going through my engine start. Minutes later I taxied out onto Runway 4, positioned myself on the centerline and blasted off.

My track had been carefully designed so that I would reach zoom apogee directly over Edwards AFB. This was where all the official radar antennae and cameras had been installed, ready to photograph and record my exact altitude the moment I went over the top.

Success hinged upon having several things happen and each at the proper moment. I needed to obtain optimum speed, then burn off just the right amount of fuel at the right location at the start of my climb. The magic formula for setting the record was deceptively simple: The less fuel I had left onboard, the lighter the plane; the lighter the plane, the higher I'd go. But with one very important *caveat* remaining. I had to have enough fuel left in my tanks to make it back to Palmdale and land the plane.

✈ ✈ ✈

I was climbing. The clear, cobalt blue skies gave Palmdale, California, no cover. Landlocked and naked, the city stood at the mercy of the same sky that gave my F-104A life. I couldn't help but laugh to myself. I was getting paid to do something Michelangelo probably would have given his right hand for! Me, Scrappy Johnson, a Kentucky boy, soaring with the eagles and not frying chickens for Colonel Harland Sanders. Me, Grandma's "Golden Boy" at the controls of the Air Force's newest and best performing fighter plane ever.

As I headed for the coast and Santa Barbara, I gently coaxed the little aircraft up to 43,000 feet, turned over Santa Barbara and made a beeline for Edwards. Nailing the course, I moved the throttle lever into afterburner. The bird leapt forward. The airspeed indicator moved up rapidly until it showed I was ripping through the air at Mach 2.23. The only sound I heard was my own breathing.

Scrappy in the cockpit of his F-104A at Palmdale, CA, just prior to takeoff before setting the world's altitude record (courtesy of USAF).

I carefully eased back on the stick, pointing the little plane's nose to the recommended 52 degrees. It hammered the air from 50 to 60 thousand feet. Then, just as predicted, at 63,000 the afterburner cut out and at 67,000 the engine quit. Not enough oxygen. I was now in a glider. My pressure suit inflated. The Starfighter kept climbing, a rocket whose fuel had been exhausted yet still continuing upward.

I blasted through 70, then 80 thousand feet. The ailerons that help stabilize the wings were losing effectiveness as I soared higher and I was now having trouble keeping the wings level. The moment I went over the top I glanced down at my airspeed indicator. Whoa! Thirty knots.

As I peaked out, the sky became a dark purplish blue and I could make out the curvature of the earth. They later said I could have seen as far away as Salt Lake City had my eyesight been good enough and if I had found the time to look. I didn't. The stick shaker horn in the little plane was buzzing. I should have experienced the stick kicker, but it had been disabled by maintenance.

(L to R) Charles S. Lodgsdon, representative from the National Aeronautic Association, watches as Scrappy is congratulated by Tony LeVier, Lockheed's legendary test pilot, on his record-setting flight, 1958 (courtesy of USAF).

On the way down the radar operator at Edwards told me over the radio that I had reached 91,249 feet. (27,813 meters). Oh my god! I had just broken the world's altitude record by over 14,000 feet!

Continuing my gliding descent, I turned back toward Palmdale, anticipating my getting to a low enough altitude to air start the engine and get the pressure suit deflated. At 47,000 feet I was able to start the General Electric J-79 engine without incident and I raced toward Palmdale where a large contingent of Lockheed executives anxiously awaited the results.

I entered the traffic pattern at Palmdale with less than 400 lbs. of fuel and had barely enough to taxi to the parking area. Tony LeVier, Lockheed's chief engineering test pilot, climbed up to the cockpit, reached in and shook my hand. I was mentally and physically drained. Such an opportunity as this does not come often into anyone's life, and had I muffed it, I would have surely regretted it for the rest of mine.

I was elated things had turned out so well, and deep inside I felt that this had been a not too shabby a feat for a pilot with only thirty-three hours in the airplane. Lockheed personnel had a special interest in this record. They wanted to sell the F-104 to other nations—such as Japan—and the NATO countries.

That afternoon we boarded a chartered bus and headed for Los Angeles, guests of the Lockheed Corporation at a celebratory dinner party to be held that evening in a private upstairs room at the world famous Chasen's Restaurant.

When the festivities came to an end, a group of us were not quite ready to call it a night, so we decided to take the party over to the Beverly Hills Hilton where a suite had been reserved for Jim, Walt and me. Our noisy group clambered down to the restaurant foyer only to find the front door had been locked. Smartass Scrappy Johnson jokingly suggested breaking it down. One of the Lockheed pilots took me seriously and stuck his fist through the stained glass top of the door. I jumped back like a scalded cat. Holy shit, fella, I was just kidding! The door remained locked; he got a nasty cut on his hand, but at least the commotion had aroused the staff and a waiter came running to let the band of brigands out.

We arrived at the Hilton and swooped into the main lounge, a loud and obnoxious bunch of revelers. After several near-fisticuffs with other patrons, some in our party staggered off to our suite. By this time the patience of the barroom staff had worn thin and a King Kong of a bouncer made his way over to our table. "Ever since you guys came barging in here you've caused us nothing but trouble. There's another bar on the second floor, so why don't you go up there?"

No argument from us, so we did as he suggested. After downing another drink which none of us needed, we made our way up to the suite to find all our beds filled with snoring Lockheed test pilots. The only thing I could find for myself that halfway resembled a bed was a chaise lounge in the middle of the living room.

Just before falling asleep I heard someone calling room service for a bottle. I smiled. After the ruckus we'd caused I knew they weren't about to send one up. A short time later the front desk called and said, "Will that guy with the bleeding hand come down and let us get it sewn up. He's bleeding all over our carpets."

A Lockheed public relations liaison had told me early into the evening's festivities that there would be a press conference in the morning, so somehow I managed to heave myself off the uncomfortable chaise at seven. While dressing, I discovered the pilot with the cut hand had apparently draped his arm around me sometime the night before and had left a blood smear on the only uniform jacket I had with me. After unsuccessfully trying to get housekeeping to arrange for a fast cleaning job I made a command decision to wear my shirt and tie without the jacket.

For more than an hour I endured the onslaught of print media folks barking their questions at me, and after it was over a newspaperman sidled up next to me and asked, "You ever done anything like this before, Major?"

I shook my head. "Nope, first time. Why do you ask?"

"Thought maybe you had some experience with the press since you were so calm."

I wasn't about to confess that I still numb from all the booze I'd sucked down the previous evening!

After the news conference the PR guy and I made the rounds of the network studios where I was interviewed for the evening news shows. The footage was then to be duped and sent out by planes to stations all over the country. I finally made it back to The Beverly Hilton where I found Walt, Jim, and a couple of Lockheed hangers-on sitting around in their underwear eating chicken sandwiches and chugalugging champagne out of paper cups.

At 4:00 P.M. we went to the airport and boarded the C-123 that had been sent back from Hamilton to take us home. Major General Parker, Commander of Western Air Defense Force, Dorie, John Bennett and several others were on hand to greet the conquering hero. A lot of pictures were snapped before I was able to take Dorie home. And in the confusion of the moment, no one thought to inquire why I wasn't wearing my uniform blouse.

I made the front-page of just about every newspaper in the country except those in Los Angeles. Clark Gable upstaged me there. Seems the King had been granted another divorce that same day.

For a few months I felt like a celebrity. I made a lot of speeches and personal appearances, but after a while I got tired answering the same dumb question, which was: "How come you were the one chosen to make the flight?"

Scrappy and Dorie share a special moment at Hamilton AFB after Scrappy set the world's altitude record the day before, 1958 (courtesy of USAF).

So I started using a canned answer. "The truth is the Air Force knew that afterwards there'd be a lot of photos taken, so I was picked because I'm the best looking fighter pilot in the country."

That usually shut them up.

One incident that helped ground me in reality—especially at those times whenever my head would really start to swell—was a comment made by Tony LeVier when we were posing together for pictures shortly after the flight.

"Scrappy, you'll be in the limelight for a month or so then it will all fade away. So enjoy the moment while it lasts."

Was Tony ever right.

My squadron mates had a special coffee mug custom made for me, inscribed with the following in big, bold, gold letters:

AT A PARTY OR IN AN AIRPLANE,
NOBODY GETS HIGHER THAN SCRAPPY

A couple of weeks after my historic flight I took off in an F-104 on a routine test hop. Immediately after liftoff—and while still in afterburner—the red fire-warning light flashed on as bright as the noonday sun! Nooooo, say it ain't so! Why couldn't this shit have happened at altitude? I came out of afterburner as called for in the emergency procedures section of the Dash-1 flight manual. All I could see in my mind was an image of the recently killed Colonel Evans. Was this an omen saying I, too, was about to die? I radioed the tower.

"Hamilton Tower, Blackjack Three Zero. You guys see any fire or smoke coming from me?"

"Negative Blackjack Three Zero. Say your problem."

"I've got a fire warning light."

"Understood, Three Zero. You have an indication of fire on board. What are your intentions?"

"I'm going to attempt to land. Request a closed pattern."

"Roger, Three Zero, closed pattern approved. You have no other traffic. Fire rescue has been alerted. Good luck."

"Roger, thanks."

I still had the fire warning light as I manhandled the Starfighter into a closed pattern. The emergency procedures now called for my ejection if the fire warning light was still on.

I had some damn strong misgivings about this procedure. Reason told me it was probably a false alarm because the tower could see no evidence of a problem, so I flew the closed pattern and landed. I came to a stop on the runway, and because I still had that big red light on, I stopcocked the throttle and jumped out of the airplane. This was not as dangerous a feat as it sounds because the F-104 was small and not all that high off the ground.

Before the fire engines pulled up, I began making my way around the plane, fully convinced I had experienced a false alarm. As I approached the tail I discovered a huge hole in the right rear side of the fuselage. Holy shit! One of the afterburner spray bars used to insert raw fuel into the afterburner was pointing out instead of in. It had been spraying burning fuel onto the plane's skin and had I remained in afterburner even a couple of seconds longer it would have burned a large enough hole to cause the tail to fall off! And that would have definitely been curtains for one Scrappy Johnson.

Colonel George Ceuleers, the wing commander, put me in for an Air Medal for saving the plane, but ADC Flying Safety nixed it because I had acted contrary to the instructions in the flight manual. They said that I should have ejected. Assholes!

Two months later I was appointed a member of a panel commissioned to review the F-104 manual at Lockheed, in Burbank. After a lot of back and forth, we agreed to change the manual to coincide with the action that I had taken, which is how it should have read from the beginning.

"If a pilot could confirm by the tower, by an airborne aircraft, or any other way that there was no fire or smoke, he should try to land the aircraft."

On May 17, 1958, Walt Irwin went back to Palmdale and set a new world's speed record for an airplane. Great job. Of course, that called for another round of celebration!

A week later General Partridge, Commander of the Air Defense Command, visited the base, accompanied by retired Lieutenant General Jimmy Doolittle. Walt and I met the two generals on the ramp and I was thrilled and honored to have my picture taken with both. General Doolittle had always been one of my heroes. As I smiled for the camera, I thought back to the only other time I had met him—at the aircraft storage depot in Walnut Ridge, Arkansas, when he had come to retrieve his B-25 of Tokyo Raid fame.

I also received a note from Steelie. "Congratulations, Scrappy, but I'll pass on the 91,000 mark. I'm married again and life is good. The only problem is her kids and my kids keep beating up on our kids!" Steelie had four, she had three, and together they had two. I was really glad my old friend was okay. Years later I heard he had become a salesman and, with his great personality, I'm sure he did very well.

✈ ✈ ✈

About two months later a Major Garriet from the ADC Tactical Evaluation Team (Tac Eval) visited the squadron. He ferreted me out to ask if I would like to become his replacement. Seems he had just received orders mov-

Scrappy (left) explains to Lt. General Jimmy Doolittle and Captain Walt Irwin how he broke the altitude record (courtesy of USAF).

ing him onward and upward. Now, as I've already written, wild horses couldn't usually pry me out of a fighter squadron, but this day I was smart enough to understand that a Tac Eval slot was understood by anyone not brain dead to be a very prestigious assignment, so I said yes.

And besides, in this new job I would get to fly a whole bunch of different airplanes—including the F-104.

14

The Collier Trophy

Air Defense Command (ADC) Headquarters was located in Colorado Springs, Colorado. I had no sooner arrived and unpacked when I was called back to Hamilton on temporary duty orders. Once there I was told that there was a flap brewing in the Pacific and that the chief of staff had ordered the 83rd Squadron and their hot new F-104s to the island of Taiwan.

It seems Mao Tse-tung was making threatening noises again so the Starfighters were dispatched in a show of force, not unlike what we did earlier with our F-80s from Clark. This time the brass wanted the pilots to fly some high-speed runs down the corridor between China and Taiwan at Mach 2 so that when the commies tracked them on their radar screens they would sit back and scratch their heads in awe.

The F-104s were flown over in double-decker C-124 Globemaster IIs. With a wingspan of only 22 feet, and with one wing removed, our little interceptors fit easily inside a Globemaster.

I thought I was going to be sent to Taiwan to harass commies, but General Parker had other ideas. He personally had requested ADC send me back to Hamilton to command—and possibly build up—what was left of the squadron. Okay, I could handle that, but after being there for a couple of months, the buildup never happened. The Air Force had decided that the 83rd's visit to Taiwan wouldn't last long enough to warrant any such changes.

For one reason or another, ten planes had been left behind, but with very few maintenance personnel to take care of them the odds of any one being flight worthy on any given day was kind of a crapshoot. This made flying time scarce to none, so the wing commander graciously made a T-33 available for me to fly back to Colorado Springs every weekend. That magnanimous gesture sure made my temporary assignment more than passably palatable.

One weekend the wing got a request to provide an F-104 for a static display at an air show being sponsored by the Arizona National Guard at the Tucson Municipal Airport. My boss agreed, so I checked out a plane and flew to Colorado Springs Friday afternoon, the plan being I'd zip down to Tucson the following morning.

On takeoff from The Springs early that Saturday, I got a red warning light on the oil system. Shit! This meant not enough oil was getting to the engine, a strong indication I had an oil leak. This was definitely not good! Failure of the oil system had been the primary cause of a recent spate of fatal crashes, all of which only added to the airplane's fast-growing bad reputation. I called the tower, told them my problem, then gingerly flew the bird around and re-entered the landing pattern. Everything went fine until I was at about 200 feet and sinking fast that I began to run out of throttle. The thin air at the 5000-foot-plus altitude of Colorado Springs, coupled with my full fuel load and fully extended flaps, left me woefully short on thrust. I momentarily toyed with the idea of going to afterburner but quickly nixed that thought. The inevitable delay I would experience between the eyelids opening and the burner taking effect would have caused me to lose thrust at a most critical moment. Luckily my airspeed held until I was just past the runway threshold and I managed to grease her onto the pavement. What had seemed like an eternity was in reality something that had lasted less than four minutes.

My problem now was finding anyone who knew how to fix the plane. Then to add to my woes, the commander of the Air National Guard in Tucson tracked me down, got on the phone and began whining because my F-104 had been touted as being the mainstay of his show, and it now looked like I was going to become a no-show! I told him to hang in there.

By eleven I was finally able to find a Lockheed tech rep who promised to drive over to the base and check out my problem. Within moments he found a popped circuit breaker and no oil leak. Then in a real friendly manner he suggested I should have flown around at a safe altitude to burn off some fuel, then taken the time necessary to see if I really did have an oil leak. He put into words what I instinctively knew: it was not a good idea to have landed with a full fuel load on any runway, especially one at such a high altitude. In fact, it was a very bad idea! I was just so damn glad to be alive that I whole-heartedly agreed with his astute reasoning.

Colonel Victor "Vic" Milner was the chief of ADC Tactical Evaluation—a man blessed with a wonderful personality and a great sense of oratory. Shortly after my arrival the group sponsored a dining in for some reason or another—maybe simply because Colonel Milner wanted a party. Whatever the reason, we had a blast! Martinis were passed around in punch bowls, and we downed them by the gallon. The many toasts rendered that night were funny and oftentimes totally incoherent.

Sometime after midnight, dining in was declared over by Milner and because the O Club bar was closed, a bunch of us decided to go downtown and rendezvous at a new nightclub which was all the latest rave. In our gang of hellions was a RAF wing commander exchange officer named Bobby Oxpring, a character of the first order. Bobby hitched a ride to town in Vic's car along with a young lieutenant and me. Vic sort of slid through a changing red light in front of the nightclub and immediately a flashing red light appeared behind them. Out from an unmarked car stepped a man dressed in a double-breasted suit who politely introduced himself as the commissioner of police. Vic immediately went into overdrive and began praising the commissioner on heading up such a fine police department. He had just about talked the man out of giving him a ticket when Oxpring, who'd been dozing, suddenly sat up, stared through dulled, red-rimmed eyes at the commissioner, wrinkled his nose and said in a most disdainful British accent, "I say, Victor, old boy, who is this insipid little colonial peering through your window?"

Well, that did it. The insipid little colonial promptly handed Victor a twenty-two dollar ticket for running a red light.

The boss told me the next day that Bobby Oxpring enjoyed diplomatic immunity because he was theoretically in our country as a British Embassy staffer. He went on to explain that since his many shenanigans were never really serious breaches of law, his relationship with the local constabulary was a now never-ending source of amusement to the men in blue. Nights when he had been in town and drinking too much, Bobby would simply abandon his car and grab a cab home. Then next morning, when he couldn't remember where he left it, he would call the police, order them to find it, then order them to call him back with directions on how to retrieve it!

Bobby and I shared desks that were butted up against each other in a cramped office barely big enough to hold one occupant, far less two. One day as he was opening his tattered old leather briefcase to retrieve some papers, I said in a humorous voice, "Wing Commander Oxpring, when are you going to break down and buy a new attaché case? You know, sir," I continued, just full of myself, "we're all embarrassed to be seen in public with you. Really, it's a bloody disgrace."

But Bobby didn't smile. He looked at me not unkindly, then said in a strange, faraway voice, "Scrappy, this case belonged to my best chum, and I'll never replace it. You see, we both flew Spitfires during the Battle of Britain. Well, one afternoon Terry got shot down by the Hun right before my eyes. The poor blighter landed in less than twelve feet of water, but was unable to get out of his cockpit because he was wearing a damn cast on his left leg, don't you know. He drowned while I circled overhead and there wasn't a bloody thing I could do about it."

"Jesus, I'm sorry, Bobby." I felt about two inches tall.

"Ah, not to worry, lad. You'd have really liked Terry. Fact is, you kind of remind me of the silly bugger in a lot of ways." He looked at his watch. "Tell you what. Let's go to the club to tip back a couple of pints and I'll tell you some stories from those days. Guarantee you, Scrappy, I'll make your toes curl."

And he did. With stories that held me spellbound for hours. Seems this Limey prankster had shot down 18 German airplanes during World War II, a feat eerily similar to that of his father who had shot down an identical number in the First World War. Oxpring was one of the "few" whom Winston Churchill had immortalized in his famous speech praising the heroics of England's young airmen during the Battle of Britain.

When his six-month tour with us was up, Bobby was the guest of honor at a farewell dining in hosted by the ADC commander. After the meal a three-foot-long scroll from the Colorado Springs Police Department was unfurled and read aloud by Mister Vice, the junior second lieutenant in attendance. After some six minutes of laudatory writings, mostly tongue-in-cheek, the summation declared: "Bobby, you are a great guy, but all of the officers in this police department are glad to see you go. God speed, God bless, and God save the Queen! And may the Creator protect our brother officers in Great Britain upon your return."

A very spiffy, very proper, very British Wing Commander Bobby Oxpring received a rousing standing ovation from over one hundred colonials that night, and I do believe I was seated close enough to see his eyes turn to water.

🛧 🛧 🛧

Since I was supposed to keep current in both the F-86 and the F-104, I flew a T-33 to bases that were equipped with them. While on one such trip to Hamilton AFB, I found myself sitting in the 83rd Squadron Operations Center one Saturday morning waiting to fly. The only other pilot in there was Captain "Gris" Griskowsky. Gris was a skinny, cocky kid who reminded me of "Hotshot Charlie" of cartoon fame during World War II. Gris didn't look good at all, so I asked him what the trouble was.

"Last night I went to beer call, had a few, went some place else, got involved in a party and didn't get home until sunup," he replied. "My wife was waiting for me at the front door and she was in a real foul mood."

"'Where have you been all night?' she wanted to know.

"'I ran into George Scofield,' I answered immediately, referring to an old friend from way back. 'We talked until the bar closed and then stopped at Bergies (an all night hamburger joint) and talked some more.' Then he shook his head. "Scrappy, she looked me right in the eye and said, 'Oh, really! Why is it I seem to remember that Bergies burned down two weeks ago.'"

"Oh, shit!" was all I said.

When Gris first came to Hamilton he was assigned to the 84th Squadron which was still equipped with those godawful monsters called F-89s. He drove by the flightline and saw them for the first time, then looked up the ramp and spotted the sleek F-104s in front of the 83rd. Without even stopping to sign in, he continued on past the 84th Squadron, the 78th Fighter Group, the 78th Fighter Wing and the 28th Air Division before finally coming to the WADF Headquarters.

He entered the building, marched directly to Major General "Lefty" Parker's office where he told the secretary he wanted to see the general. When he was ushered in, he said, "General, I'm supposed to be assigned to the 84th Fighter Squadron and they have F-89s. Sir, I don't want to fly those beasts; I want to fly the F-104."

General Parker was truly one of the great guys, and instead of throwing Gris out of his office, he granted the request on the spot. And when Gris reported to the squadron where all of the pilots had been handpicked, none could believe that he'd actually pulled it off.

✈ ✈ ✈

One evening while the 83rd Squadron was deployed to Taiwan, the pilots arranged a dinner with some Chinese officers on the base. The men set it up so that Lt. Col. John Bennett found himself seated next to a Chinese officer who outranked him. They had earlier asked the Chinese gentleman to offer a toast to Bennett, then down his drink, which meant that in order to be polite, Bennett had to do the same. This ritual is known as *gumbai*, and it's a favorite among Orientals.

Well, Bennett was no drinker and this little game got to him, and fast. He barely made it back to the BOQ where he passed out cold on his cot. Soon afterward, some of the pilots came and carried him and his cot outside where they attached a condom to the end of a garden hose, turned on the water, but only just enough so that the condom filled gradually. They then laid it on his groin and waited. When the thing finally burst, they snapped several great pictures which were roundly admired by everyone in the squadron.

✈ ✈ ✈

One of the colonels in Tac Eval was a real popular guy named "Swede" Jensen. Swede had been the leader of the Air Force aerobatic team prior to its being called the "Thunderbirds," but now he was grounded because he had become blind in one eye. Consequently, whenever we went out on inspections he'd always fly in the back seat of one of the base T-33s. Whoever was flying that particular bird, he would always let Swede make the landing, which he always did, and did well. It sure seemed to me that if Swede could do this, then why in the hell was he grounded in the first place? This didn't make a lot of sense, especially in light of the fact that no one could see worth a damn from the back seat of a T-bird anyway!

Soon after Bobby left, I received a phone call from the Chief of Staff's office in The Pentagon informing me that I had been chosen to be that year's recipient of the prestigious Collier Trophy. Holy cow! I was completely tongue-tied! It seems that I was to be honored along with Captain Walt Irwin; Clarence L. (Kelly) Johnson, the man who'd designed the F-104; as well as Neil Burgess and Gerhard Neumann, the two General Electric designers of the J-79 engine. The Collier is awarded to a person, or persons, who had made significant achievements in the advancement of aviation in the year just passed. The voice on the other end told me that official orders would follow, directing me to come to Washington, DC.

That night at dinner, between bites of Colonel Sanders' fried chicken, I casually informed Dorie of the news. Then, waving a drumstick under her nose I asked, "You want to come with me to meet President Eisenhower at the White House, or would you rather stay here for your regular Wednesday afternoon bridge game? Your call, Dorie. And if you say you can't go, heck, I'll understand."

Dorie balled her paper napkin and heaved it at me, hitting me squarely between the eyes. "Just you try going off to see Mr. Eisenhower without me, Buster!"

We both laughed at her antics and her mock-serious threat then huddled for some serious trip planning.

We decided to take some leave in conjunction with the TDY so we drove, and as we passed through Louisville left Ted and Carol with their grandparents. Dorie's mother informed us that she was in the middle of making arrangements to have a big party in my honor when we returned, and had begun inviting friends from as far back as our grammar school days.

Before leaving Colorado, I'd heard through the grapevine that the Air Defense Command had actually recommended me for the Harmon Trophy but that General Curtis LeMay had been given the nod over me for what was being called a trumped-up deal. LeMay and a select crew had quickly flown a KC-135 down to Buenos Aires, Argentina, in November 1957, specifically so he could qualify to become that year's Harmon Trophy recipient. Seems The Strategic Air Command had no intention of being upstaged by a couple

Collier Trophy presentation by Vice President Nixon. (L to R) Capt. Walt Irwin, Scrappy Johnson, Lt. Gen. Jimmy Doolittle, VP Richard M. Nixon, General White, Neil Burgess, Gerhard Neumann, Clarence L. "Kelly" Johnson (courtesy of USAF).

of unknown line pilots from ADC. And that marked the first time I had ever heard anyone use the phrase "It's all about politics." But it sure wasn't the last.

The day after we arrived in Washington I attended a luncheon hosted by the sponsors of the Collier Trophy and I found myself seated between General LeMay, now the Air Force Vice Chief of Staff, and the world famous aviatrix, Jackie Cochran. After our dessert plates had been removed and the coffee poured, a rumpled reporter came over to our table and without preamble asked LeMay what he thought the future held for the aircraft carrier.

LeMay yanked an unlit cigar from his bow-shaped mouth and a dark, angry look creased his jowly face. "Young man, if you don't know the answer to that asinine question then you're beyond anyone's help." LeMay then turned to me, his left eyebrow arched in a big black question mark, obviously seeking the support of a fellow Air Force pilot. I just nodded, hoping that I, too, was coming across as a very sage visionary on the unique role of strategic bombers, and silently berating the clod for asking such a stupid question. It was all I could do to not spray a mouthful of coffee all over the starched white tablecloth.

It was customary for the President to present the Collier Trophy, but President Eisenhower was in Europe that day, so Vice President Richard Nixon stood in and did the honors. The ceremony was held in the Capitol Building and attended by a score of dignitaries, including Generals Jimmy Doolittle and Thomas D. White, the Chief of Staff of the Air Force.

Mister Nixon could not have been more warm or cordial, and he took the time to ask me several well-thought-out questions about my record-breaking flight. The man really impressed me that day, and I was genuinely pleased when he finally became president. People always seem to paint him as being stiff and wooden, but he certainly didn't live up to the billing in my presence. He was totally at ease. While we were standing around chatting prior to having our official picture taken, he leaned close and confided that the movie actor John Barrymore had once told him back when he was a freshman congressman in 1947, "Dick, whenever I'm about to have my picture snapped I just say 'ssshheee-iiit.' I've found it makes for a much better smile than saying cheese, and folks looking at the picture just seem to know you're having a whale of a good time."

We both said "ssshheee-iiit" in unison and the photo turned out great. In 1975 I sent it to President Nixon to have it autographed, and several weeks later it was returned with a warm message and signed Richard Millhouse Nixon. I still treasure that picture.

Chappie was stationed at The Pentagon at the time so I made sure he was invited to the luncheon and ceremony. A reception followed in a nearby hotel, and when it was over we snuck out, found a bar and proceeded to down a few for old time's sake. While we were playing catch-up, a public relations captain came in and basically ordered me to go to another room in the hotel to have my picture taken with LeMay. Partly because I was enjoying my reunion with Chappie, and partly because I resented the way LeMay had gotten the Harmon Trophy, I blew him off and stayed to finish my reunion with my friend. I never did have my moment of glory memorialized with General LeMay. In later years, I came to realize that Chappie would not have been so buddy-buddy. He would have zipped upstairs to have his picture taken with the Chief of Staff of The Air Force in a flash.

The drive back to Louisville was treacherous, especially going through the mountains of West Virginia and Eastern Kentucky. It was foggy, cold, and water seeping down from the slopes collected in large puddles on the roadways which than turned into ice as the temperature dropped into the teens.

When we finally arrived back in Louisville, Dorie's mother threw the big bash as promised. I had a fabulous evening strutting like some puffed-up peacock, the center of attention and devoid of all modesty. Throughout the night's festivities I would often overhear Ruth Holder bragging about my accomplishment to her friends.

✦ ✦ ✦

One busy Monday morning less than a month later, my assistant came into my office carrying a telex from the USAF deputy chief of staff for public relations. The gist of the three-page message read: "Send Captain Walt Irwin to the Netherlands to fly Queen Juliana in an F-104 orientation ride." Lockheed had pulled out all the stops for this one and was heavily promoting the flight worldwide because they wanted to sell their hot new interceptor to the Netherlands.

This would have been fine by me except for one petty little detail. Walt had been transferred to an F-102 squadron several weeks ago and was no longer current in the F-104. To bring him up to speed would take at least a couple of weeks, an impossible task seeing how the flight was scheduled to take place in six days.

"Colonel, how about I just submit your name instead? Heck, you're famous, just like Walt."

"That's alright by me," I replied, wondering what Dorie's reaction would be when I told her this latest piece of news at dinner.

The Air Force public relations folks had other ideas. A return telex arrived less than an hour later. "Major Johnson does not cooperate. Submit the name of another pilot."

What the hell, screw you! I was miffed, but I suggested Lieutenant Colonel Jim Jabara, one of our squadron commanders. Jim had been the first American jet ace in Korea, so in many respects it was an inspired choice. And anyway, I didn't really give a damn about flying the Queen of Holland around her Tinkertoy Kingdom anyway.

✦ ✦ ✦

One night I was awakened from a sound sleep by a ringing phone. Can't be good news, not at this hour, I thought, picking up the receiver. It was a very drunk Chappie James and Harlan Ball. They had been downing a few and decided it would be a hoot to roust me out of bed. I peered at my watch. 1:00 A.M. This was another bad habit that fighter pilots shared. After a snootful it would be, "Let's get Ol' Scrappy (substitute any other name you want right here) out of bed." But Dorie was fast becoming truly pissed, and just before she erupted, I got some really good news. Chappie whispered that he had seen my name on the lieutenant colonels' promotion list. "Don't tell a soul you heard it from me, Scrappy. My bosses find out, I'll be court-martialed for sure." He was still at The Pentagon and had access to the names on the list days ahead of the commanders in the field.

I nudged a still-trying-to-get-some-sleep Dorie to ask her how it felt to be snoozing next to a lieutenant colonel. Like some spring-loaded toy she shot upright, instantly wide-awake. We grabbed one another and hugged, then decided that piece of news deserved a celebratory toast. We crawled back into bed an hour before dawn, tired, but thoroughly happy.

And Chappie was back in her good graces.

Members of Tac Eval were chosen not only for their flying ability, but the winnowing process included a weighing of other traits that might set them aside from other pilot officers. Even so, some turned out to be real characters, and among this select group were Vic Milner, Richard "Steam Boat" Gariet and Bobby Oxpring. Another was Major Frank "Bones" Dietrick, a skinny guy with a great personality. Bones was also a terrific piano player and just plain fun to be around. The man could play everything from pop to classical—a huge plus in any Air Force unit because fighter pilots love to sing!

Upon leaving Tac Eval, "Steam Boat" was sent to the Air War College, and at the end of the course had to write his thesis on any famous battle in history. He chose "The Gunfight at the OK Corral." His thesis was accepted by the staff and he received an excellent grade.

Vic Milner was replaced as head of Tac Eval and promoted to a wing commander's slot at Goose Bay where Air Defense Command now had a composite wing. ADC's commanding general had a policy that if you had an aircraft accident in your wing, you had to come and explain it in person the following Monday. Of course, being called on the carpet in such a public fashion was meant to embarrass the wing commanders and motivate them in accident prevention. Unfortunately for Vic, his wing had a C-47 accident shortly after his arrival, so he had to brief the general the following Monday, then assure him it would not happen again. Vic was snake-bit because he had to make a repeat call the following Monday. Seems he had tried to stretch the fuel in his T-33 flying back to Goose Bay after the first briefing and had run into some really heavy-duty headwinds. Bottom line: he was forced to belly-in a mile short of Goose Bay! Ouch!

My promotion to lieutenant colonel became official the same day my boss, Colonel William "Bill" Schaefer, had to attend a meeting at another base. He had informed the support group personnel office that we needed a new secretary since ours had just been promoted up and out. Before leaving Schaefer said, "Scrappy, a gal's coming over for an interview but since I'll be gone, I need you to go over her qualifications with her. If you like what you see, then offer her the job."

Five of the other guys in the office overheard this conversation and as soon as Bill left we all began to speculate whether or not she'd be a looker or not. We did not have to wait long for our answer. The minute she was spotted, bedlam reigned.

"Holy Toledo!" one of the newer captains exclaimed in an excited falsetto voice. "Ohmygod, sir, she's hired, she's hired! Oh, Lordy, would you take a gander at those headlamps!"

The rest of us followed her every step down the narrow sidewalk until she disappeared into the building, our faces reflecting the fact that we had all just seen a bit of heaven on earth.

Luckily for me, she turned out to be an excellent secretary.

In the summer of 1960, HQ USAF sent a special request down to select six F-104 instructor pilots to be sent PCS (Permanent Change of Station) to the Military Advisory Group in Germany. I wanted to get back in F-104s, and I was getting restless in my present assignment simply because so much had changed in the last year. Guys like Vic and Bobby were long gone; I felt it was time for me to move on, so I lobbied the boss hard to be one of the six guys picked from a service-wide pool. After several weeks the list was approved in The Pentagon, and the number one slot held the name Lt. Col. Scrappy Johnson. The real icing on this particular cake was that Walt Irwin and a couple of other guys I'd known back in the 83rd Squadron were also going to be accompanying me.

Moving overseas turned out to be a big production and an even bigger headache. No way was it possible for us to take all of our household goods, so a whole bunch of stuff had to be put in storage. Then we all had to get shots, and lots of them. And lastly, I had the task I dreaded most: I had to find a home for my dog, Rusty.

Rusty was my third springer. He was a large, liver-and-white male, and definitely not the most laid back dog I'd ever owned, but he was one beautiful animal, and he was my buddy.

Major Dave Wynn in Tac Eval expressed an interest in taking Rusty, so he brought his four-year-old son over one Sunday afternoon to check him out. I led Rusty into the living room and all went well until the kid went over to Rusty and lovingly laid on his back. Rusty was having none of that little game so he bared his teeth and let loose with a low, warning growl. That ended any talk of adoption.

I advertised in the paper and the following Saturday an old codger came down out of the mountains to see him. He was pleased with what he saw, but I felt duty-bound to warn him of Rusty's mercurial temperament.

"I've got to be honest, he doesn't take to strangers too well."

As the mountain man was coaxing Rusty into the cab of his banged-up pickup with a large dog biscuit, he looked up at me, smiled and said, "Sonny, that's just the kind of dog I've been looking for."

We drove to the port at Philadelphia, dropped off our car for shipment, then rode in a MATS C-54 to Germany with only one refueling stop, that being in Prestwick, Scotland. Twenty hours later and with no sleep, we arrived at our quarters in the U.S. Embassy compound at Bad Godesburg. I can't remember ever being as tired in my life. After about a year in bed, we set to the task of turning our big, roomy apartment into a home. This was by far the best military quarters Dorie and I had ever seen. It was on a par with something a four-star would have been assigned at any stateside base.

15

The Luftwaffe

I was greeted with good news and bad news. The good news was that the Military Advisory Group (MAG) headquarters was housed right inside the U.S. Embassy, a scant two miles from my new home. The bad news was that I was tasked to be the advisor to a German wing at a base called Buechel, some sixty miles southeast and through the Eiffel Mountains.

The Sunday following my arrival, the Germans held an air show and my boss, a USAF colonel, took me down there to introduce me to the wing commander. The man seemed friendly enough, but after shaking my hand he turned to my mentor and said, "When I needed an advisor you would not give me one, Colonel. But now that I don't need one, why, who shows up on my doorstep but Colonel Johnson." He was all smiles as he spoke, but the brittle undercurrent I heard in his words set the tone for my three-year tour.

✈ ✈ ✈

On Monday my group of six reported to the MAG Headquarters for three days of nonstop briefings and signings for scads of supplies we were told we'd need to perform our jobs. On Wednesday I was issued a factory fresh, olive drab, Volkswagen Beetle, and on the following day drove my new Bug to Buechel and formally reported for duty.

As I waited for the German commander to invite me into his office, I took stock of my situation. Here I was, the supposed expert on the F-104, yet this German wing was still flying F-84Fs and hadn't a clue when their F-104s were supposed to arrive. Now I had once flown an F-84G around the flagpole for less than an hour when I was stationed at Goose Bay many years earlier, but that was it. I knew jack-all about the F-84, and was having to get checked out by the very pilots that I was supposed to advise!

✈ ✈ ✈

The German wing commander was a no-nonsense guy named Lieutenant Colonel Walter Krupinski, a World War II ace with 197 victories to his credit, an impressive number in anyone's book. For the most part German pilots had amassed considerably more victories than their American or British counterparts, an anomaly which could be explained in several ways. One was that the German fighter pilots had started out flying and fighting in the Spanish Revolution in 1936, then had fought continuously until the end of the war in Europe in 1945. Second, in many instances early in the war they were pitted against a less well-trained foe flying outdated airplanes; and third, if they were shot down it was usually over friendly territory which meant they lived to fly another day. I say this not in any way to discredit their incredible achievements but merely to explain the sizeable difference in numbers of kills between their aces and ours.

There were two distinct categories of pilots flying in the postwar Luftwaffe. One consisted of the very cliquish older World War II pilots—men now in their early forties—the other, younger, freshly trained pilots in their mid-to-late twenties. Regardless of the group, the training procedures were several years behind ours.

✈ ✈ ✈

One night a German pilot crashed shortly after takeoff. The instrument departure instructions for this particular airfield called for a climbout to three thousand feet while at the same time making a two-hundred-and-seventy degree turn to lock onto a homer. The pilot's takeoff was uneventful, but during his climb to three thousand feet—and while he was in the left turn and heading to the homer—he lost control of his plane and crashed.

The German board of inquiry quickly determined that this particular pilot had not flown in over thirty days. It seems he had just returned to duty from a month's leave, and to compound the problem he hadn't flown any night missions in over six months. The board also took note of the fact he had taken off into a thunderstorm. When asked for my opinion, I told the board that he could have flown that flight under the same conditions ten times in a row and that he would have in all likelihood crashed in nine of them. This observation was met with stony silence. Needless to say, it was not incorporated into the final draft.

A short time later a second pilot crashed and was killed during a daytime flight. Even though he had a 300-foot ceiling to contend with, this particular accident should never have happened.

For as long as anyone can remember, German-built aircraft had their flight indicators manufactured with the indices scribed on the bottom of the instrument, while those manufactured by the British and Americans were exactly the opposite, as in the U.S.-built F-84. Anyway, it seems that some staff officer at Luftwaffe Headquarters had decided on his own initiative to change the flight indicators back to the old German configuration. The order came down through maintenance channels to institute the change, however, no one in the operational side of the house was told about this radical modification. The unsuspecting young pilot took off, flew into the 300-foot ceiling, immediately checked his instruments and correctly rolled over as his attitude indicator was telling him he was flying inverted. Less than three seconds later he crashed.

The German Air Force in those days had scores of other maintenance and mechanical issues to contend with. The majority of the maintenance troops were draftees, which meant they were only obligated to serve in the Luftwaffe for eighteen months. This was nowhere near enough time to be trained in such a highly technical field, but the Germans had no intention of changing the status quo. Which meant that I often found myself unable to do a whole lot of useful advising during my tour.

✈ ✈ ✈

In the summer of 1961 someone realized there were enough ADC Tac Eval alumni spread around in Europe to warrant a bunch of us getting together for a reunion. The call went out, and Dorie and I spent a week with about thirty friends at the Eipse Hotel in the Alps. This was a U.S.-managed property whose primary mission was to provide first class R&R (Rest and Relaxation) accommodations for military personnel. Somebody in our little group wrote up some fake orders which we used to get Bobby Oxpring to come over from England. Bobby had recently been promoted to group captain, a rank equal to a U.S. colonel, and my British pal was ready for some serious partying.

The man hadn't changed a whit, and the first night of our group get-together he regaled us with an interesting tale. It seems he had been tasked to lead the latest annual parade celebrating the Battle of Britain and, on the Thursday evening prior to the grand occasion, he'd held a meeting with the man who was to be his sergeant major in Saturday's big to-do. Bobby noticed the man's uniform was threadbare and somewhat seedy, so he instructed the sergeant to get another. Well, Bobby took a gander at his own best uniform and saw that it wasn't all that great either, so first thing Friday morning he went in search of a tailor who could put together a new one for him in record time. He picked up his crisp new uniform early Saturday and, while putting it on in a room near the parade ground, discovered five stripes sewn onto his right sleeve. "Crikey, there's only supposed to be four!" Bobby exclaimed, wickedly mimicking the stricken sergeant in a bang-on cockney accent. "I can't salute the Queen with five bloody strips on my sleeve; there's no such rank in the RAF!" He frantically called out to one of the Queen's Guard dressing nearby, "Get me a razor blade."

Bobby began laughing as he explained how a seven-foot-tall giant in the Queen's Guard, resplendent in his two-foot beaver hat, took off at a fast gait and returned with a razor blade and proceeded to cut off the extra stripe. Bobby made it to the parade ground just in time, and at the proper moment rendered the smartest salute of the morning to his monarch.

As for the rest of the week, I can report it was a memorable one for me, visiting with pals from my not so distant past and enjoying a libation, or two, or three.

✈ ✈ ✈

One night several months later, Dorie and I were having a quiet after dinner drink at the bar at the Von Steuben, a U.S. military hotel in Wiesbaden, when in walked Bones Dietrick, an old friend. While we were chatting and playing catch-up, three major generals in dress uniforms entered, bellied up to the bar and ordered a round. I recognized them all from my days at ADC.

After a spate of exchanged greetings, one of them explained that they were now stationed at USAFE Headquarters, which meant they spent a lot of time in their fancier uniforms because their duties required they attend so many official functions. After a few minutes of small talk, the oldest said, "Let's go to the lounge upstairs and have some fun. It's got a pretty decent piano and I'm thinking a good old fashioned American sing-a-long à la Mitch Miller is definitely in order."

We all ascended the stairs and traipsed into the lounge only to find the piano padlocked to the wall with its keyboard facing inward. By now we had attracted several bystanders, all eagerly awaiting the music to start, so one of the generals sent the bartender off to get the manager to come and unlock the piano. The man returned and with a long face reported that no one could find the key. That bit of news failed to deter the general. "Then go get something to pry the lock open," he ordered. Off the man went again and returned with a crowbar.

Bones played and we sang until we were all hoarse. It was well past two o'clock in the morning when the group decided to call it a night.

The one thing fighter pilots love most, next to flying and drinking, is singing songs—especially songs about flying, and drinking!

✈✈✈

One really big plus about being stationed in Germany was that we were able to visit so many famous places. Dorie, the children, and I went to Paris several times, London twice, and once to Spain for a truly memorable vacation. Now I'll be the first to admit that I'm not all that keen on sightseeing, so on many of those trips I would remain outside the museums or churches in the various cities and watch the world pass me by while Dorie took the children inside and loaded them up on culture. I did go on one tour—reluctantly, to be sure—but was totally turned off when some jerk tried to sell me a fistful of pornographic postcards right on the steps of Notre Dame Cathedral, for Christ's sake! And not a gendarme in sight!

✈✈✈

After a year and a half of flying the F-84F, the wing was finally notified of the pending arrival of our first F-104Gs, prompting the Luftwaffe to start sending pilots to the Lockheed plant at Palmdale to get checked out. Since I hadn't flown the Starfighter for almost two years, I arranged for the U.S. Air Force to send me along with the first group. Six Germans and I went to California and spent the next ten weeks flying the F-104G. It was great being back in the Starfighter; I hadn't realized just how much I'd missed it. While there, I discovered that the Air Force didn't have a lock on goofy characters. Lockheed had its fair share of zanies as well.

One was a rather long-in-the-tooth test pilot who was flying the navy version of a T-33 one morning when he suffered an engine failure while making the turn onto final. There was no way he could stretch out his glide so he came down real hard just short of the runway threshold. He survived the impact and was limping around the site when the crash crew arrived along with several other company pilots.

One rushed over to the guy and yelled, "What the hell happened, Charlie?"

The man just shook his head and replied, "How should I know, I just got here myself!"

✈✈✈

The Luftwaffe also had a base just across the Mosel River, which was equipped with Canadian Sabres. As soon as I got back to Germany after being checked out in Palmdale, I flew the Starfighter every chance I got (sometimes in formation, sometimes alone). On those days when I flew alone, I would have a great time messing with those Sabre drivers. Often I would spot eight or ten of them mixing it up, then I'd fly up to a point just below their contrails, accelerate to about Mach 1.3, make a hair-raising pass through the lot of them then hightail it out of there. I would look back and laugh myself silly at all those contrails trying to catch up with me. The Germans would follow me for ten or fifteen miles until they acknowledged the futility of it all by breaking away and heading back to their practice area. I would lurk well below until they were engrossed in their games again then repeat the process. Toying with those guys was a helluva lot of fun.

Later in my career I often wished that I hadn't volunteered for that advisor's job. I'm not the diplomatic type, and I came to realize that I would have much rather spent those three years in an American fighter unit.

Looking back, though, I must say that the highlight of our tour in Germany was the birth of our son, Billy. He joined the Johnson clan shortly after our arrival, and Dorie and I couldn't have been happier.

16

The Tactical Air Command

My tour in Germany ended in August 1963 and I returned home to my follow-on assignment of choice: I was joining the 479th Tactical Fighter Wing at George Air Force Base, California. This renowned wing was equipped with F-104Cs and Ds, and its primary mission was air superiority. I was anxious to get on board, and upon arrival was delighted to learn that my old friend Walt Irwin was also assigned to the same squadron.

My first order of business was to become combat ready, which meant I had to qualify in air and ground gunnery, low-level navigation, dive-bombing and rocketry as well as in-flight refueling. No question this was a full plate, yet I handled all but that last item with ease. In fact, after my first attempt at air-to-air refueling I wasn't at all sure I would ever be able to master the skill. The F-104 was refueled on a basket-like contraption, and staying hooked to the tanker was no easy chore. Wind currents tended to push my small fighter away from the basket and I found it necessary to constantly cross control the Starfighter just to keep it in the correct position long enough to on-load fuel. On that first mission I flew wildly: in and out, up and down, going everywhere except where I wanted to be. I had an IP (instructor pilot) in the back seat of my D model, and I felt badly for him because of the rough ride he was getting. But the guy was a real cool head, and he gave me scores of valuable pointers. After a couple of practice missions I got the hang of it and was soon refueling without all the gymnastics.

When I turned forty I discovered I had to start using reading glasses, and by the time my forty-third birthday rolled around I was having considerable difficulty dialing in the correct radio channels, especially at night. I began practicing changing the channels by feel, but there were times this makeshift maneuver didn't work.

One such occasion was when Captain Dick Quigley and I ferried a couple of F-104s to Myrtle Beach, South Carolina, where one of our squadrons was deployed, We arrived over the East Coast about nine o'clock at night only to be greeted by a large thunderstorm over Myrtle. No landing here, we were told by the tower, so we diverted south to Warner Robins, in Georgia. Dick was flying lead because I was still in training, which meant I would be landing on his wing. During the descent and approach, I completely screwed up when it came time to change radio channels, forcing me to land without radio contact. Dick said nothing after we landed, but I knew this problem couldn't last much longer or there'd be some serious consequences.

A week later during a visit with the flight surgeon, the man floored me when he replied to my confession, "No big deal, Colonel, we'll get you fitted with bifocals, that's all." That's it? For some dumb-ass reason I'd been living under the misapprehension that if the day ever came when I needed bifocals, then that would be sayonara for me and I'd become permanently grounded.

I was fitted with my new glasses and a new world opened up right before my eyes.

I was now a seasoned lieutenant colonel and had hoped to become a squadron commander. I knew I was ready, but all of the squadrons already had commanders, so instead, I was made a squadron operations officer. At times it seemed I was destined to fill that job for the rest of my career, but each time I felt this way, I cheered myself by remembering this was far better than being a PX officer.

General Sweeney commanded Tactical Air Command (TAC) in those days. He was an ex-Strategic Air Command (SAC) boss who had brought with him all his big bomber management procedures which included such nitpicking crap as having to inform the TAC command post that you'd be incommunicado for even the few minutes you had to go to the john! And you sure as hell could forget about going out to the base on any Sunday morning, kick the tires then fly off into the wild blue as Don Scherer and I had done on so many Sundays back in the Philippines. No sir! Each flight had to be scheduled at least a week in advance, and if you missed the scheduled takeoff by more than a few minutes—regardless of reason—then you lost brownie points bigtime on Sweeney's rating system. And wing commanders whose wings showed up at the bottom of this rating system two months in a row were usually looking for another job by the end of the following month.

✦ ✦ ✦

In the winter of 1963–64, our squadron was tasked to deploy for three months to Moron, Spain. The squadron commander, Lieutenant Colonel Howard "Howie" Dale, wanted us to fly non-stop from George to Moron, in spite of the fact that the standard procedure was to fly to a base on the east coast, rest, refuel, then island hop to Bermuda, the Azores then into Moron. This really was a clumsy way to doing things. If anyone had a maintenance problem pop up during any of these refueling stops then it either caused long delays for everyone, or the decision had to be made to leave the problem airplane behind.

Before TAC would consider signing off on our non-stop flight, Howie and I had to go to Langley AFB and brief General Sweeney personally. Howie was to do the actual briefing and I went along to hold the pointer and flip the charts. We flew to Langley in a two-seater, and the day the briefing was scheduled Sweeney was off visiting some base or another in Florida. His vice commander, a three-star, listened to the briefing, asked a few probative questions, then said to Howie, "It sounds good to me, Colonel, but I have to call the boss and get his okay." I couldn't believe my ears. This three-star general was not permitted to make a simple decision; this was a guy who could be commanding a numbered Air Force in his own right, for Christ's sake! That, unfortunately, was typical of the way Sweeney ran his command. While Howie and I cooled our heels, the vice commander explained our mission plan in detail to Sweeney, and after about ten minutes of yakking back and forth, he announced, "General Sweeney says it's a go." The oracle had spoken!

The flight was to last about eleven hours and called for six in-flight refueling hook-ups. We took off from George about 9:30 P.M. on a Monday, with me flying in a wing position because I had not yet made an ocean crossing. (This was another of Sweeney's rules.) The weather en route was supposed to be good except for a front that seemed to be forming over the mid–Atlantic.

We had two sets of tankers assigned to the mission: one tanker for each flight of F-104s. We picked up our first set of flying gas stations over Kansas, refueled without a hitch, repeated the maneuver over Ohio and then again southwest of the coast of Maine.

It was a piece of cake until the third hook-up. The night was hazy—not cloudy—yet visibility was low. As I approached my tanker I inexplicably experienced a severe case of vertigo. It felt as though the behemoth and I were flying along with our left wings pointed toward the ground. This had happened to me once before and I had been able to overcome it, but experiencing vertigo while refueling with a basket in the middle of the night was a whole other matter.

I elected to hold off, and told numbers three and four to refuel ahead of me, hoping that the whirling motion would pass. I lucked out big time. As number four backed off the tanker and I approached it again—full of apprehension, I might add—a very thin line of light appeared in my windscreen signaling daybreak. Suddenly, we were both flying straight and level again and the refueling went off without a hitch.

Soon after, we joined up with our second set of tankers and headed out over the Atlantic, hitting the front about halfway across as briefed. It took about forty minutes for the group to penetrate that weather system, but it didn't interfere with our refueling.

We all wore rubber "poopy suits" under our normal flying gear for protection from the cold waters of the North Atlantic in the unlikely eventuality we had to punch out. These things are miserable to wear, and shortly after dawn I made the decision to cut the tight wristbands on mine in order to get the blood flowing back into my hands. This little bit of tailoring meant that the suit would leak, but fortunately I didn't have to test its usefulness.

The most difficult part of the flight was sitting in that small cockpit for so long. We'd each been given six white pills from the flight surgeon before departing George, which we called our "go pills." One of the greeters on the ground at Moron asked me after landing how I felt after such a long flight. I just grinned and said, "If I had six more of those little pills I could fly around the world."

✈ ✈ ✈

The squadron enjoyed an excellent tour of duty at Moron. Our mission was simple: provide air defense for the SAC wing stationed there. I'd performed similar missions at Cape Cod, Thule, Goose Bay and Castle, so to me this assignment was a piece of cake.

Although far from home, we still had problems with General Sweeney's rules. Even though we were now under the operational command of United States Air Force Europe, (USAFE) TAC still insisted we complete our flying training by filling all the squares on our TAC checklist. One glaring problem was that we did not have a bomb/gunnery range at our disposal to complete that particular phase of the training syllabus, so we sought assistance from USAFE Headquarters. They had little sympathy. Their thought was that since our mission in Europe was air defense, then any bombing and ground gunnery training should be waived. I sure as shit couldn't find fault with their reasoning, and neither could Howie, but Sweeney's rules still dogged us, so I looked elsewhere for a solution.

Two days later we learned that the Spaniards had a range near the base at Zaragosa, so I flew over there to get permission from the local commander to use it. The Spanish colonel in charge was only too happy to have us use his range, but said that as a formality we would need to ask the civilian political leader in Zaragosa to approve the deal. Dale and I met with a very distinguished gentleman, and after some ceremonious conversation, he, too, gave his blessings for us to work on the range.

Soon after that we sent our first detachment to Zaragosa to start training. One day later our squadron gunnery officer reported back that the range was very primitive and that he didn't think it would work. I flew back up to take a look. The man was right. It was even difficult for me to ferret out the boundary markings, targets, etc., and I had the devil's own time distinguishing the range from the rest of the arid Spanish countryside. It was so poorly marked and maintained that no one could possibly distinguish pull-up points and other critical markings. Nonetheless, I decided we would go ahead with the training. I also convinced Howie to record the results and send a report to TAC Headquarters which would reflect scores accomplished on a decent range, or, as Steelie Eyes back at Hamilton AFB would have so aptly put it: Fake it. The bottom line was this: when given a recognizably impossible, stupid task, fighter pilots will always figure out a way to beat the system.

I made several flights from Moron to Zaragosa during the time we were completing our training. While flying back to Moron from one of these trips, and still under the control of Zaragosa's radar, I just happened to switch to our local radio channel and overheard a conversation between the ADC's alert flight and the ground radar folks at Moron. Boy, did I ever get an earful. I caught the sneaky flight leader in the process of arranging an intercept on my plane.

I quickly decided to turn the tables. I knew that when I was eventually handed off to the radar site at Moron for letdown and landing, all my flight information would be passed along on a ground telephone line: air speed, heading and altitude. I timed it so that my air speed would be duly noted as being six hundred knots. And it was. But only for a couple of seconds. I then poured on the coals and accelerated to Mach 1.5—or about one thousand miles per hour—then turned the radio back to the channel on which I had heard the scheming conversation and listened as the intercept attempt unfolded. This was showtime, and I was enjoying the view from my very own front row seat!

When the controller turned the interceptors towards me they did so at a speed to intercept me at six hundred miles per. Suckers! I was already over the homer at Moron before they even came close, and made a fast descent and landing. Those interceptor pilots didn't have a clue what happened until I cornered them on the ground and gloated as I explained how they'd all been snookered by little old Scrappy. These kids didn't know about all those dirty tricks I'd learned from Captain Pappy Hood in the Philippines.

Howie Dale had deployed previously to Moron with other squadrons and the pilots had willingly contributed money to a nearby Catholic orphanage. Shortly after we arrived on base the orphanage sent a representative who handed us a piece of paper which essentially said, "Your contribution this time is one thousand dollars."

The entire squadron took umbrage at the audacity of this blatant demand and the group decision was not to give anything.

A short while later we came to relish our resolve.

During a night mission, one of our two-seater airplanes developed an engine problem and the pilots had to eject. They landed unharmed near a small town high up in the mountains of northeast Spain. We deployed a detachment to remove what was left of the airplane, fill in the hole and make the appropriate monetary compensation to the landowner. A captain from our squadron spent several days on-site, and when he came back he told us he had found the perfect place for our charity donation. He said the local school badly needed books, pencils and other school supplies for the kids, so we all dug deep. He took almost a thousand dollars worth of supplies back up to the school. The grateful staff was overwhelmed with our generosity and he said they couldn't stop thanking him. That made us all feel really good.

Walt and I took a two-seater on a cross-country training mission back to my old Luftwaffe base at Buechel, Germany. From there we hitched a ride to Bad Godesburg and had a rip-roaring good time visiting old friends for the better part of two days. We returned to Buechel only to be informed that all of the French air traffic controllers had gone out on strike which now meant all flying over France was verboten. Walt and I shrugged our shoulders in unison. So what? This didn't bother us since we were operating on an American clearance anyway, and the Germans didn't give a damn when we announced our intention to go.

Things went fine until we were midway over France and ground control started giving us a hard time. The more we ignored them the testier they got, until in a fit of pique they declared war and threatened to send up Mirage interceptors to force us to land. Oh, no, not Mirage interceptors, especially not ones flown by France's best aviators!

"Watch this," I said to Walt over the intercom, and before those earthbound Frogs sitting in front of their phosphorescent screens could make good on their threat, I had us heading out of their airspace at Mach1 plus, plus.

Within minutes I was initiating our descent into Zaragosa for a pit stop, both of us laughing hysterically all the way to the ground like a couple of deranged kids.

After our Starfighter was serviced, Walt accidentally struck his head on the sharp, leading edge of the wing while performing his walk-around inspection for the final leg of our flight to Moron. He let loose with a startled yelp, and backed away from the plane sporting a large, ugly, bleeding gash on his forehead. Despite his protests I got him admitted to the base hospital and flew on without him.

After three months of thoroughly enjoyable duty, another squadron from the wing flew over to replace us and we returned to George in the bowels of a cargo plane. That was one interminably long and thoroughly miserable trip, but everybody agreed it was sure good to be going home.

General Sweeney wanted to impress upon the Army that the Air Force in general and TAC in particular was serious about its mission of providing close air support, and that we were an integral part of the bigger team. So he decreed that we in TAC would wear green army fatigues on Fridays. We began calling them "Sweeney Greenies."

I really doubt that any of those army grunts were too impressed with our Friday look. All they really wanted was good air support. I'm sure they could have cared less whether or not we wore fatigues or pantyhose.

In the summer of 1964 the commander of the 436th Squadron was transferred, and so after eight years of waiting and cooling my heels, I finally got to be a squadron commander. I had never wanted the job in order to enhance my career or to help me get promoted; I just wanted to be a squadron commander. And now my dream was finally being fulfilled.

The 436th was the primary alert squadron for the wing, which meant we had to be prepared to go gear-up, heading for any place on earth with only three hour's notice. This also meant we had to keep a bag packed at all times. Didn't bother me, I was firmly ensconced in fighter pilots' heaven.

The 436th Squadron's logo was "The Black Aces." In the past they had called themselves "The Proven Professionals," that is, until the squadron next door started calling them the "PeePees!"

Alas, I was not to be squadron commander for long.

One day a couple of months later while I was strapped in my cockpit busily preparing for a cross-country flight, Colonel Darrell Cramer, my wing commander, drove up to the plane and got out of his staff car. He climbed up the side of my jet until he was at eye level, then without a word took off his flight cap and threw it into my cockpit. Not knowing why he had done this, I politely picked the cap up and handed it back only to have him toss it at me again. I shook my head. I hadn't a clue what he was trying to say. Dumb me! Cramer was in fact telling me he had just received word that I had been promoted to full colonel!

Now, most of the time Air Force officers are keenly well aware of pertinent promotion board meetings, and if one's eligible for consideration to be promoted to the next higher grade, then it's fingernail-biting time for that man, or woman, until the appropriate list is made public. I didn't realize I was even being considered for promotion, or that that year's colonels' promotion board had even convened. And unlike the "Blue Flamer," John Bennett, who had wanted so desperately to get a squadron so that he could get promoted, I was genuinely wistful when it happened to me because it meant losing something I had wanted for so long.

That same afternoon the base grapevine reported that the division commander, Colonel Robert Worley, was on the new brigadier general promotion list and that he had just received orders transferring him to TAC headquarters at Langley AFB, Virginia. His new assignment: TAC deputy for operations. Worley was a good guy, and I was happy for him. It was a hell of a nice step-up, and he would undoubtedly earn a couple of more stars before retiring. A few days later he called me into his office and told me that he was having orders cut for me to go with him as second in command in the TAC command post.

This was definitely not the kind of news I wanted to hear. "Colonel Worley, I don't want to work in the TAC command post," I blurted out.

Worley was quick with his reply. "I know you don't, Scrappy. Hell, if I thought for one moment you wanted the job and was an eager beaver to go to TAC, then I wouldn't want you. But the fact of the matter is I need you, so you're going. Generals can do that to colonels," he said with a conspiratorial wink. "Dismissed," he added, but not unkindly.

That evening I went to the club and had some martinis to drown my sorrows before going home to tell Dorie to pack our bags. Colonel Cramer happened to be there, and between gulps I whined and cried on his shoulder, telling him how I didn't want the job at Langley.

As the days passed I heard no more about the command post job. Worley processed out and headed east, so I just assumed he had changed his mind about me. Later, Walt Irwin told me that he had overheard him telling another colonel before he left that I had pulled strings with the TAC personnel officer to weasel out of the assignment. This was not true, but I never had a chance to tell him that. General Worley didn't stay long at TAC, and later that year was killed in an F-4 crash in Vietnam. I barely knew the TAC personnel officer and certainly did not have any pull with him to change an assignment. I never knew how I got off the hook, but years later it dawned on me that in all probability it might have been Colonel Cramer's doing. He definitely knew the TAC personnel officer and he had witnessed firsthand how upset I was that night in the O Club. He could easily have been my savior. Made sense to me then; makes better sense to me now.

✈ ✈ ✈

The wing now had a full colonel on their hands they didn't know what to do with—namely me—so I was temporarily assigned to the made-up job of assistant wing deputy for operations. Three months later the DO moved on to a new assignment and I was promoted into his slot. Hot damn, this was a second dream come true, and all this had taken place in the space of a half-year!

✈ ✈ ✈

Tactical Air Command held an exercise every spring in conjunction with the Army at McChord AFB, Washington. It was code-named "March Hare," and 12th Air Force was tasked with pulling off the flying side of the mission. I was picked to command the blue-suiters, and was given 12 F-4s and 12 F-104s to work with.

While I was at McChord—and in the middle of our exercise—the base opened a newly renovated fighter pilots bar. But in the mad scramble to get it up and running for the newly arrived visitors, someone made the ultimate, unforgivable mistake. A telephone had been installed in the bar. Such a blunder is a bigtime no-no because custom dictates all telephones are off limits, never, ever, to be installed in a stag bar. The reason is simple. No phones keeps wives from calling up to say: Johnny, get your ass home this instant, thus causing some unfortunate jock to quickly upend his drink and slink off into the night, embarrassed beyond words in front of his vulgar, raspberry-tossing friends. Yet every married pilot knows in his most manly heart of hearts that but for the grace of God, on any given night he could find himself standing in that unfortunate Johnny's flying boots.

Late one night, and after a few drinks, one of my junior pilots brought the phone over to my table and put it down next to my just-freshened martini. "Colonel, you had a long-distance call, but I cut the frigging line." He then handed me the useless receiver with its trailing cord and began laughing his fool head off. I never did learn if he was kidding or not about there being a call, but I laughed right along with him and everybody else at the table, then gulped down my chilled potion and ordered another.

Soon after this we were tasked to send pilots and four F-104s to Alamogordo, New Mexico, to participate in some sonic boom tests. One of the pilots was Captain Al Bache, a good pilot and great guy, but Al could be a little overzealous at times.

The tests were finished and a panel was assembled in the base operations building for the final critique. A civilian scientist who was a staunch believer that sonic booms were not all that bad was conducting the briefing and just as he was reiterating his position to the other members of the panel, an airplane whizzed by at about 200 feet. And it was flying supersonic! The sonic boom blew out a huge window in the front of the room, knocked all of the pictures off the walls and in general raised hell with the attendees.

In reconstructing the events leading up to how such a thing could have happened, it seems that flight line maintenance had prepared this particular airplane for its flight back to George AFB, but it needed a test hop before being released. Just prior to takeoff, the crew chief had asked Al to fly a low pass down the runway before landing. Al agreed that would be a cool idea, and with the test hop completed, got permission from the tower to make the pass. He lined up with the runway but had no intention of going super sonic. However, at Mach 9 plus, all a pilot has to do is drop the nose a little and any F-104 will slip through the sound barrier.

After Al Bache's pass that day, the panel had to alter its findings for the final report.

I was extremely happy and thoroughly content in my job as the DO of a shit-hot TAC fighter wing equipped with F-104s, one whose primary mission was air superiority. And because I was happy, so, too, were Dorie and the kids. Life was indeed grand. Unfortunately, the good times lasted less than a year.

17

Hell

Like the proverbial lightning bolt striking out of the blue, I found myself blindsided one Monday morning with orders transferring me to the USAF Inspector General's Staff. My base of assignment: San Bernardino. I was benumbed with shock for the couple of minutes it took for this terrible news to sink in, and then my hands trembled from anger as I read every word in every block of my orders. Here was the one posting that trumped the dreaded PX position and every command post job I had wheedled my way out of. Later that day I was told by a source who shall remain nameless, that I'd been earmarked to head up the Tactical Air Command's ORI Team but that certain powers at HQ USAF had nixed the deal by saying they needed me in their Inspector General's office. He also confided that my name had popped up because I'd been in the ADC inspector's office back when tactical evaluations had been moved out from under the operations side of the house: a move initiated to make sure all inspections remained free of even a hint of impropriety or favoritism.

Well, Howard C. Johnson wasn't nicknamed Scrappy for nothing, so at the crack of dawn the following morning I was in an F-104 heading for The Pentagon. I landed at McConnell Air Force Base in Witchita, Kansas, to refuel and grab a sandwich, then pressed on to Andrews AFB, aptly nicknamed, "The Gateway to the Nation's Capitol."

I flew eastward at my designated altitude of thirty thousand feet, moving in concert with the earth's rotation and under a bright sun, but well above a solid cloud cover which blanketed the nation from left coast to right coast. I knew when I was passing over Louisville because of my radio aids, so I looked down and recalled the many pleasant times that I had enjoyed in that fair city of my youth. There were those idyllic summers when I had played tennis and swam at the Lakeside Swimming Club, my first girlfriend, and so much more. For several minutes I waxed nostalgic on my trip down memory lane, but quickly brought my thoughts back to reality and the urgency of my mission.

When I arrived over Andrews, their approach control cleared me for landing, and that's when I began rummaging around in my flight bag and through the many zippered pockets on my flight suit. Oh oh, I've got a bit of a problem up here, Andrews. I had to ask to be directed through my letdown, approach and landing because I had left George AFB in such a hurry that I had forgotten to pack my letdown book for the East Coast. I suspect the con-

lem up here, Andrews. I had to ask to be directed through my letdown, approach and landing because I had left George AFB in such a hurry that I had forgotten to pack my letdown book for the East Coast. I suspect the controller had already figured this out, but he was a true gentleman and refrained from uttering any caustic remarks for everyone on the channel to hear.

Early the following morning I appeared at the door of the Colonel's Group in The Pentagon, the section that handles all O-6 assignments exclusively. My hopes soared when I spotted a sign on the door in huge block letters which said: IF YOU DON'T LIKE YOUR ASSIGNMENT WE'LL CHANGE IT TO VIETNAM. I actually let loose a huge sigh in relief. That was exactly what I was going to ask them to do!

First, I talked to a major who listened to my tale then said I would have to speak with the colonel in charge of the office, but it could take a while because the man was busy with previous appointments. Okay, I could wait. When I finally met the boss some ninety minutes later, I quickly cut to the chase and mentioned that I wanted what the sign on his door was offering. He was taken aback and began to tap-dance around the issue for several minutes, making it obvious that he didn't have the power to get my assignment changed. The sign was only so much bullshit! Dejected, I flew back to George AFB after stopping over in Columbus, Mississippi, for the night where I drowned my sorrows in the O Club bar. This was worse than the dreaded PX job. It was a three-year tour, and there weren't any ordained minister Lieutenant Colonel types around to bail me out.

The following week I came up with a new plan of attack. Maj. Gen. Ben Greene—one of the three generals from the songfest in the Von Steuben—was now the USAF Chief of Personnel, so with nothing to left to lose, I flew to Randolph AFB, Texas, and pleaded with him for any assistance he might offer. The man was sympathetic but elected not to intervene, thus sealing my fate.

I had spent but such a brief time in heaven, but for some unknown reason the gods had turned on me and I was now about to pass through the portals of hell.

✈ ✈ ✈

My orders read to report to the IG on a date that fell on a Friday, so I called the office and asked the colonel in charge if I could take two days leave and report on Monday. He said that that would be all right.

San Bernardino was only a fifty-minute drive from my home in Apple Valley, so I decided to commute rather than move the whole family out of a community they enjoyed living in. I bought a 1957 Corvette from a fellow going overseas, a good move on my part, because it seemed to make the daily drive shorter than usual. And besides, it was a whole lot of fun to drive. This model year Corvette had an unusual gear arrangement which, for some unfathomable reason, caused the car to take about two minutes (I exaggerate just a tad) to hit 40 mph; but once past that magic number, she took off like a rocket.

When I reported for duty on Monday, I found that my immediate boss— and inspection partner—was a prim and proper colonel who answered to the name of Willie I. Williams. Now, I had always prided myself with being able to get along with any boss, including those infamous "Blue Flame" squadron commanders, but it was obvious from my first moments with this man that I had hit a brick wall. My task was going to be difficult at best, impossible at worst.

He started out not with a welcome aboard speech and a handshake, but instead he wanted to know why I hadn't reported for duty on Friday. Are you for real? I quietly explained my telephone call to his boss, and when I asked him where I needed to go to sign in, he actually accompanied me to make sure I didn't forget to account for the two days of leave time. This really torqued my jaw because for many years I had lost leave days that I hadn't been able to take, or, as was also often the case, days I'd simply elected to forego. And, moreover, the two days in question had fallen on a weekend when his damn office was closed! I would have recorded the leave time without him hovering over my shoulder like some sort of designated Keeper of the Universal Military Leave Record Book. It sure didn't take me long to find out why most folks called Willie I. Williams, "Piss Willie." His was the perfect moniker!

And talk about pouring salt into an open sore, this was a non-flying assignment to boot. I was so miserable I just wanted someone to take me outside, un-holster his gun and end it all Instead, I waited until I got home where I downed several stiff martinis. Dorie matched me drink for drink, and we commiserated with one another until it was time to go to bed.

✈ ✈ ✈

Dorie and I had plenty of friends in the 479th Fighter Wing, Lt. Col. Harlan Ball being one. Harlan and I had served together in the 18th Group in the Philippines and Korea, and now he had been chosen to take over my squadron. And our longtime buddy, Chappie James, was stationed on the other side of the state line at Davis Monthan AFB, in Tucson, Arizona.

Harlan thought it high time we had a little reunion so he asked Chappie to fly over and give an inspirational speech to his squadron one Friday afternoon during Commander's Call. Of course, Chappie jumped at the opportunity, so I upped the ante by suggesting I host a dinner party at my home on Saturday. The invited included Harlan and his wife, Betty, Walt and his wife, Chris, and, of course, the man of the hour, Chappie James. Walt had never met Chappie and I remarked several times how he'd enjoy being introduced to my friend.

Well, Chappie arrived late and was well oiled by the time he crossed my threshold. Seems he'd made a little detour by way of the O Club bar. The short version of a long story was that Walt—and everybody else for that matter—was less than impressed by Chappie's overblown opinion of himself that night. The man spent the entire evening monopolizing the conversation, droning on and on about how Colonel Robin Olds was getting a wing in Vietnam and how he was begging Chappie to come with him as his deputy commander for operations. And listening to my friend only served to reinforce my own feeling of abandonment at being stuck in a frigging, dead-end IG billet.

A buddy at Lockheed had given me four tickets to the pro-bowl game to be played in Los Angeles the following day and the plan called for Chappie, Harlan, Dorie and I to attend. Well, Harlan was so pissed at Chappie for his boorish behavior the evening before, he flat out refused to go. So Dorie, Chappie and I went without him, and I handed the extra ticket to Chappie to give to a clean-cut black kid I'd spotted hanging around outside the stadium. Turned out he was obviously no football fan but an up-and-coming entrepreneur, because just as the game began some middle-aged guy waddled over and plopped himself down in that fourth seat.

Ten months into my sentence on Devil's Island a message came down from USAF Headquarters, one which damn near reduced me to tears. Tears of joy, that is, because buried inside the third paragraph were the words, "Thus, any officer who wishes to volunteer for a Vietnam assignment will be released from his three-year controlled tour...." Holy shit! I immediately hightailed it over to my desk and dashed off a letter volunteering for a tactical fighter wing assignment anywhere in Vietnam. Then I hand-carried it to Piss Willie who was compelled by regulations to forward it up the food chain. I wanted my request acted upon before another message came telling everyone to ignore the first one because it had been sent in error. Talk about the stuff of nightmares! Anyway, my action only served to deepen the already barely checked animosity that existed between Piss Willie and me.

My present assignment was so unbelievably bad and I was so utterly miserable working for Piss Willie that I had actually contemplated retiring from the Air Force. I saw it as my only way out. And Dorie, true trooper that she was, said she'd support any such decision. But now that I had spotted a rainbow on the horizon, I crossed my fingers and waited.

While on an inspection tour some ten days later, Piss Willie invited me to go bowling after dinner on our last evening. What the hell, why not? We walked from the O Club over to the base bowling alley and bowled two games. And strike me dead if I'm lying when I tell you I bowled the two highest consecutive scores I've ever bowled—before or after. The first game I managed a 226; the second, a 227. Piss Willie spent most of his game watching his ball roll down the gutters and barely broke a hundred both times. That was sweet, but in no way did it repay me for the miserable year that I'd been forced to spend in his company. The next day he told me he had received word that my request to be transferred to Southeast Asia had been approved. I was being sent to an F-105 wing in Thailand. I almost passed out from sheer joy upon hearing those words, and didn't even think to give him a hard time for not telling me the good news sooner!

My last inspection was finalized at TAC Headquarters several days later, which signaled that I was finally free to return to the real Air Force. Halle-frigging-lujah! My old wing boss, Colonel Cramer, was now director of operations for TAC, so I got on the phone to tell him of my assignment. After congratulating me, he noted that I hadn't flown for the better part of a year. Not good, so he quickly cut through a ton of red tape and arranged for me to go TDY to Nellis AFB, Nevada, and get ten familiarization and orientation rides in the F-105 Thunderchief. Without his help I would have been sent to war without any time in the bird, which in all likelihood would have meant I'd be transferred lickety-split into some utterly useless staff job at headquarters where I'd rot for the next twelve months of my life.

Cramer was my savior and I owed him as much as I did the young lady at the University of Kentucky who provided me with the answers to the cadet entrance exam a quarter of a century earlier. The only difference between the two was the lady was a damn sight prettier!

18

Thailand

Orders were cut making me the vice-commander of the 355th TAC Fighter Wing at Takli, Royal Thai Air Base, Thailand. But that all changed before I left the States. I was handed a new assignment: director of operations for the 388th TAC Fighter Wing at Korat Royal Thai Air Base, Thailand. The mission for both wings was the same; each was built around the F-105 Thunderchief.

Because I hadn't flown anything faster than a desk for the year I was in the IG job, I reported to Nellis Air Force Base in Las Vegas, Nevada, for F-105 orientation school. After five hours and a check ride in a T-33, I flew my required ten flights in the Thud. Rules are rules. Fortunately, flying is much like riding a bicycle—damn hard to forget once you've learned how it's done.

While at Nellis I ran into an old friend, Jim Jabara, the guy who was chosen as my replacement to fly Queen Juliana of the Netherlands on her orientation ride in the F-104. Jim was now also a colonel and he was on base for recurrent training in the F-100. He had recently been handed orders to take command of an F-100 wing in Vietnam and he couldn't wait to get into the thick of things. Sadly, that was the last time I saw Jim. Shortly afterwards he was killed in a tragic auto accident while riding with his newly licensed sixteen-year-old daughter in her Volkswagen.

When the day finally arrived for me to leave for war, it was as difficult a parting as any in memory. Since I had to be up and gone by four o'clock in the morning I murmured my goodbye to six-year-old Billy when I tucked him into bed the night before. Tired but happy, he innocently asked, "See you in the morning, dad?" My reply was a fleeting smile then I turned off the light and closed his door softly behind me. That's a scene I've replayed over and over again in my mind in the intervening years and I always arrive at the same conclusion: where were my head and my heart that night? Not only would my little boy not see me come morning, but possibly he'd never see me again. That is one moment in time I wish I could live over, because my son deserved so much better from me that chilly October night in 1966. Of course, he knew from conversations around the dinner table in the evenings leading up to my going away that something was up; he just didn't know what. I should have taken the time to explain the where and the why for my leaving, and I should have told him how much I would miss him and how much I loved him. Sure, Billy got over it pretty quickly because Dorie was able to console him in the days that followed, as only a mother knows how. But it's something I still regret these many years later because it's exactly what my own father would have done to me!

Dorie and I were unable to sleep that night, so we lay in bed those last few hours going over the last-minute details of things to do during our year-long separation. And we refused to dwell on the obvious: that my assignment was fraught with danger and that I could be shot down and captured—or worse. Then it was time to go. We whispered our goodbyes, kissed and held each other tight. By pre-arrangement Dorie stayed in bed while I tiptoed my way through the darkened house and out my front door.

✈ ✈ ✈

I flew out of Travis AFB, California, on an Air Force contract airliner—destination Bangkok, Thailand, via Anchorage, and Tokyo. On the ground in Bangkok I learned there was a shuttle that flew a daily round robin to all the bases in Thailand, so I was able to hitch a ride to Korat. The shuttle had two routes. It flew in one direction one day, then flew the reverse on the next. This day Korat was the last stop, so I got to eyeball each of the other bases on a flight which took the better part of the day.

Colonel Bill Chairsell, the wing commander of the 388th TAC Fighter Wing met me on the ramp. He was happy to have me aboard but quickly voiced his concern that I only had the mandatory minimum ten orientation/checkout rides in the F-105 under my belt.

"Scrappy, I'd feel a lot better if I can send you to Kadena to get ten more rides before you start flying any missions, okay?"

I figured I could hack the program with what I had, but since he was the boss, I went along with it.

On Okinawa I was assigned to the 67th Fighter Squadron of my old 18th Fighter Group. Major Matt Mathews—better known as "Black Matt"—was the commander. Black Matt later became infamous in Air Force circles when he led a flight of F-105s over the Air Force Academy during a graduation ceremony. He took the flight supersonic at low level and smashed a goodly number of very expensive stained glass windows in the newly built chapel. I introduced Matt to a friend a few years later and recounted Matt's memorable academy flight.

Matt gave a crooked little "aw shucks" grin and said, "I won three wars single-handed, but that's what people will always remember me for." He also knew he was damn lucky the Air Force didn't make him pay for the damage he caused that day because he'd still be in hock! And it's not as if there weren't any witnesses.

I flew those ten missions, which included some ground gunnery and dive bombing work, thus learning how to turn on all the gun and bomb switches. During this training I flew several times with Matt and we became fast friends. The evening after my tenth and final run, I popped into the stag bar to celebrate with a martini. Some forty minutes later Matt walked in, came over, joined me in a drink then invited me to his house for dinner. I tried to beg off because I had already downed two stiff ones, but he wouldn't hear of it. I finally agreed to go but only if he would let me bring along a captain I'd been talking to, an F-104 pilot I'd known in the 479th at George AFB. Matt said fine with him, then invited one of the jocks from his squadron to come along for some grilled steaks. His wife wisely elected not to join us.

Halfway through the dinner all hell broke loose. Chairs were suddenly pushed back and what followed was a flurry of pushing and shoving. We all wound up outside on the patio. No blows were struck but Matt and I ended up in a squared-off stance, as did the two younger guys. I decided it was maybe past time for the young captain and me to shag-ass out of there. In our haste to get to my staff car we knocked over the still-hot barbecue grill causing smoldering coals to scatter everywhere. We drove back to the club for a nightcap.

"What the hell happened?" I asked over the rim of my glass.

The captain shook his head. "Damned if I know, Colonel, but things sure went to shit in a hurry."

Nothing lasting came of it. Matt and I remained good friends and later had a lot of laughs remembering that evening.

I returned to Korat confident in my ability to fly the Thud. I was ready for war. That first night back and while standing at the bar and discussing the wing mission with one of the pilots, the man became suddenly quiet. The faraway look in his eye told me he had mentally withdrawn to a different place—somewhere I couldn't go and wasn't invited. It lasted for only a few moments then he said, "Colonel, there ain't no way," meaning there was no way a pilot could fly an F-105 one hundred times over North Vietnam and realistically expect to live through it. This saying was commonplace throughout the wing at the time. I made a decision then and there to do something about it.

The next day I gathered all the pilots together and dropped the hammer.

"There ain't no way I want to hear anyone in this wing say 'there ain't no way' ever again." I stared long and hard at the group before me. "There *is* a way, dammit, and we're going to find it." Without another word I stormed out of the room as they all scrambled to attention.

✈ ✈ ✈

The Pentagon had sliced North Vietnam up into six areas called route packages, but the pilots referred to them just as packages. Package 6 was further split into 6A and 6B, with Package 6A being assigned to the Air Force and Package 6B to the Navy. The pilots of the 388th Wing were flying two missions a day into Package Six, an area which included the heavily defended capital city of Hanoi. These missions were built around sixteen ships, flown in flights of four. And the flights were timed to hit the targets at five-minute intervals. This was beyond stupid because after the first flight hit, the North Vietnamese knew there would be three more, following at five-minute intervals. Naturally this precision on our part gave them ample time to prepare to engage. The air order of battle had been approved at higher headquarters and was built around tankers and radar jammers instead of around us, the fighter/bomber pilots who were doing the job. We were accommodating them instead of them accommodating us and, even worse, these procedures did not allow us to implement tactics for hitting the targets with the least number of casualties.

Because I did not see combat in World War II, I made it a point to listen to the guys who did, and one thing I heard them all say was, "You don't make a second pass at an airfield, because if you do they'll shoot your ass down." I remembered this time-tested piece of advice now because of the way we were attacking North Vietnam. It was in direct contradiction to all the rules of good sense.

True, we were not attacking airfields, but the targets we were hitting were similarly defended. The pilots were dejected and morale was terrible. And just how low the morale had sunk was demonstrated by the following incident.

Prior to a mission, I was being briefed on the local procedures—refueling, target areas and such—by a captain wearing a strained look on his face. Midway through the briefing he excused himself and hurried out of the room. When he returned, he wore an entirely different look. This changed man let loose a deep sigh of relief then said, "I can relax now, Colonel. I don't have to go into Package Six today because the mission's been scrubbed due to weather."

Most of the pilots in the wing shared his feelings.

Several nights later I was talking to Major Ralph Bowersox, an officer I'd known previously, and Bowersox tried to convince me that the morale of the pilots at Korat did not properly reflect the tactical situation in the air. "Colonel, it ain't that bad," he said by way of summary.

The wing vice-commander had been the DO prior to my arrival. He and I shared a comfortable trailer together, a far cry from the squad tents we'd used in Korea more than a decade earlier. It had been his custom to attend all the Pack Six briefings, and the early morning mission briefings were usually held about 4:00 A.M. This particular morning he woke me and asked if I was going to attend.

I propped myself up on one elbow and squinted at my watch. I shook my head. "No, I'm flying with the afternoon mission."

"You going into Pack Six?" He couldn't hide the shocked look on his face. He hadn't flown into Pack Six himself; indeed, none of the colonels in the wing had been there.

I was wide-awake now, so I swung my legs over the side of my bunk and sat upright. "I decided the first day on station that I wasn't going to be a sender. You see, the leadership isn't pulling its weight around here, and that's a big part of the reason why morale is in the tank. We colonels aren't leading by example, so, yeah, I'm going into Six."

The look he gave me spoke volumes. He was not at all pleased with my answer.

I had flown five missions into Laos and two into Pack One when I told the squadron ops officer to schedule me on a Pack Six mission. The adrenaline flowed as I taxied that big warbird out, but I quickly settled down once airborne. The mission target was a railroad yard just north of Hanoi and because it was partially obscured by clouds we had to dive almost straight down through a hole to hit it. As far as I know, I was the first full colonel to fly a mission into Package Six from the 388th Wing at Korat. While joining up and heading out of the area, a SAM hit an F-105 ahead of me and the pilot had to eject; there goes another guest for the Hanoi Hilton, I thought, as I tried to catch a glimpse of a chute. The rest of us made it back to Korat without further incident, but on the ride home I could not help but remember that pilot back at Warner Robbins who had returned from F-80 school, and his remark about flying F-80s being for young guys. And he was only twenty-nine at the time. Here I was just completing a pretty hairy mission dive, bombing a railroad yard near Hanoi, then pulling about seven or eight G's coming off the target, and doing it at the not so tender age of forty-seven.

I discovered that afternoon there was nothing more exhilarating than returning in one piece from a successful mission over Hanoi.

As the Christmas season unfolded the wing found itself overrun with civilian VIPs. They were coming in droves to Bangkok to buy presents, but in order to justify the boondoggles they had to first visit us and get a ticket-punching briefing to show the folks back home that this was hard work. Now, giving a briefing was never a favorite pastime of mine—and no way I could handle this load by myself—so I set up a special team for the job to be led by my assistant deputy for operations, Lt. Col. Mervin Taylor. We briefed dozens during this period—from the president of the Daughters of the American Revolution (DAR) to congressmen, senators, and even one Under Secretary of the Air Force.

The season came, the season went, and I survived, just barely.

The U.S. Air Force command structure governing air operations in Thailand was not just unusual, it was unique. Operationally, we were all under the command of 7th Air Force in Saigon, but we looked to the 13th Air Force in the Philippines for logistical support. This arrangement was tricky at best, because officially we were not even supposed to be in Thailand to begin with! Sometimes directions from these two headquarters were contradictory and downright confusing. For starters, we were stationed on a Royal Thai Base and not on a USAF facility. This meant there could be no civilian media folks on the base, thus all news stories regarding our mission or accomplishments were released to the newspapers by Air Force public affairs officers.

The 13th Air Force commander at the time was a fire-breathing dragon named Lieutenant General James "Whip" Wilson. Whip had no peer when it came to raising hell about people and things that pissed him off. LeMay was no longer the competition since he had retired a few years earlier. Invariably, a royal ass chewing followed, or for those offenses he considered beyond the pale, wing commanders and group commanders were fired on the spot. Nobody liked to be told that Whip Wilson was coming to town.

He flew over to our base shortly after the start of the New Year, inspected the airmen's barracks and definitely did not like what he saw. He lit into Colonel Chairsell in front of the staff and finished his tirade by saying he expected results, and expected them fast. Chairsell called him the Alligator.

True to his word, Wilson sent a representative back a month later to see if progress had been made to his satisfaction. The liaison's verdict was no, and Chairsell caught a stronger dose of flak and snapping jaws from the Alligator. There's an old saying in the military that shit flows downhill, so I was about to catch my share of it, too. Chairsell hauled me into his office.

"I don't want to hear another word about those frigging barracks! Now get somebody to fix those damn buildings, and, Scrappy, I don't give a shit what it costs!"

The base finally fixed the airmen's barracks to the satisfaction of the 13th Air Force commander and Chairsell got to keep his head. And I got to keep mine.

From the very start of my tour I sensed that there was tension between Col. Chairsell and the 355th Wing Commander at Takli, Colonel Robert Scott. I never knew when, where, why or how it had started, but knew that it existed and that it was palpable. Whenever I had to contact anyone from the 355th I always tried to be as cordial as possible and did everything I could to stay far removed from the problem.

In December of 1966, Colonel Robin Olds, Commander of the 8th TAC Fighter Wing held a tactics conference at Ubon Royal Thai Air Base. Representatives from the various wings, along with staff members from 7th Air Force were split into small groups to tackle a host of problems. The one on the front burner dealt with how difficult it was for Olds' F-4 pilots to properly give the F-105 flights attacking targets in Pack Six the proper MiG coverage when our flights were being strung out in five-minute intervals. This was one helluva sore point with me also, because I had already decided it was stupid for us to fly the missions with our flights rolling onto the target in such predictable intervals. In my mind it was a bigger mistake than making repeated passes at a target. All it did was give the gunners a breather between flights and time to reload.

In order for us to effect a change, we had to get all our supporting units—including the tankers and radar jammers—to change their tactics. We agreed that this meant the tankers would need to drop us off in closer proximity to each other, and do so in a manner whereby we could form up and ingress in squadron formations as we wanted to do. We wrote up our recommendations and the 7th Air Force staffers dutifully took them back to Saigon. That was the last we heard of the matter.

I became aware of a trend developing among the pilots, one that really bothered me. It arose from the fact that the completion of one hundred missions over North Vietnam for all pilots was a magical number. Once reached, a pilot did not have to fly north again. Sometimes, flights returning from a mission inside North Vietnam were directed to a tanker for refueling where they'd top off then return into North Vietnamese airspace which meant they were immediately eligible to log an additional counter, for a total of two missions over North Vietnam instead of one. I found this scenario occurring when something unusual was unfolding, like a pilot was down, or a hot target needed to be hit at once.

There was nothing intrinsically wrong with this except the concept was being abused. I had heard flight leaders calling Cricket—the airborne command post—and ask permission to be refueled so they could pop back into Package One in North Vietnam for no particular reason other than to get a quick—and for the most part—easy counter. I decided it was time to put a stop to this practice so I put out the word in plain English that this was now an immediate "be no."

Two days later I was a part of a flight being led by a major from the 13th Squadron. Our target was in Package One, a comparatively safe area. On the way out the major started calling Cricket, requesting a tanker and another target. I could not believe my ears, but said nothing until we were back on the ground. I reminded him of my directive restricting this sort of thing only to hear him admit that, yes, he was aware of it, but had chosen to disobey. I also knew that he had been on his 98th mission and told him it seemed to me he intended to get his 100 counters in this fashion. Forget it, I told him, you just shove off and go home with 98. I directed his squadron commander to send him home two counters short.

On another flight I was scheduled as number three in a four-ship into Package Six. Our target was a bridge over a small stream on an obscure road between Hanoi and Phuc Yen Air Base. Again, it was a major from the 13th Squadron leading the flight. All went well until we were in the target area when the major had difficulty finding the bridge. His solution was to circle until he could spot it. This was an unbelievably dumb decision since part of his circling maneuver was putting us smack over the southern perimeter of Phuc Yen Air Base, and its gunners were already beginning to zero in on us. Luckily, he spotted the target and we rolled in on it before any of us were shot down. After the flight returned to base I raised holy hell and ordered the squadron commander not to ever allow him lead a Pack Six mission again.

Some guys really did have shit for brains!

For most of my tour as DO I faced a chronic problem of having either too many or too few pilots. To backfill for the latter, Colonel Chairsell had an arrangement with the 18th Fighter Wing commander on Okinawa that when we found ourselves short the 18th would send us over some guys on temporary duty. One such pilot was a young captain with a great sense of humor. He brought along a professionally carved teakwood plaque he'd had made, showing the front end of an Edsel mounted on a pair of command pilot's wings. Even the village idiot could recognize this as a slam against Robert

McNamara for his role in the manufacturing of the Edsel, the biggest automotive flop of the 1950s. Now, as secretary of defense, he was the lead drumbeater for the production of the F-111 Aardvark, which at that time was experiencing all kinds of problems. The plaque clearly suggested the F-111 was a flying Edsel. The captain asked me if he could hang his plaque on a wall in the club. I told him he could, and everyone loved it.

Soon after it had found a home in our O Club, we were told by 7th Air Force to expect a visit from Secretary of the Air Force Harold Brown. Chairsell got on the phone and ordered me to hide the damn thing until the secretary was all the way out of the country.

We also had some great young officers assigned to the wing, and First Lieutenant Karl Richter was one such guy. Karl had already flown a complete hundred-mission tour then asked for, and was granted, permission to fly another. He was well into his second hundred-mission tour when I showed up. Not only had he proved himself in combat, but was also as dedicated a young man as I ever had the privilege to know. Chairsell, too, was rightfully proud of this officer and arranged for a one-on-one meeting between him and Secretary Brown, thinking some of Karl's knowledge, enthusiasm and honesty would rub off on the secretary. Polite to a fault, he simply said to us after the encounter, "We were on different wavelengths."

Chairsell was not pleased with Brown's dismissive attitude so immediately upon hearing the secretary was "gear up" and had cleared Thai airspace, Chairsell called me to told me to get the Flying Edsel plaque back up pronto.

Like every other wing in Thailand, the 388th had a mascot. Ours was a mutt named Roscoe: a sixty-pounder who like the proverbial eight-hundred-pound gorilla did whatever he wanted whenever he wanted. The pilot who had brought Roscoe to Korat had been shot down, so, now an orphan, Roscoe ended up being everybody's dog. He would faithfully attend the early morning briefings and lie in the wing commander's chair when Chairsell wasn't there. The pilots would say it would be a safe mission if Roscoe slept through the briefing. And I think most of them believed it. Roscoe lived like a king. He was fed from the tables at the Officers' Mess, and he would only accept rides around base from drivers of his choosing. One morning he was sitting outside the club when I was getting into my staff car to go to the morning briefing. I whistled and held the door open, but Roscoe was having none of it. He actually got up, turned around until his butt was facing me, then plopped back down again. I laughed and slammed the door, wondering what had I done to piss him off? Half an hour later he sauntered into the briefing room, walked past me without so much as a glance, hopped up onto the commander's seat and proceeded to lick himself. Obviously he'd found a driver more to his liking that morning.

Base security had orders to shoot any stray dogs because of rabies. This order worried the pilots so they banded together and made sure all the guards, U.S. and Thai alike, were supplied with "Roscoe Posters." To many of the guys Roscoe was a talisman and they were not about to lose whatever slight edge they thought he brought them. In fact some of them tried to bring him back to the States in 1973, but the immigration authorities put their foot down on that one. Sadly, in 1975, one of Roscoe's many admirers while visiting Korat found his little manicured grave near the Officers' Club. A stone marker held the following inscription:

> "Here lies Roscoe. Came to Korat 1965. Died here
> on 13 September 1975. I spent all my life waiting
> for my master, but he never returned from North
> Vietnam. Now we are together and I am happy
> to see him again. Only God can part us now."

During the first part of my one-year tour we had to pattern our tactics to counter SAMs (surface to air missiles), MiGs and ground fire. Then we received jamming pods, which allowed us to fly at higher altitudes and thus partially avoid the most serious threat—namely, ground fire.

One morning I was scheduled to fly the early Package Six mission, but when I stepped out of my trailer I found myself standing in the middle of a real pea souper. I could barely see six feet in front of me. The air was heavy and my station wagon's windows were dripping with moisture. I slow-crawled my way over to operations.

A first lieutenant gave the weather briefing and I couldn't believe my ears when he said the fog would lift in time for us to fly. No frigging way this fog was going to lift until after the sun had come up and burned it off! I called 7th Air Force operations and asked them to delay the takeoff. Some weenie there asked to speak with the weatherman. The lieutenant told him the same thing: the fog was going to lift in time for the take-off, so 7th ordered us to go. We trooped onto the flight line, got into our cockpits, fired up and taxied out. I could barely see 20 feet in front of the plane's nose, making it difficult to even stay on the taxiway. We sat lined up and waiting for takeoff for over an hour before 7th Air Force finally called it quits. As I suspected, the fog did not break up until about an hour after sunrise. The aircraft now needed to be re-serviced, and by then it was too late. The mission was scrubbed.

After breakfast I called the lieutenant into my office and said, "Lieutenant, I'm not allowed to tell you what weather to predict, but even an idiot knows that the fog is not going away until the sun comes up and burns it off." When I finally ran out of words, he saluted and left, and I felt a whole lot better.

During my year at Korat, the base was constantly seeing new construction projects springing up all over. One was a beautification plan to sod the entire base with new grass—an undertaking requiring the effort of hundreds of Thai nationals, and to my mind, it was a giant waste of time and money. I couldn't keep my big mouth shut, so one day I asked Chairsell, "Why not just have them plant some grass seed and let nature take its course?"

His reply surprised me. "Scrappy, it's cheaper to pay them to sod the place rather than to plant a thousand acres of grass by hand." I found out later why this was true.

The United States had just finished building a highway from Bangkok to the northern border of Thailand. It was called the Freedom Highway and we had paid for grass to be planted on both sides of the entire length of this roadway. This was the sod the Thais were digging up and selling back to us.

My duties as wing DO lasted twenty-four hours a day and I was never able to get enough sleep. I was either scheduled to fly the early morning missions or I monitored their briefings then went outside to watch the takeoffs. Usually there would be an hour's break between the briefing and takeoff, so I'd catch a forty-minute nap on a large leather sofa in my office. But there were plenty of days in 1967 when I knew and felt every one of my forty-seven years.

After a few months, sleep deprivation finally caught up with me. One night at the club I was drinking martinis when Chairsell came in and asked if I would like to join him for dinner? I turned down his invitation, proceeded to get blasted, and ended up going to bed pie-eyed and without dinner.

At seven-thirty the next morning Chairsell came into my trailer, woke me up and kind of ordered me to join him at breakfast. He said nothing regarding my indiscretion the night before, but instead suggested I knock-off for a few days and grab some R&R.

Major Lash Lagreau, Captain Frank Smith and I took off for the Philippines together on R&R. We rode to Bangkok in the base C-47 then grabbed another military plane to Clark AFB. From there we got base transportation to the mountain resort in Baguio, and played golf for four solid days. But we damn near missed getting out of Thailand altogether because some idiot

MATS lieutenant colonel in Bangkok insisted we needed visas to go to the Philippines. That was beyond ridiculous since we were traveling on military orders, but he threatened not to let us on the airplane without this little stamped appendage to a passport. It was seven o'clock at night and there was no way we could get a visa. I was steaming, but managed to control my voice when I asked him if there were still empty seats on this departing aircraft? He said, "Yes." I replied that we were combat pilots on official R&R, and that if the plane took off without us and had empty seats when it went gear-up at the end of the runway, then General Momyer, the Commander of 7th Air Force, would hear about it come sunup. "That's not a threat, colonel, it's a promise," was how I ended my little tête-à-tête as I stood nose to nose with the man.

That remark got his attention. He quickly agreed to let us on the airplane if I would sign a paper stating I would be responsible if the Filipinos found us trying to enter their country without visas. Such a scenario was highly unlikely since we were arriving at Clark AFB in the middle of the night, so I signed his paper then shoved an unlit cigar into my mouth. He actually helped me carry my bags out to the plane.

At the foot of the ramp he saluted then asked, "Would you really have called General Momyer, sir?"

I took the unlit cigar out of my mouth, pretended to flick some non-existent ash on his shoes, returned his salute, and said, "Are you for real? I like being a bird colonel, but if I was ever stupid enough to even think about calling Momyer over something like that, then, hell, I'd deserve to get busted back to your rank." I shoved the cigar back into my mouth and mumbled, "See you on my way back." I grabbed my bags and hustled onto the C-54.

✈ ✈ ✈

Come spring, the Thais celebrate a holiday called "Di Mai" which entails squirting or pouring water on others as a friendly gesture. One of the prettier waitresses at the club got it rolling on base by pouring a glass of water over me while I was eating lunch. I'm sure more than one of the pilots talked her into it. Well, this fast set the stage for a bigger and better celebration, so I moved it outside. Moe Seaver and I jumped into my station wagon, and with me driving and him sitting in the rear with a fire extinguisher filled with water, we drove over to the operations building and thoroughly doused a bunch of the pilots on their way out.

The fever spread. One of the pilots we had hosed down, a Major George Rowan, filled a bucket of water and stood on a corner of the main intersection which had a four-way stop. A young army lieutenant in full dress uniform pulled up in an open jeep and spotted George standing there with bucket in hand, wearing only shorts, a hideous sports shirt, and an evil grin. The lieutenant looked at him and yelped, "I order you not to throw that water!" With that George let him have the full load. As the lieutenant drove off, thoroughly drenched, he screamed at the top of his lungs, "You're one of those … those … pilots, aren't you?"

Hollywood couldn't have done it better. I just love native customs!

And also come springtime, the farmers in Laos, Thailand and Vietnam burn off their rice fields to ready them for a new planting season. It's been this way since the dawn of recorded time. However, this practice creates extremely low visibility, lasting for days until the burning is over. Not only did it make for hazardous flying during takeoffs and landings, but it made our dive-bombing runs true hair-raising events.

I was leading a flight of four to a target—a small bridge on a minor road—in Package Two near the Laotian border one morning. I found the target, rolled in from 10,000 feet, lined up, released my six 750-pound general-purpose bombs and started a pullout at about 3,500 feet. Everything was working fine for a moment or two, but as I pulled the nose of the F-105 up past the horizon in all that smoke, I found myself going on instruments. I had pulled up so steeply that my flight instrument showed a steep climb, but with no indication of just how steep because it was topped out. Luckily, I broke out of the haze at about 9,000 feet and before I stalled out completely was able to regain control of the aircraft. That escapade sure left some skid marks, and needless to say, I didn't do any more dive-bombing that day!

In late February, Washington decided the bombing campaign would be directed against North Vietnam's major industrial targets, and the bureaucrats further decided the Thuy Nguyan steel mills should be first on the list to be hit. February was also the month a man named Captain Bob Pardo was assigned to Ubon Royal Thai Air Force Base. Bob found himself scheduled to fly against this target on the first day of March. However, bad weather kept the rather sizeable force he was a part of from reaching the target that March morning, but his group continued to be fragged for this same mission for several days running. And still the weather wouldn't cooperate. But naturally, the North Vietnamese who by now had now figured out our single-minded game plan used the time to build up their defenses to the point where the survivability of all the aircrews had been decreased by a factor of ten. These were not good odds.

If the commanders at 7th Air Force had had the authority they could have easily fragged another important target, one whose defenses had now been drained for the buildup up at Thuy Nguyan. Those mills weren't going anywhere; they could have been re-fragged for a later date when their defenses were diminished, but this kind of logic had too much merit for the wheels in Washington to fathom. All such authority remained in the hands of President Lyndon Johnson and Defense Secretary McNamara, and their attitudes were: Either hit the steel mills now or they would be taken off the list.

✈ ✈ ✈

On March 10, 1967, Bob Pardo and three other pilots were involved in what was to become one of the most heroic acts of the Vietnam air war, and has since become known as Pardo's Push.

It started when a formation of F-4s began their bombing run on those steel mills. They first flew into an ungodly barrage of flak, then several MiGs came up to join in the fray. And an already bad—and worsening—situation was further exacerbated by the weather.

Bob Pardo and his backseater, Steve Wayne, were number three in the last flight in the formation: the most likely spot for a ship to get hammered. As the flight approached the target, number four, Captain Earl Aman, and his backseater, Bob Houghton, got severely pounded. Then pulling off the target Pardo's plane took an antiaircraft round to the belly.

As the flight climbed out and the defenses diminished, Aman began falling behind, prompting Pardo to make the decision to hang back with him. Aman jettisoned everything possible in the hope he could stay aloft longer, but was also very concerned about the MiGs which were still in the air and hunting for cripples.

Soon both Aman and Pardo found themselves below bingo fuel, but Pardo, ever the optimist, assured everyone they would make it to the tanker. He didn't want Aman getting unduly upset at this point; he figured his pal had enough on his hands just keeping his damaged Phantom flying. Pardo's assurances were not enough. Aman, now dangerously low on fuel, knew he would never make the tanker, yet Pardo, with his own fuel falling fast still refused to abandon his friend and make a dash for the tanker alone. He was formulating a last-ditch effort of a plan in his mind—something so unconventional, so preposterous, that no other pilot in the annals of flight had ever thought it of.

He suggested Aman jettison his dragchute, which he did, opening up a sizeable hole in the tip of his tail. Pardo peered into the void, then said, "Earl, I might be able to give you a push." He began to inch his way closer, but found there was so much wash coming off the stabilizer and wings that it was impossible to get into a position to shove.

Desperate circumstances call for desperate measures, so Pardo further refined his plan. He told Aman to drop his tailhook, and with it down was able to place his plane up against the dangling hook. He started to give Aman a series of small pushes, and through trial and error found a spot on the nose just below his windscreen where the hook wouldn't keep sliding off. He then began pushing in earnest and kept it up for the better part of ten minutes, Aman's hook resting against his plane just in front of the windscreen. And then Pardo got an engine fire warning light signaling his own left engine was on fire. And to add to his woes he was rapidly losing fuel.

By now both men had reached the same conclusion—neither plane would make it to the tanker, but by pushing Aman's plane, Pardo had doubled the distance that his friend was able to glide and had vastly increased Aman's and Houghton's chances of being rescued.

All four pilots were forced to eject, all four were rescued by choppers, and all four suffered serious injuries. But Pardo's were the worst. He was plagued with severe neck problems from a very hard landing: painful injuries that have dogged this hero still.

But the Air Force was none too pleased with Pardo for staying behind, pushing his friend and ending up also losing a Phantom. The action was quickly written up as a "be no" in case others should attempt such a stunt in the future. But in the end cooler heads prevailed, and twenty-five years later, with a strong nudge from Texas Senator John Tower, the Air Force finally recognized this man and his extraordinary feat of airmanship. For his heroism, Bob Pardo was awarded the Silver Star, as were the other three.

When asked why he did it, Pardo said without hesitating, "It just seemed like the thing to do at the time. How could anyone just fly off and leave a buddy? Besides, we've got lots of airplanes."

19

In the Beginning

Late in the spring of 1967, Johnson and McNamara decided to stop our bombing of North Vietnam—again. Their skewered logic suggested this action would somehow signal America's good faith and thus lure the North Vietnamese to the negotiation table. How utterly naive. All it did was give Ho Chi Minh the time he needed to put more lethal and accurate defensive weapons systems in place to shoot us down. With each new bombing stand-down, the NVA built more SAM sites, more radar posts, and more antiaircraft gun emplacements, and it gave them time to train more technicians. These bombing halts were heaven-sent for the enemy, and Old Ho probably laughed his ass off each time one was announced in Washington.

It was during one of these stand-downs that the second tactical conference was held and, as I mentioned earlier, this was when The Red River Valley Fighter Pilots Association (River Rats) was born.

While our tactics meeting was profitable in many respects, unfortunately, it didn't solve all our problems and definitely not the one we agreed was our thorniest—the theater-wide problem we all had with the aerial refueling tankers. For some unknown—and never explained—reason, these SAC (Strategic Air Command) flying gas stations were firmly under SAC's control which meant they did not have to answer to the folks at either 7th Air Force Headquarters in Saigon, or to the commander at 13th Air Force in the Philippines. These tanker guys had reams of regulations explaining their other regulations for god's sake, which made it damn difficult for us fighter pilots to accomplish our missions. What we were asking of SAC was really rather simple: we want all of our flights to be refueled simultaneously then dropped off within sight of each other. How hard could that be? Well, SAC said no because their regulations contained specific restrictions on how close tankers could get to any receiving aircraft while off-loading fuel. No shit? So how about changing the reg to conform to life in the real world? Luckily for us though, after our conference the word got around among the SAC crews and on the QT many acted upon our request which meant ignoring their own reg in the process. We offered daily prayers of thanks for these tanker drivers, because if they had been caught giving the finger to their regs, we knew they'd land in a heap of trouble.

Anyway, after a weekend of storytelling, drinking and partying (and, yes, there were serious moments, like those mentioned above) a planeload of us boarded the base C-47 Gooney Bird and headed off to Bangkok for three glorious days of R&R.

Mother Baader, Chappie and I spent the time together, kind of a reunion of the "Ferocious Four" in spite of the fact that Spud was no longer with us. After checking into our hotel and stashing our bags, we went outside to a rain-washed sidewalk where a group of men hovered close to their line of taxicabs, jibber-jabbering in high-pitched, singsong voices. We zoomed in on one particularly animated fellow and asked what he would charge to work exclusively for us for the next three days. "Ten bucks apiece," he replied in a flash, then grabbed our hands and began pumping them wildly, sealing the deal before we could change our minds. With each up and down stroke he repeated through a silly grin, "You call me Sam. Me your number one, okay?"

That evening Sam took us to an upscale nightclub that had a dozen pretty ladies to dance with. Jim Redding, Chappie's roommate from our days in the Philippines, was now stationed in Bangkok, so he came over to join us. He quickly became drunk and rather obnoxious so Chappie had Sam take him home.

The three of us drank and danced until closing time. Sam took us back to our hotel where we told him to be outside at nine in the morning, then we each trundled off to our respective rooms. I must say, the girls we had danced with were gorgeous and, I'm told, if a guy had played his cards right, why, it was possible he might have persuaded one to spend the night with him!

The first mission I flew after getting back from Bangkok—after the stupid bombing halt had been lifted—was as leader of a flak suppression flight. It was a four-ship, which meant we were armed with CBUs. I liked leading these flights simply because they allowed me more flexibility in making rapid-fire decisions in an ever-changing battle environment. That particular day we were part of a larger sixteen-ship group and our target was 20 miles northeast of Hanoi.

In keeping with the inevitable chaos resulting from the political micro-management of this war, Washington selected all of the targets in Pack Six and the pilots were only allowed to hit them when cleared to do so by The White House. Deviation from these strict rules of engagement was granted only to the flak suppression flights and allowed the pilots to drop their bombs on targets that were actually shooting at them. Sometimes, when the approved targets were close by the Phuc Yen Air Field, the flak suppression four-ships would roll in and drop their CBUs on the airfield because the bad guys would

Photograph taken from the rear of Scrappy's F-105. Here he is pulling up from a low level bombing run against the Ho Lac Air Base in North Vietnam in 1967.

actually be shooting at us from there—or because someone in the flight would announce he definitely saw muzzle flashes. And that was the only authorization we needed to unleash holy hell on the enemy.

    On this particular day, my number two had to abort at the end of the runway. This was no big deal. The wing always had a couple of spare Thuds armed with the proper mission ordnance and with their engines already lit just waiting for any such mishap. I radioed for backup and within minutes a new number two taxied into the correct position and seamlessly joined my flight.

As we approached the target I spotted an 85mm gun emplacement at eleven o'clock, and, by god, it was firing at us for real. Big black bursts appeared all round us. Very close. So close that I could feel and hear some of the blasts. I looked down at what was a classic Russian Army Manual setup: six big guns in a circle and rotated their firing sequence. Rolling in, I dropped my load of cluster bombs and as I pulled off the target, out of the corner of my eye I noticed the spare guy was tucked in real close on my wing. Instead of CBUs, the spare carried Lady Fingers, five hundred pound GPBs since it was not known who he'd end up being a spare for.

We flew these missions with our cameras pointing rearward so that when we dropped our bombs we could assess the damage once back on the ground. I was pumped that day as I reviewed the footage: not only had my CBUs carpeted the target, but my wingman had dropped his bombs at the same time and had nailed it dead center. I studied that film over and over again, even playing it in slow motion to savor the moment. We had annihilated that 85mm site, and I remember my feeling of utter satisfaction that day knowing that the people manning those guns would never shoot down another USAF fighter-bomber. Too bad Jane was off that day.

Our ops building at Korat was way too small and guys were constantly tripping over one another. My office—which was the size of a broom closet—was situated in the middle of this bedlam which meant it was next to impossible for me to get any serious work done. Something had to give, so I asked Colonel Chairsell to approve my putting up an adjoining structure so I could move some functions over to the new building. He studied the blueprints the CE folks had drawn up and noted there were to be several large glass windows facing the flight line as well as a small glass-enclosed tower with a UHF radio and telephone set up. I have to admit this was not an original idea but one I had borrowed from Colonel Leon Gray and my days at Otis AFB. He had installed such a radio setup in his office so that he could listen in on the traffic both on the ground and in the air. I thought that was a pretty sharp rig then, so I wanted one of my own now.

Colonel Chairsell pooh-poohed the idea but grudgingly let me have my way. Later, he was thankful that he had because one day a plane landed and blew a tire while still on the runway. In the greater scheme of things this was no biggie, except it now closed our runway for however long it would take to tow the plane away. Several vehicles belonging to the crash crew were parked

"Why we won the Cold War." Scrappy in front of his F-105, sporting his fighter pilot's mustache, Korat RTAFB, 1967 (courtesy of USAF).

around the cripple when a four-ship radioed they were coming in on low fuel, and that, no, they couldn't make it to Takhli, their alternate field. I heard the whole thing unfold on my office radio and sprang into action.

The wing had an emergency plan for just such a contingency and it called for allowing planes to land on the parallel taxi strip, especially those declaring emergencies. I grabbed my phone and told the tower to put the plan into effect immediately. The four-ship flight landed safely. If I had not had access to a radio that day, there's a good chance we would have lost four F-105s.

One afternoon I was given a heads up that one of our planes had gone down in Laos. That's all we know, the command post told me. Further information coming some fifteen minutes later revealed it was Moe Seaver who had punched out. Ah, shit! Since there was absolutely nothing I could do, I went to the Club and began drinking coffee by the gallon. I took along my ground radio so the command post could keep me updated, and as I sipped, my mind went into overdrive, conjuring up the worst kind of images.

It was not unusual for one of our pilots to be shot down on any given mission, but those odds would really ratchet up if a mission was going "downtown" as we euphemistically referred to Hanoi. To get there and back we would have to overfly Laos, and oftentimes on those return flight pilots would be forced to bailout of Thuds too chewed up to make it home, or at least as far as the Thai border and safety.

Laos was a land shrouded in mystery, home to many disparate tribes and factions, with each ruled by a warlord more vicious, more evil, than his neighbor. It was a place where people disappeared without a trace. And true to form, many of our pilots ejected over Laos with the majority never being heard from again. The thought of having to punch out over Laos was a frightening possibility, and it haunted us all during every mission.

After sweating for almost an hour and a half, I was told that the rescue chopper (a Sikorsky CH-3C Jolly Green Giant) had gotten Moe out, and that he was alive. I knew the chances were good he was badly injured, so I was on the flight line when the helo landed and my friend jumped down unaided onto the tarmac. He looked like he'd been dragged down the road and through the brush while tethered to a rampaging elephant, but when he spotted me he managed a big grin and a solid thumbs up before being whisked away for a medical checkup. He told me later that a whole bunch of Laotian bad guys had chased him all over the map before the Jolly Green rescue pilot figured a way to get him out. "It wasn't a clean pickup," he said, meaning that he damn near didn't make it, "but who in the hell cares? Not me, Scrappy, because it's the results that count!" The only thing that mattered was that Moe was alive and safe, albeit badly shaken, but at least he hadn't come back in a body bag. Needless to say, there was a helluva celebration in the club that night!

But I'll be damned if Moe wasn't forced to eject from another F-105 a short time later. He was on a test hop when his engine flamed out and he couldn't restart it. He bailed out inside Thai airspace and was able to communicate via his radio that he was okay. The waiting this time around wasn't quite so bad, and three hours later the rescue chopper brought Moe safely home. Hard as it was on me that day, I'm sure Moe found the whole situation a hell of a lot tougher to deal with.

During the latter part of my tour I chose to fly most of my missions with the 44th Squadron. Moe was the operations officer and Lieutenant Colonel "Fritz" Trez was the squadron commander. Fritz was a very able pilot and a fun guy to fly with. In fact we flew several Package Six missions together and became fast friends.

Lieutenant Colonel "Swede" Larson, the commander of the 469th Squadron phoned one afternoon to say he had a problem and asked if he could make an appointment to speak with me. I figured it was something serious, so I told him to come right on over. He didn't waste my time with a bunch of small talk. He cut to the chase and told me about a Lieutenant Colonel Tipton who had aborted on every occasion when scheduled to fly into Route Package Six. Swede went on to tell me that the guy had sworn he'd never go into Package Six regardless of the consequences. But the thing bothering him the most was that some of the other pilots in the squadron were now wise to the guy and Swede had begun to sense an undercurrent of resentment. This was a major problem and it needed to be taken care of fast.

"I'll see Chairsell as quickly as possible, Swede, and we'll decide what to do. But give me a couple of days to get back to you, okay?"

The following day the wing received a request to send five pilots over to 7th Air Force Headquarters in Saigon to serve on its operations staff. I gave each of my squadrons a quota and told them to submit some names. Meantime, I had informed Colonel Chairsell the evening before about the reluctant flyer as I had promised Swede I'd do, so he suggested getting rid of the problem by simply putting the guy on the list. I did, but later I really regretted it. I should have told Swede to put the son of a bitch up for a Package Six mission with me on his wing and if he had aborted then, I'd have damn well court-martialed his ass. Years later Swede roundly criticized me for not doing just that. I can honestly say, though the criticism stung, it was deserved.

✈ ✈ ✈

"Fritz" Trez had a Captain Davis in the 44th Squadron. Now Davis wasn't the greatest pilot in the 44th, so Fritz submitted his name for the transfer to headquarters. I knew Davis by sight, but that was it. I had never spoken to the man, and I didn't see him very often in the O Club after the duty day.

The following morning my first sergeant came into my office to tell me that a Captain Davis wanted to see me on an urgent matter. I told the sergeant to send him in. Davis entered, stood at what he mistakenly though was "at attention" and rendered a pathetic excuse for a salute. His uniform was a disgrace, and I found myself starting to seethe. What the hell did this sad sack want? Oh, yeah, let me guess.

"What's your problem, Davis?" I asked in a voice cold enough to freeze a vodka martini in Miami.

"Colonel, I'm a reservist. I own a drugstore back home and it's costing me a heap of money to be over here. But I volunteered to come and fight because I believe it's the right thing to do. We have to stop the commies here and now, because if we don't, they'll take over the entire region, then after that, who knows. What I'm trying to say, sir, is this: I don't want to serve the rest of my tour in some flunky-ass staff job. I just want to fly my hundred counters and go home knowing I did a damn good job for my squadron and for my country. I want to leave holding my head up high."

You could have knocked me over dead! He finished his speech and stood waiting for my answer. Talk about judging a book by its cover. Was I ever wrong!

I found myself moved as I studied this man before me. Here was a guy who didn't have to be in this place at all, a guy willingly putting his neck on the line because he thought it the right thing to do. For some inexplicable reason my mind flashed back to the final scene in the movie *The Bridges of Toko-Ri* starring William Holden and Fredric Marsh. Holden had played the part of a reserve navy carrier pilot who was shot down behind enemy lines in Korea then executed by the commies—just like what happened to my friend Spud. Marsh was the two-star task force commander, and he looked on Holden as a surrogate for the sons he'd lost in World War II. Well, anyway, when Fredric Marsh is finally told that Holden had been executed by the enemy during a rescue attempt, the audience can physically see and feel his anguish. With the weight of the world resting upon his shoulders, the admiral looks out over the carrier's flight deck from high up on the Flag Bridge and poses this poignant question: "Where do we find such men?" It was powerful, heart-stopping stuff.

I snapped out of my reverie. "Don't worry, Captain, I guarantee you'll stay and finish your hundred missions." I sent William Holden back to his squadron and told Fritz to send me up another name. I knew the answer to Frederic

Marsh's rhetorical question. These men come from the heartland of the greatest country on earth!

When Captain Davis flew his 100th mission, Fritz let him lead the flight. He asked me to fly with them both, and I was proud to do so. I flew number two, Fritz flew number three, and a squadron pilot-buddy of his joined us as number four. Everything went fine until we came in to land. Fritz had given Davis permission to lead us in a diamond formation flyby down the runway with Fritz was on one wing, me on the other, and number four in the slot position.

We were in our descent, readying to make the pass down the runway when Captain Davis looked over at Fritz and gave the hand signal for opening speed brakes. As he turned towards me I heard Fritz scream into my ear, "No, no, Jesus, no!"

God and Fritz were sure looking out for the number four—indeed, looking out for all of us—that day. It was impossible for him to have seen Davis' hand signal and he would have flown right up Davis' tail pipe. In all likelihood all four of us would have gone down, a crash that would have definitely been heard around the world!

On the first day of August I led the wing on a very successful strike against the Bac Ninh railway yard siding. The weather was crappy and we had to bob and weave our way in and around the clouds to reach the objective. Luckily, the target area was clear when we arrived and despite some heavy flak we managed to destroy scores of railway cars. And we chewed up a lot of track. But best of all we pulled off the mission without a single loss. Colonel "Cleo" Bishop, the new wing vice commander, flew this mission and during the debriefing told me how impressed he was with the professionalism of the pilots. I was pleased that he had noticed, and I agreed, adding that I believed they were the best of the best. Cleo was the replacement wing vice commander and he now shared the mobile home with me.

Chairsell was not on base when we flew that mission. He had recently been promoted to brigadier general and was off on a TDY somewhere for several days, which meant Cleo was in charge.

The next afternoon Cleo and I were sitting in a staff car at the end of the runway waiting for a pilot to come in from his 100th mission. Getting one hundred counters was a big deal for everyone, and we always made a production out of those events. The colonels would meet the lucky pilot at the end of the runway with lots of honking horns then have an impromptu parade back to the ramp with a fire engine leading the way spouting plumes of water high into the air.

Well, on this particular day the pilot decided to jazz up the occasion, so instead of just landing, he scared the living crap out of us by buzzing the runway from an altitude of about 20 feet. Believe me, having an F-105 fly over your head at that insanely low altitude scares the living shit out of you! This was about as big a "be no" as anyone could ever commit, and if Chairsell had been there he would have had that young hotshot's ass for dinner.

Cleo asked me what punishment I thought he should mete out. Remembering like it was yesterday what Major Gibson had done to me at Clark Field for committing the same offense, I said, "How about we tell his squadron commander to hold him here until General Chairsell gets back and see what he wants to do?" (It was customary for a pilot to head home ASAP after flying his 100th mission.) "Cleo, let the kid cool his jets until the last moment then tell him to vamoose just before Chairsell lands. He'll be a nervous wreck, but, by god, he'll sure have learned a valuable lesson!"

Captain Dramsi of the "March Hare" exercise at McChord AFB reappeared as a replacement pilot in the 388th. I went out of my way to let him know how pleased I was that he was part of the wing. He flew only a few missions before being shot down on a mission into Pack One. When I heard the news on the radio in my office I went kind of numb, like maybe it was a mistake, that it wasn't Dramsi who had gone down. I hoofed it over to ops for the debriefing. The flight leader told me that John had made it safely to the ground then had gotten on his radio and began directing the flight to bomb and strafe his position which he said was being overrun by the enemy. He did this with complete disregard for his own life. Later, I heard he had managed to escape from a POW prison and had evaded the NVA for several days before being recaptured.

Captain John Dramsi was a very special kind of a guy.

Fighter pilots are always looking for ways to get into trouble and Cleo and I were no exceptions. We decided to set our sights on pulling one off on Colonel Chester Jack, the base commander. Jack was in charge of building a swimming pool behind the O Club and had promised General Chairsell he'd have it finished prior to his rotation, which was now only days away. Chester was already a nervous wreck but we decided to make his life even more miserable, so we cornered him one night at the bar.

"Chester, I hear you're planning to put up a puke-ugly chain link fence around our beautiful new pool. Please say it ain't so," I needled, in a whiny, mock-falsetto voice.

"Well, it is so, Scrappy, because that's what the damn regs call for. A fence that will keep all the kids out."

"Chester, you'd be right on the money if this was a stateside base and there were a bunch of kids around. Maybe I'm blind, but how many little darlings did you see today?"

The man had had it with my tomfoolery. He slammed his beer mug down on the bar's countertop and through clenched teeth began to rip me a new one. "Go get frigging well laid, Scrappy. The frigging pool is getting a frigging fence because I'm following the frigging regs, so how about you shoving off and leave me frigging well alone." I told you Chester was pissed!

A couple of nights later Fritz and I were in the club, pumped and primed from having flown another successful mission that afternoon. Well, one thing led to another and before we knew it we were heading to the pool. We found a bunch of posts lying in a pile on the ground, so we loaded them into my station wagon, drove over to Chester's mobile home and heaved them underneath.

The next day at lunch a still-pissed off Chester cornered me at the club. "Scrappy, where did you put my goddamn fence posts?"

I figured the man had suffered enough. Wearing a look of shocked innocence on my face I answered in a butter-wouldn't-melt-in-my-mouth voice, "Why, Chester, they're safe and sound under your house."

Chester got his fence erected and the swimming pool filled just two days before General Chairsell's scheduled departure. On the morning of his leaving, Chairsell and I sat down for breakfast at a table next to a window overlooking the pool. I did a double take. Ohmygod, Chester's pool was empty! We both hurried out to see what had happened.

Oh, oh, from one end to the other, a large crack ran the entire length leaving maybe a thimble's worth of water next to the drain. Chairsell just shook his head as he stared down at that ugly gash, probably wondering where a hundred thousand gallons of water could disappear to so fast. As for me, I was at least smart enough not to open my big trap with some inappropriate quip.

I actually felt sorry for Chester that morning. By the time he got that crack repaired and the pool re-filled, General Chairsell was long gone.

20

Korat Confidential

When I arrived at Korat I began flying my missions with the 13th Tactical Fighter Squadron. After flying about thirty counters with them, I switched over to the 34th and flew another 25 missions before hooking up with the 44th. And upon my arrival at each of these squadrons I gave the commanders identical orders: schedule me like you would any other new pilot. That meant I'd start off flying a wing position, move up to flight commander, and finally, the force commander. I firmly believed that when it came to flying lead, combat experience in the skies over North Vietnam counted for a hell of a lot more than rank. But when it came time to choose a force commander, I would slip on my director of operations hat and approve the selectee, but always making sure that I spread the task around amongst those pilots most qualified. But there was also another factor which influenced my wanting to rotate the force commanders, a factor that was definitely a tad more pedestrian. Medals were awarded to folks leading those flights, and some force commanders earned Air Force Crosses for demonstrating superior leadership qualities under particularly hair-raising conditions. This was my way of spreading the opportunity for certain officers to stand apart from the crowd, something I deemed crucial for inclusion in their annual fitness reports. Medals and difficult missions flown as force commanders carried a lot of weight with promotion boards.

I had an F-105 assigned to me so I decided to have it customized. I named my Thud the "Liger," and had a picture painted on the side showing an animal with two heads; one a lion's, the other a tiger's. Now, I know this is not what a liger is in the real world, but I liked the finished product. It was my good luck mascot, and to me that's all that mattered. For you curious readers, know that the liger really exists: it's the result of crossbreeding a male lion and a female tiger, and the offspring possess the features of both parents. And as a general rule, it tends to be larger than either of them, and it's thought by some to be the meanest animal in the jungle.

Anyway, one day when I was tasked to fly a mission I found myself studying the scheduling board so as to get a mental rundown of who would be flying and in what position when I saw that my plane had been assigned to someone else! (The tail number was my clue.) "Nothing doing," I said in a voice loud enough for everyone in the room to hear. "That's my frigging airplane." The other pilot quickly switched birds with me.

But that wasn't the end of it. When I got to the ramp and stopped in front of my Thud, instead of my lucky "Liger" painted on the side, the plane was now sporting a picture of a goddamn bumblebee and some asinine words pronouncing it a "Bumble Bee Bomber!"

Well, it didn't take me long to find out what the hell was going on. Someone in maintenance had turned my plane over to Moe's squadron a couple of days earlier and then someone there had assigned it to him! Of course Moe had no idea this was my Thud, so he had told the local artist to go ahead and put his logo on it. I flew the Bumble Bee Bomber that day, but I was honked.

That day, July 28, 1967, also turned out to be a particularly bad one—but for another, far more serious reason. I lost a young friend named Karl Richter. Although Karl was only a first lieutenant, he was a pilot's pilot, and this day he was flying his 198th mission into North Vietnam. What made the loss all the more difficult to accept was the fact that this should have been a fairly easy mission—even for Karl—because our wing always tried to schedule pilots for the less dangerous missions when they were down to their last five counters.

The target that morning was in Package One, an area nowhere near as hot and dangerous as any of the other five packages. But all was for naught because Karl got hit, and hit hard, by antiaircraft fire while making a strafing pass on an AA site. Knowing Karl, I'm sure he had probably pressed the issue to the max and then some.

He was able to nurse his cripple into Laotian airspace before being forced to eject—and that's when his luck ran out. He got a good chute, but came down in a very rugged mountainous area and was fatally injured when he slammed into the side of a jagged karst. The rescue chopper got to him as soon as it could, but he died of multiple and massive injuries a short time later while en route to the base hospital. Karl Richter was only twenty-four-years old.

Losing Karl affected me deeply, as it did everyone else in the wing, and although I hadn't known him long I admired him for his courage and airmanship skills. He didn't need to be there that day. He had fulfilled all of his mission requirements months earlier, but instead of going home he'd volunteered for a second 100-mission tour. There's no doubt in my mind that had Karl lived, he would have one day worn general's stars.

On June 13, 1992, a statue of the forever-young Karl W. Richter was unveiled at Maxwell Air Force Base with a poignant inscription at its base recounting the words of the prophet Isaiah: "Whom shall I send, and who will go for us? Here I am. Send me." How fitting a tribute.

✈ ✈ ✈

On August 18th, 1967, Robin and his Wolf Pack hosted another Red River Valley Fighter Pilots meeting at Ubon. We flew over there in the base C-47, and I loaded it with all the pilots I could squeeze in it. Before landing I had the pilot overfly the base and we dropped dozens of rolls of toilet paper to ensure the place was appropriately decorated for our arrival. Once on the ground we had a parade, only this time the chosen transportation was water buffaloes instead of elephants. Chappie was the MC at dinner that night and after all the rah-rah speeches, for the finale I presented Robin with Karl Richter's pet monkey. I had meant this to be a joke because that monkey was one mean little bastard and would sink his razor-sharp teeth into anyone who

The "official" River Rat emblem was designed by the 469th TFS from Korat. It grabbed everyone's attention for its sheer simplicity, and its catchy nickname has endured until today.

got close enough to try and befriend him. Turned out Robin grew fond of that simian devil and he later told me he would have brought him back to the States except for all the red tape.

We partied late into the night, most of us already suspecting that this could easily morph into something of a more lasting nature, something with regularly scheduled gatherings. And it was during this bash that our official emblem was born, selected from several imaginative entrants submitted by squadrons representing several in-theater wings. One particular emblem—submitted by the 469th TFS from Korat—grabbed everyone's attention for its sheer simplicity. Theirs was a solid black shield with two words written in red across its face: River Rats. It was declared the hands-down winner by a solid majority and its catchy nickname has endured until today. Indeed, a few of us had already decided that the Red River Fighter Pilots Association would definitely become a permanent organization.

✈ ✈ ✈

One day the wing was fragged to bomb the Than Hoa Bridge. This was the second most important bridge in North Vietnam and one of the most important targets we were sent against during my year at Korat. The 44th

Squadron was tasked with the mission so I told Fritz I wanted to lead it. I had been force commander on several other Pack Six targets but this was far and away the most significant.

I had planned for us to take the route down "Thud" Ridge simply because it was the most practical for hitting targets around Hanoi. Everything went well until we neared the target area.

Flying at 12,000 feet across the ridge I could see in the distance that the valley in which Hanoi was situated was covered with a broken overcast at around the 4,000-foot level making identification of our target damn near impossible. When we got to within ten miles of Hanoi I reluctantly made the decision to abort. I had fifteen F-105s on my wing, and no way, no how, was I going to have this many planes circling over Hanoi while I had my eyes peeled looking for the target. This was not the time or the place for that kind of a dumb-ass stunt.

At the debriefing ninety minutes later I apologized to the guys and said, "I didn't want to put you in the position of orbiting the target while I was looking for it. We would have probably lost two or three of you and it sure as shit wasn't worth it to me."

Had we hit the target and brought the bridge down I would in all probability have been awarded the Air Force Cross. But I still vividly remembered the major I'd fired for turning me into a sitting duck, circling over Phuc Yen and getting my ass shot at.

Scrubbing that mission was a huge disappointment, but all these years later I'm still comfortable with the decision I made that day.

✈ ✈ ✈

We had our smart bombs, or, in this particular case, smart missiles. The missile in question was Martin's AGM-12, nicknamed the "Bullpup," and it was sent to us to be used against targets in North Vietnam. To say the results were a disappointment would be the understatement of the year. The missile was hung under the wings of our F-105s and wired to some fancy optical guidance doodads in the cockpit. Once released, the pilot guided the Bullpup by using a small joystick to visually line it up onto the target then keep it there. It sounded great in theory, but in practice this was a whole 'nother smoke. Literally. And that's because the Bullpup gave off a smoke trail, but in order to properly guide the thing the pilot had to fly down that smoke trail until the missile hit the target. Well, hell, the North Vietnamese gunners wised up fast to this fact of life and the word got around that all they had to do was fire into the smoke trail, and before they knew it the following Thud would fly right into their withering wall of fire.

After losing a couple of planes real fast we decided the Bullpup could only be used against lightly defended targets—like secondary bridges up on the northeast railroad, but definitely not against any targets downtown.

Several USO shows came through Korat that year, including Bob Hope's fabulous troupe. On this particular occasion it was Brenda Lee coming to town, so the base commander sent the C-47 to Bangkok to pick her up, along with her band. Turned out Chester Jack had a birthday the day she came to Korat, and even though everyone knew she was there primarily to entertain the enlisted men, Chester inveigled her to come over to the Officers' Club for a party some buddies were throwing for him. She made a brief appearance, but when Chester put the squeeze on her to sing a special song for his birthday, Brenda Lee politely refused. Well, this really pissed off Chester, so next day when it came time to fly the troupe back to Bangkok he grounded the C-47 and made them ride the bus back. Yes, sir, old Chester was a real world-class gentleman!

I flew my hundredth mission north in the middle of September, but because my year's tour wouldn't be up for another month, I led one more mission after that into Package Six.

It was a replay of Robin Olds' successful "Bolo" mission. (That was the time he had led his F-4s in a formation that painted the planes as a bomber force on the enemy's radar screens. He had planned this in the hopes of enticing the enemy's MiGs to come up and engage—which they did.) We went in as though we were on another run-of-the-mill strike force mission, except this time we only carried fuel tanks, sidewinders and cannons.

Now, the F-105 could not turn as tight as the F-4, but we had awesome cannons, which were a mighty big plus in our favor. The F-4 relied on missiles for its defense—some of which were well capable of hitting targets at quite a long range—but for the most part these were useless in environments where the pilot had to visually identify his target before blasting it.

We were truly loaded for bear that day, but alas, the MiGs never rose to take our bait.

I stayed a few days extra after my tour officially ended, hoping I'd get the chance to lead a strike on the Phuc Yen Air Base. Rumor was that Washing-

Scrappy on his way to getting tossed into the officers' club pool after completing his 100th mission over North Vietnam, Korat RTAFB, 1967. He finished the whole bottle of bubbly by himself! (courtesy of USAF).

ton was about to give us permission to hit it, but then they kept delaying until I couldn't postpone my departure any longer. Permission to hit it was later granted but by then I was long gone. I found out many years later that the delay had been caused because some Russian biggie had been promised by Washington it wouldn't be hit while he visited there.

✈ ✈ ✈

In summary, I had flown 101 missions over North Vietnam and 16 noncounters into Laos—in my mind they were to make up for those I did not get in Korea—making a total of 117. I felt good.

But when I got my orders all the feeling good quickly vanished. I was going to an Air Defense Command wing at Kinchloe Air Force Base in Sioux St. Marie, Michigan. And I was going as the DO. There was no hiding the

Scrappy on the flight line with his F-105 Thunderchief at Korat RTAFB after a mission over North Vietnam, 1967 (courtesy of USAF).

✈ ✈ ✈

fact that this was a real menial, dead-end job since the wing only had one fighter squadron. I was crestfallen. Later I found out why I had been chosen for this particular slot.

After I left Korat the North Vietnamese gunners had a field day picking off colonels. My roommate, John Flynn, the wing vice commander, got shot down, followed in short order by the wing commander, Colonel Edward Burdett, and then James Bean who had come to Korat as my replacement. All three went down within a month of my leaving.

21

Stateside Again

I took a thirty-day leave and returned home to Dorie and the children who were still living in Apple Valley. The month flew by and before I knew it I was off to Kinchloe and my new assignment.

Colonel Bill Brierty was the wing commander, my boss, and one hell of a good guy to work for. I had known him—but not that well—back during my days at San Bernardino. He had been in the Air Defense shop while I had worked for the IG. Looking back, I sure wish I had worked for him instead of Piss Willie.

The lone squadron at Kinchloe was equipped with the F-106 Delta Dart, a terrific airplane with a delta-winged design which it shared with its cousin, the F-102 Delta Dagger. Its mission was to intercept and shoot down big bombers but it would also have made a great air-to-air fighter if someone had just put a cannon on board and given it a canopy a guy could actually see out of! The Air Force had streamlined its external tanks thus increasing the range to about 1600 miles. Let me tell you, that single engine dart could zip along at a mighty fast clip.

One day, out of the blue, I received a call from my old boss from Korat, General Chairsell. He asked how I was doing, and then after some more small talk he mentioned that he had checked my efficiency reports. I suppose he had been curious as to why I hadn't received a far better assignment coming off an excellent year in Thailand. He had given me a rating all the way to the right, meaning it was as high as could be. He then told me that Piss Willie had given me a really bad report and strongly suggested that I immediately take steps to get it purged from my personnel folder. Well, it didn't take long for me to discover that such an undertaking was well nigh impossible. A major general had rubber stamped Piss Willie's career-ending OER (Officer Effectiveness Report), and I was told by one of the more friendly paper pushers at Randolph that once a general officer had added his signature to such a document, only an act of congress would get it purged. When I finally I got ahold of the OER Piss Willie had written on me, I had to agree with General Chairsell; it was the worst efficiency rating I'd ever seen, and I mean for anybody! No wonder I had been sent from such a high-profile war zone combat assignment to such a career-ending one as the DO at Kinchloe!

During this time Robin had been recently promoted to brigadier general and was now the commandant of cadets at the Air Force Academy. Talk about the right man for the right job at the right time! He was definitely an inspiration for every cadet who ever dreamed of flying fighters.

One afternoon Robin called to say he had a speaking engagement in Chicago and that he wanted to fly up to Kinchloe on the way and spend the night. He also said that before we started to party too heavily he needed to set aside some time to discuss the possibility of forming a permanent River Rats Organization. Yes, sir!

I met his T-33 at base ops and dropped him and his pilot off at the BOQ. After a shower, the two came over to my house for dinner. I'd also invited Lt. Col. Jerry Mau and his wife, Ruby, because they had been previously stationed with Robin. I'd also known Jerry since my days with the 12th Fighter Squadron in the Philippines and Korea. He had been my assistant DO at the time, and was an all round great guy. Ruby liked the social life at the club and Jerry had no problem with this except he couldn't drink a lot, and the worst thing he ever did was fall asleep. One night Ruby, Jerry, Dorie and I were at the bar in the O Club. It was about midnight and we were all talking and having a good time when Jerry suddenly fell off his barstool. Apparently he had dozed off, and when he realized what happened, he got up and sheepishly said, "How about that, sports fans?"

Robin and I discussed the River Rats while still sober, then proceeded to drink a lot of booze, and although we both agreed at the end of the night that the Rats should become a permanent organization, nothing definite came of it. It was not until several months had passed—and only after Larry Pickett got involved—that a specific plan for making it happen finally came into being.

I was at Kinchloe for a year before the Air Force deactivated the fighter wing and moved the

F-106 squadron. I was out of a job, but not for long. A week later my new assignment came down: I was being transferred to Perrin AFB, at Sherman, Texas. Perrin had an F-102 Delta Dagger training wing, and again, I was going as DO. But what the hell, at least it was a flying job. I had now been an operations officer in four fighter squadrons, and the DO for four fighter wings. That

(L to R) Brig. General Robin Olds and Scrappy on the flight line at Kinchloe AFB, Michigan, 1968 (courtesy of USAF).

had to be some kind of a record, especially as it pertained to the number of lateral transfers for a colonel.

Bob Hardee was the wing commander at Perrin. I had first met him in ADC when I was with TAC EVAL and I'd just broken the altitude record. We'd both been tasked to brief the graduating class at the Air Force Academy on the merits of snagging an assignment with Air Defense Command.

All the instructor pilots at Perrin were old hands, which meant they knew how to do their jobs, which in turn, made mine that much the easier. The wing had two squadrons and, as always, there was intense competition between units. And they delighted in playing tricks on each other. One night someone decided to up the ante and played a gotcha on the entire base. When folks arrived for work the following morning they were greeted by a garbage can perched atop the flagpole. Of course, no one could figure how it got there, but worse, no one could figure out how to get it down!

The base CE (civil engineer) put his best eggheads to work on the problem but none could figure out how to bring the offending can down. Finally, after three days, the wing commander declared a truce and demanded whoever was responsible to step forward and get the damn thing off his flagpole. One of the instructor pilots did just that and lowered it the same way he had put it up. In front of an enthusiastic crowd of almost fifty people, he attached the head of a broomstick to the line used to hoist the flag, ran it up until he'd snagged the garbage can, then lowered it to a round of applause and whistles.

My boss was not the easiest person to work for, but we got along. And he was no Piss Willie! After a year he retired and a Colonel Vermont Garrison took over the wing. Vermont and I clicked. We had both been in the flying business so long we could do our jobs in our sleep, so we spent half our days drinking coffee and trading war stories. Vermont had shared a mobile home with Chappie James at Ubon, so naturally Chappie was often a part of our conversation. Our colorful friend had just made brigadier general and was touring the country giving patriotic speeches in defense of the administration's handling of the war. His was a cause we agreed with in spades, and also agreed that Chappie was a natural for such an assignment. But we often found ourselves laughing aloud at some of his stories which found their way into the press recounting his many feats of flying derring-do. Most were definitely somewhat of a stretch, but we both agreed on one thing: our pal Chappie was just being Chappie!

One of the perks which went along with this assignment was that I could sign out an airplane on weekends and fly it just about any place I wanted. On one such occasion I flew to Williams AFB at Chandler, Arizona, for a reunion of Thud drivers. Scores of old pals showed up, including General Chairsell, and I don't think any of us got more than three or four hours sleep over those two days.

On Sunday the general asked if I could drop him off at Holloman AFB on my way home. While waiting for our clearance at base ops we began talking about the god awful efficiency rating Piss Willie had given me, and we agreed that it had effectively ended my career at the rank of colonel.

Chairsell then popped the million dollar question. "Scrappy, tell me the truth, you weren't trying to make general anyway, were you?" His words were not spoken in an unkind manner, and I knew what he was really saying. Let's face it, I had not gone out of my way to attend any of the senior officer schools, like the Air War College, nor had I jockeyed for an assignment to headquarters—both musts for any officer hoping to be considered for promotion to BG.

"No, I guess not, General," I replied after a long moment, "but that goddamn report sure has made a huge difference in the assignments I've gotten since Nam."

"Can't argue with you there, Scrappy," was his last word on the matter, then tactfully changed the subject.

In 1969 I heard that Larry Pickett was also interested in seeing the River Rats become a permanent organization, so after several telephone calls back and forth, he volunteered to host a stateside reunion at which we would adopt a charter and elect a board of officers.

Meanwhile, the River Rats still stationed in Thailand had remained very active. They had managed to hold what they called "practice reunions" with the first one at Korat on May 22, 1967, the next at Ubon on August 18, 1967, then one at Takli on November 30, 1967. There was also one at Udorn on March 7, 1968, then again at Korat on June 14, 1968. A decision had been made to call these gatherings "practice reunions" and that they would continue as such until our POWs were released from the prisons in North Vietnam. Then, and only then, would we Rats hold our first "real reunion."

The first Stateside practice reunion was held in Wichita, Kansas, in April 1969. I was elected president, and Larry the vice president. The vote was unanimous because General Chairsell had chaired the election committee and we were the only candidates whose names he allowed to be placed in nomination. Membership cards were issued to all attendees on the last day of the reunion. They were sequentially numbered, and mine was card number 1. The practice of numbering the cards was discontinued the following year because there were too many arguments over who should get the lowest numbers! Thirty-eight years later I still have my original card with the words: Col. Scrappy Johnson, River Rat #1. I'm damn proud of that card!

We accomplished a lot that first year. We established the forerunner of the popular Country Store, the Scholarship Program came into existence, and we began the Bumper Sticker Program. The first issue of our newsletter, *MIG SWEEP*, was published on July 1, 1969, and we encouraged River Rats everywhere to get involved in their communities by making speeches to keep the public fully aware of our POWs' and MIAs' wretched predicament.

Those early days for the Rats were grim indeed. We had little money when we jump-started the bumper sticker program, and we struggled mightily just to sell enough stickers so that we could buy more, but a short time later the program took on a life of its own. It rapidly snowballed to such an extent, that by mid–1972 it seemed we had bumper stickers on half the cars in the States. The sticker read:

POW/MIA
DON'T LET THEM BE FORGOTTEN

We started our Scholarship Program for children of those POW/MIAs. That first year we were only able to award three $1,000 scholarships, but we all agreed that a good start. The program has grown many-fold over the years, and much of the credit must go to Lt. Col. Fred Dennis, who was my assistant DO at the time.

✈ ✈ ✈

In 1968, the pilots of the 388th TFW at Korat pooled their resources and had a Freedom Bell cast in a local foundry. The bell was then hung in an impressive Asian mount, and the men decided that the clapper would be immobilized only to be rung for the first time at the official reunion following the POWs' release. It was then crated and shipped off to the States, where it somehow made its way to my office. As association president, I was to be its custodian.

✈ ✈ ✈

In August of 1969, I was invited to come to the Officers Training School at Lackland AFB, near San Antonio, to be the guest speaker for the graduating class. The original plan had called for the ceremony to be held in the Cadet Officers' Club, but someone soon realized the main room was not large enough to hold the entire class at one time, so I was informed I would have to give my speech twice. The back-to-back events were scheduled for Monday and Tuesday nights.

Dorie and I drove down to San Antonio the Saturday before, managing to work in a mini vacation en route. We checked in to the base BOQ, an old World War II barracks just recently renovated. Memories stirred, a fog lifted, and I began to nosey around. The more I did the more I told myself the place sure looked familiar. So much so that for my opening remarks that Monday night, and before segueing into my speech, I said:

"On August 18, 1942, I was among forty Aviation Cadets that moved into the first barracks built on the hill at the San Antonio Aviation Cadet Center. Tonight I am staying in that same barracks. They have jazzed it up and are now calling it the VIP Quarters." This got a rousing response from the class because it was true! The remainder of the speech was a breeze, something I was truly thankful for, because public speaking was never something I volunteered to stand in line to do.

✈ ✈ ✈

In September 1970, USAF Headquarters sent me to Air University at Maxwell AFB, Alabama, to lead a team of six officers in a writing of the history of the air war over North Vietnam from 1963 to 1968. This was a sizeable undertaking and it took us the better part of a year to complete. I was able to arrange it so the wing at Perrin would send a T-33 down to pick me up on Friday evenings and fly me back on Monday mornings. Except for being away from my family, it was a pretty good duty. I had a suite in the VIP quarters—the real VIP quarters—and the O Club was only a short walk away.

They had a great library at Maxwell, so we spent the better part of the first month researching our subject. We were all veterans of the air war over North Vietnam and none of us were happy about the way it was still being waged. The Maxwell crowd was afraid we would insert these feelings into our writing and we were cautioned not to do so. Well, that was then and this is now, and I refuse to allow myself to labor under any constraints as I write this memoir.

Secretary Robert McNamara masterminded every facet of the operation of that war. His qualifications for such a daunting undertaking? Turns out just one. He was a low level supply officer during World War II. And it was President Johnson who loved to boast: "They don't hit an outhouse in North Vietnam without my approval." I'm sure he thought the statement was cute—fact was it was downright stupid. But sad to say, it was also true. And it was the root cause why the war lasted ten years without a win for our side. His misguided policy of calculated escalation allowed the North Vietnamese to build up their forces when and where they needed, and it only served to intensify their resolve. And his running of the war from Washington cost us many, many lives.

The air wings operating in South Vietnam and Thailand were given JCS (Joint Chiefs of Staff) targets to hit, and if they were not completely destroyed on the first mission, then the pilots would have to return day after day until they were. This took away any advantage of surprise that we might have had. Overnight the North Vietnamese re-deployed both their SAMs and antiaircraft batteries to cover these targets because they knew we would be coming back. The Thuy Nguyen Steel Mill was a good example of such folly. Our commanders ordered us back to this target day after day for fear it would be taken off the approved list.

The way we conducted the air war over North Vietnam was in direct conflict with established and approved U.S. Air Force doctrine, which clearly called for hitting airfields, communications networks, command centers and other important targets as soon as hostilities broke out. All those things that would help the enemy fight his war his way had to go, and go fast. Confederate General Nathan Bedford Forrest was bang-on when he said that the key to winning was to "get there first with the most men." It was true then, and just as true today. And I'd heard all the reasons why these things weren't done in Vietnam: The Russians might come in; the Chinese might come in; if we hit their airfields they'll just move their planes to China. Well, who the hell cares? These things should have been considered long before starting the fight in the first place. In summary, my feelings are as follows: The Vietnam War as it was handled by President Johnson and Secretary McNamara will live forever as a classic textbook example of how not to fight an air war!

✈ ✈ ✈

Our next River Rat practice reunion was held in San Antonio, and George Jessel, the comedian—not the long-dead British jurist of the same name—was our guest speaker. Mr. Jessel brought his own introduction with him, and it was a short one paragraph. Later I learned why this experienced speaker did so. The ramblings of an inept introducer can really set the stage for a lousy performance.

These were troubled days for the State of Israel and Jessel, affectionately known as "the Toastmaster General of the United States" showed up in an Israeli uniform. He was a rabidly patriotic man, both for Israel and the United States, and his humorous stories kept the guys rolling in the aisles. A funky band followed him, and after several forgettable tunes he jumped up and berated them for not playing patriotic music!

During this gathering I made myself an election committee of one and elected Robin Olds to succeed me as president and tapped Captain Bruce Miller, USN, to serve as our vice president. I felt badly for not giving Larry the president's job, but I did not want the Rats to be seen as an F-105-only group. I understood that making Robin our president and Bruce the vice president would go a long way toward keeping the F-4 drivers and the Navy guys involved, and we very much needed their support. Much later, Larry was voted in as president, done so by popular acclaim. I wrote scores of letters to friends on his behalf and was delighted when he was finally made our president. No one deserved the honor more.

Robin, our newly elected president, had to leave early on Air Force business, so the new vice president made the obligatory speech in his stead. Once started, Bruce really warmed up to his task, so much so, that after a while, Jessel began digging me in the ribs and saying in a loud voice, "Tell him to sit down, Scrappy."

I was not about to start a war with the Navy after I had gone to such ends to keep them involved, so I whispered to the funny man that I didn't have the cajones to intervene! Jessel thought that was a scream.

As the last piece of business, I left myself in charge of administering the Scholarship Fund. Doing so made me feel that I was still an active part of the organization.

I packed up the Freedom Bell and sent it to Robin. As president he would keep it until his term was up—or even better—until it could be rung. Instead of placing it in his office Robin decided to put it on public display at the Air Force Academy where it was seen by over a million people during the time it was there.

Robin hosted a River Rat board meeting a couple of months later, and it was here that I met a truly wonderful person, a man named John Verdi. John was a Marine Corps lieutenant colonel, and as their representative, he was indeed an inspired choice.

I would get to know a lot more about John Verdi later.

22

Punchin' Cattle

I made it through the year at Maxwell and returned to Texas full time. I became interested in the cattle business. Dorie and I bought a small fifty-acre plot and started a small cattle operation. After all, we were in Texas!

When I was little my dad took me to the cinema on Saturday mornings to see cowboy movies featuring such heroes as Bob Steele or Tom Mix. Then during the following week, we kids would play out the plot. The West had always fascinated me.

I knew little to nothing about raising cattle, but two pilots working for me had grown up on ranches, so I hired them as my advisors. Yet even with their help we still managed to make lots of mistakes. Our spread (I loved calling it that) was near Whitesboro, Texas, about 20 miles from the base, and I'm probably the only person who regularly checked on his cows from the cockpit of an F-102!

That first winter we left our stock in the field not realizing that they had to be fed hay because there was no grass for grazing. Where in the hell were my "professional" advisors, you ask? Good point. And we also soon learned that cattle needed constant care—like shots and other stuff—and that you had to have a corral and chute in order for these chores to be done. We had neither. Greenhorn and tenderfoot are two words that come to mind whenever I describe my initial foray into this newfound profession, but I was no quitter.

My plan was to retire in the area, and even though I dearly loved being in the Air Force and considered my job flying fighters a privilege, the time had come for me to move on. Simply put, I wanted to make money.

✈ ✈ ✈

Before I retired I would sit in my office and dream for hours about the big ranch I was going to own. My vision was crystal clear: I knew my spread down to the last detail. It had a pair of humongous wrought-iron front gates with a sign that read, "20 miles to the ranch house." And I would count calves, then buy 'em. Lots of 'em! I would start with 30 and hold on to half the herd each year, repeat the process the following year and tote up how many head I'd have in ten years, then twenty years. On paper it seemed real easy, and I just knew I was a shoo-in to become a cattle baron. I soon found out that it wasn't quite the way of my dreams when it came to life in the real world. The King Ranch was sure spared my encroaching on their title of being the biggest spread in Texas!

Dorie and I found another spread—seventy-three acres this time—close to Lake Texoma, on the Red River. (The Texas Red River, that is.) It was a beautiful piece of land with lots of trees—just what we wanted. We crunched some numbers, found it was doable, then hired a builder to erect our dream home. We moved in even though I had not yet retired.

In 1972, Robin held the River Rat Practice Reunion in San Diego, and he snagged famed World War II Marine Corps ace—and Medal of Honor recipient—Joe Foss, to come as our guest speaker.

I found myself seated on the dais beside a well dressed, very distinguished looking bearded gentleman. He was introduced to the gathering as a retired Australian admiral, a man whose career we were told, was legendary Down Under. Well, when the guest started to speak we realized he was drunk. I mean the man was toasted! It seemed everyone could see he was gassed except him, and he plowed ahead with his speech. He had us all in stitches as he stumbled from one topic to the next, oftentimes not even finishing his sentences. His powers of concentration were zilch. Folks were laughing so hard they had tears streaming down their cheeks, and still the old gent continued to talk, oblivious of the commotion he was causing. When he finished some fifteen minutes later, he burped, almost fell off the stage as he lost his balance, then staggered back to his chair and plopped himself down beside me. He turned a glassy eye my way and winked, then started to nod off, catching himself in the nick of time then feigned an interest in what Robin was saying.

We learned a few minutes later that we had just witnessed a performance by an up-and-coming comic named Foster Brooks. The applause was thunderous! I didn't realize just who he was until later that evening. Foster Brooks and I were from the same hometown. In fact, I clearly remember listening to him when he was a local disk jockey, and I knew his brother, Pleasant Brooks.

I retired from the Air Force in September of 1972, with zero fanfare. I declined the offer of a formal ceremony, so I just said my goodbyes and left.

One of the guys at work asked me on my last day what I was going to do when I retired and I said, "I plan on spending the first couple of years getting my ranch the way I want it, then I'll play golf." Fourteen years later when I sold it, I was still working on getting it the way I wanted it, but I was able to work in a lot of golf! I had replaced all the fences, cross-fenced it and built a steel corral. Most people in Texas would have hired a bulldozer and driver to clear their land, but I cleared mine all by my lonesome. I selectively cut my trees, leaving the ones I wanted to keep—which were most.

I had several close calls during those years, either with death or serious injury, and I later read that farming and ranching was near the top of the list of the most dangerous occupations. Boy, could I ever relate. Oftentimes when I found myself in a pickle I'd think: I flew fighter planes for thirty years and I faced combat in two wars without busting my can, but I've almost done myself in a dozen times while operating a tractor and a chainsaw, to say nothing of trying to coax a fifteen-hundred-pound bull into doing what I wanted him to do!

The weather was always a huge factor in our daily lives, much the same way as it was in flying, except this was different. In the Air Force, I always wanted the weather to clear so I could go punch holes in the sky. In ranching, I always wanted it to rain so my grass would grow and my cows could eat for free. 1976 was such a dry year that I had to start feeding hay to the herd as early as the first part of July. This setback completely wrecked my financial life because there was so little hay to be had anywhere in Texas, and what was available was very expensive. My stock pond went dry by early summer, but thank God my well didn't. It literally kept my cows alive.

The River Rat officers took the Scholarship Program out of my hands in 1973. I was told it would be administered in Washington because one of the Rats there was affiliated with a stock brokerage firm which could better invest the money. You can imagine how this sat with me. But I went along with the board's decision.

After pussyfooting around for ten years like some third-rate, backwater, pseudo-power, the United States finally had enough of the North Vietnamese politburo's bullshit and commenced bombing the living daylights out of Hanoi and Haiphong. This was an around the clock, all-out effort employing our B-52s (we called them BUFS, which stood for Big Ugly Fuckers) and the campaign was known as Linebacker II. President Nixon finally got it right; he declared that nothing was to be off limits. As a result of this shellacking, the North Vietnamese scurried to the peace table in Paris and signed an accord in January 1973—agreeing to basically the same conditions they had rejected in 1968. Our POWs were released from their hellholes in several groups over the next few weeks.

Everyone I know in the military agreed that this all-out bombing campaign should have taken place back in 1964.

In August of 1973, we held our first real reunion in Las Vegas, Nevada. All the returning POWs were invited as honored guests along with their wives and families. This was our shining moment. President Nixon had been invited as our guest speaker but at the last minute he bowed out and sent General Alexander Haig as his representative. This was right in the middle of the Watergate mess, and a siege mentality had overtaken the residents of the White House West Wing. More than 2,600 people attended our big splash, and most of the stars performing on the Las Vegas Strip stopped by to pay their respects to our returning heroes, sing a song or two, or simply crack a few jokes for a very appreciative audience.

Mr. Ross Perot, a true leader who had worked tirelessly year after year for the prisoners' release, honored us all with his presence that weekend. Dorie and I were selected to be his escort. We picked up Mr. Perot at his hotel, walked him over to the convention center and sat with him during dinner. What a rare individual. And to think: we were fellow Texans!

During dinner a few folks spontaneously began tying together the yellow dinner napkins which adorned every place setting. Soon scores joined in and began tying their napkins, and next thing I knew everyone was in on the act! All rose from their seats and joined an impromptu conga line, the line snaking between the tables while hundreds of dancers held aloft a wonderful band of yellow ribbons. And three thousand voices belted out Tony Orlando and Dawn's cult classic, "Tie a Yellow Ribbon Round the Ole Oak Tree." It was a moment never to be forgotten. This has since become a custom at our reunions, and while the tables are still set with starched napkins, each table also has a supply of yellow ribbons. I often think that whoever had to untie those 2,600 yellow napkins that memorable night in Vegas could not have been too pleased!

Prior to the dinner and during the part of the program where the speeches were made, the Freedom Bell was to be rung for the very first time. General Alexander Haig and I were called upon to do the honors. Our initial attempt was far from successful so the general and I tried to ring it a second time by swinging the attached rope. Still no luck, because the bell was hung on a swivel and it just moved along with the clapper. After a third, and then a fourth try, several boisterous River Rats—far rowdier than a now worked-up General Haig and I physically picked the bell up off the ground—stand and all—and managed to elicit a dull thud. But that's all the folks needed to hear. The audience broke out into a loud and lengthy cheer.

The clapper's malfunction that night is still remembered by many River Rats as an omen. Some hold to this day that there were MIAs who had been "sold out" and left behind, and feel in their hearts that was the reason the bell didn't ring as it was meant to that night. They believe God's hand stilled that clapper.

Prior to 1973, our River Rat practice reunions had all been stag affairs, but because this reunion was being held to honor the recently released POWs who had been separated from their wives and loved ones for so long, the board had decreed this reunion would be coed.

After the ceremony I found myself standing in the hall with Robin congratulating ourselves on such a splendid night when he suddenly whispered, "Scrappy, let's go in there right now and have a MiG sweep!"

Even I knew better than that! I looked Robin in the eye wondering if maybe I hadn't heard right. Nope, I do believe he wasn't kidding.

"No, Robin, we can't. There are too many ladies in there!"

I had been one of the strongest advocates that our reunions should always remain stag affairs, but I know now that the change was not only for the best, it was actually necessary. The River Rats have endured and prospered these many years, and I don't think this would have happened had we remained a stag organization. It turns out that many of the wives are our most active and ardent supporters, and their presence has sure kept us from getting into any real trouble, such as the infamous Navy Tail Hook scandal at the beginning of the nineties.

✈ ✈ ✈

The mere mention of Jane Fonda's name will send a River Rat into a rage.

Few of us can ever forget the photo of Jane Fonda in *Life* Magazine, taken near Hanoi when a lot of us were getting our asses shot at, and shot off. The photo shows her seated at the controls of an antiaircraft gun, wearing an idiotic smile on her face and an enemy helmet. It's difficult for us to forget this image of her willingly giving aid and comfort to the enemy when so many Americans were dying in Vietnam. And it is impossible to forget that she said, "There's no reason to believe that U.S. Air Force fliers are being tortured by the Vietnamese," and how she then went on in her next breath to brand us as "professional killers." But the utmost in stupidity was brought home for all to hear in her remarks in 1970 to a crowd at the University of Michigan. "I would think that if you understood what communism was, you would hope, you would pray on your knees, that we would someday become communists."

Fonda's was the face of all treasonous folk of like ilk, and our members have vented their righteous anger at this woman in association newsletters and at River Rat reunions. Our anger has not diminished with time and after her public apology for her conduct, the River Rats National Board released the following statement:

> The River Rats attitude concerning the Jane Fonda "apology" is that we deem it totally unacceptable in context and sincerity. It is not acceptable to our association or to us as veterans of the Vietnam War. Neither do we believe it should be acceptable to our nation nor to the American people.
>
> Jane Fonda's actions and statements maligning United States servicemen—even to the extent of categorizing them as war criminals, during her visit to Hanoi in 1972—were at the very least, detrimental to the conduct of the war. More importantly, and of a much more serious nature, they caused grievous bodily injury to our men held captive in North Vietnam. These actions and words could be considered outright traitorous, even to the most casual observer. Jane Fonda did not take enough time to reflect on the possible consequences of her actions prior to her trip to Hanoi in 1972, and she obviously still has not reflected on those actions, nor is she concerned with the consequences today, except for their affecting her career. No simple apology or disavowal of her reported statements could so easily rectify the heartache and pain she so willingly inflicted upon our fighting men and this great nation. Feeble attempts to rectify or clarify all the wrongs she committed only serve to further aggravate this association. If Jane Fonda really wants to get serious about an apology, we recommend she demonstrate this fact through action as well as words. Our fighting men, whom she chose to degrade, demonstrated their patriotism through their actions, and Jane Fonda should be held to the same standard. She should use her influences and resources to assist our government in obtaining a full accounting of our MIAs, in reconciling the uncertainty and hardships they have endured over the years, and giving aid and comfort to our needy veterans rather than to the enemy. Only through such actions and deeds, and the publicity associated therewith, can Jane Fonda again achieve status with this association.

It was obvious we did not accept her apology.

And as late as March 2005, Fonda finally acknowledged that it was a "betrayal" and "the largest lapse of judgment that I can even imagine," she said, referring to the infamous picture of her taken seated at the controls of the North Vietnamese antiaircraft gun. But in her next breath the woman resolutely continues to defend her leadership role and reprehensible conduct during the antiwar movement, including her radio broadcasts on Radio Hanoi. Of course, this came in a television interview as a prelude to the release of her memoirs!

The nearest base to our ranch was Shepherd Air Force Base, located at Wichita Falls, Texas, a boring two-hour drive away. Dorie and I went there about once a month to stock up on dry goods at the commissary and to pay the obligatory visit to the Base Exchange.

It was during one of these visits that Dorie noted her ID card was going to expire in about five weeks, so we decided to save ourselves a trip and get a new one now. We went to the office that handled ID cards and approached a young airman wearing two stripes on her sleeve. We explained the situation, gave her Dorie's old card and asked her to please issue a new one.

She looked at the card, mulled the request for a long minute then said, "The regulation says that I can't issue you a new card until 30 days prior to the expiration date of the old card. Sorry."

We went through the explanation about the two-hour drive but she wouldn't budge. I was just as persistent in letting her know that I found her answer to be unacceptable, so finally she said in a voice loaded with contempt, "My sergeant will be back in one hour. Come back and talk to him."

We left and returned in an hour and were greeted by a staff sergeant. We explained the situation about the two-hour drive, which he thought about for all of a microsecond and asked Dorie for her card. She handed it over. He whipped a pair of scissors from his desk drawer and cut her card in half, then halved the halves. Dorie's card now looked like confetti. He grinned as he admired his handiwork. "Ma'am, I can only replace this card within thirty days of its expiration, or if it's damaged." He pretended to study the little pile of detritus in his hand, then exclaimed, "Why, I do believe your card is definitely damaged!" He turned to the two-striper and told her to fix Dorie up with a new card.

That's why noncommissioned officers are the indispensable backbones of every military service in every single country on earth. These guys and gals know instinctively how to cut to the chase and get a job done!

✈ ✈ ✈

Our golf club was home to an assortment of personalities.

There was John Warren who at the age of 75 could shoot his age every day. John had been a track star at the University of Texas and he once told me he had taught "Babe" Dedrickson how to get out of the chocks, meaning he had helped contribute to her great athletic career. I once said to him as a result of something that he had said to me, "Nobody likes a smart ass." His reply? "Smart asses don't care!"

Then there was Dwight Nevell, the club pro. He had been on the professional tour and had enjoyed a few successful years. His only problem was his temper. I once saw him blow a good score in the Byron Nelson Classic in the Dallas Preston Trails Tournament by hitting three balls into the water on 17 when the hole placement was fifteen feet from the front of the green. This really bothered me at the time because I had a ten-dollar bet saying he would beat Miller Barber—and he was ahead at the time.

Otha Denham was another special character. He was a successful businessman and a scratch golfer, but he, too, was somewhat temperamental. His longtime hobby was making golf clubs, and Otha had a fine collection.

The eighteenth hole at Tanglewood bordered a large lake. One really off-day, he threw a set of custom-made clubs worth about $1,500 in 1980 dollars into the lake in a fit of disgust. One of his friends wordlessly hustled off to a nearby marina, returned with a magnet and retrieved most of them for Otha.

Then there was Gerald Guthrie, a guy who always managed to keep us in stitches. One day he was playing with a member who was a known stickler for the rules. Now Gerald was certainly not one to cheat or to knowingly break any rules, but this guy had pulled a couple of nit-pickers on Gerald and he was getting miffed. On the seventeenth hole, each hit solid second shots, both landed on the green, but then both of their balls rolled off the back side and came to rest within 10 feet of each other. Gerald got to the scene first and, after getting out of his cart, walked over and checked both balls. He then took up a stance behind one of them. The "nitpicker" came up and assumed that Gerald was standing behind his own. He went to the other ball and chipped it onto the green, at which time Gerald gleefully announced, "You just hit my ball, and that's going to cost you two strokes!"

We had a regular Sunday morning game which involved husbands and wives. There were eight to twelve couples, and we called ourselves the "Pros and Cons." Among the group were Tom and Jacki Gulick, a couple Dorie and I always enjoyed playing with, so when we threw up golf balls to decide who would play together, we usually rigged it so we became a foursome.

Tom was a successful Dallas businessman who had developed a heart problem, so Jacki insisted that he retire early. The four of us had a particularly memorable golfing trip to Palm Springs in the winter of 1985/86, marred only by the fact that I had to continually apologize to several residents of homes on the golf course because Tom's drives kept bouncing off their tile roofs.

In 1985 we sold the ranch for a considerable profit and bought a house in a nearby golfing community. I played every day and, for a while at least, just loved it. Dorie was an excellent golfer and had easily been one of the best women golfers at any of the clubs we had belonged to during our service days.

Later, I had mixed emotions about selling the ranch and, truth to tell,

Dorie had not liked the idea at all. However, there must have been a God looking out for us because a major dip in oil prices hit the world's markets in late 1985, and that crash caused land prices in Texas to nosedive. And the market did not recover for several years.

Another good thing about selling was that I was able to start flying again. I had gotten my commercial pilot's license during World War II but had lost it when the rules were changed during one of my overseas tours and I wasn't able to do whatever it was the FAA wanted me to do by way of updating information. I had to get a new license, which meant passing a written test and taking a flight check. No biggie there. After getting my license back, I bought a little Mooney and had a ball flying it around to my heart's content.

On July 13, 1985, the Tucson Chapter of the River Rats, led by Mr. Roman Darmer, dedicated a site on base close to the main entrance to Davis-Monthan AFB. Named Warrior Park, it was created to memorialize both the members of the armed forces still listed as missing in action—now more than a decade after the Vietnam War had ended—as well as the approximately 3,000 pilots who were killed in the skies over Southeast Asia.

An F-105 and an F-4 were placed on static displays. Darmer explained to the assembled dignitaries and guests the very special reason why these particular planes had been selected.

"Colonel Howard 'Scrappy' Johnson, one of the founders of the River Rats, is with us today, and he flew an F-105 similar to the one here. The F-4 is the same model as the one flown by then-Colonel Robin Olds, also a cofounder of that organization. And I should note that Colonel Olds was credited with four MiG kills over North Vietnam while piloting such a plane."

My name was placed on this F-105 dubbed Liger, as had my plane been at Korat. And Robin's name was printed on the side of "his" F-4.

Scattered about the park were several buildings which housed other appropriate memorabilia from the Vietnam era, such as squadron patches, photos and the like.

Invitations had been extended to several members of the Arizona congressional delegation, including outgoing Republican Senator Barry Goldwater. Goldwater received a bronze statue entitled "Fighter Pilot-Nam" and Steve Ritchie, one of only a handful of Vietnam air aces, made the presentation.

Other invitees included representatives Jim Kolbe, John McCain and Morris Udall. McCain, a navy pilot during the Vietnam War, had been shot down and spent more than five miserable years in North Vietnamese prison camps.

Darmer told those assembled that the idea for the park had its roots with

Davis-Monthan's previous commander, one Brig. Gen. Alan Lurie, a Vietnam pilot and ex-POW—and he had offered the site on base as an alternative to locating a River Rat memorial at the Pima Air Museum, southeast of Tucson.

A plaque commemorating the nation's prisoners of war and those brave souls still missing was unveiled, then Laird Guttersen, a retired Air Force colonel and an ex-POW himself, delivered the keynote speech.

I was deeply moved to have been honored in such a manner, and I still consider it one of the most endearing occasions of my life. To be so recognized by one's peers is truly meaningful, and I will never, ever, forget that day as long as I live.

Dorie and I took off on a road-trip vacation in early September 1985, our first stop being Louisville to visit her widowed mother. I knew I had arrived back home in Kentucky when I saw a roadside sign which read: FOR SALE: MATERS, TATERS AND BEANS. Leaving Louisville five days later, we headed north to the Upper Peninsula of Michigan to visit our son, Ted. He had started college there when I was stationed at Sioux St. Marie and had stayed and gotten married. We had a wonderful visit, then pressed on to the West so that I could get in some serious trout fishing. Bozeman, Montana, was my first choice, but the weather was lousy: bucketsful of rain and miserably cold temperatures. So we headed south to West Yellowstone. No luck there. The place was knee-deep in snow. The calendar was now crowding late September, so we headed even further south, stopping in Gunnison, Colorado. Strike three. It just was not meant to be. By now it was too late in the season so we packed up and headed home.

Dorie had developed a hacking cough during the trip but had shrugged it off as just a cold. I wasn't so sure, so when we arrived home I made her see a doctor.

The news was devastating. My Dorie was diagnosed with lung cancer, and it was in a very late stage. Dorie had smoked since she was sixteen. She lived another nine months and died at the far-too-young age of sixty-three. I know she would have lived many more years had she never smoked. Her father lived to be seventy-eight and her mother outlived them both, passing at the age of 96.

Previously, I had had a couple of polyps removed from my vocal chords which had caused my voice to become noticeably raspy, which in time, returned to normal. Now it was happening again. For years I had smoked cigars, but had quit the first time I had developed the problem. However, this time my larynx did not respond, and my voice stayed raspy. My morale plummeted, and for several months I moped around. I felt I had no purpose, no reason for living.

I missed Dorie.

23

Scalawag

My friends kept trying to fix me up with female companions and in the later part of 1986 I decided to do something about it myself. I called Elena O'Brien, a lady I'd met while investigating an aircraft accident many years earlier. Although I had neither seen nor spoken to her in over 15 years, I was able to find out that she was not married and I got her telephone number by going to the local library.

I made arrangements to visit her at her home in Houston, and we clicked. During the following months I kept the highway or the airways from Dallas to Houston warm in either my car or my Mooney. When flying, I'd put the Mooney's wing leveler on, then do a bunch of crossword puzzles to pass the time. This was a lot safer than reading because I could scan the sky for other aircraft between each word.

Elena was an interior designer and had built a very successful business from scratch, until the crash in oil prices in 1985. By 1986 downtown Houston was a ghost town. Half the homes in the city were for sale by the banks which had repossessed them, and office space went begging for tenants. When money's short, people consider the services of an interior designer a luxury they can forego.

In 1987 Elena and I decided to move to greener pastures. We took a trip to Palm Beach County, in Florida, where she was offered a position with a rather substantial design company. We leased a townhouse on the island of Palm Beach and lived there for the next year. After that, Elena decided she wanted to go it alone.

I had long been a devotee of John D. MacDonald's books and had read every one. He had written a series of tales about a guy named Travis McGee, and every title had the name of a color in it. Travis was an adventurous character who lived in a fancy marina just steps from the ocean in Fort Lauderdale. His home was a houseboat named the "Busted Flush" and he always seemed to have a slew of pretty women hanging around. I decided to join his world, so I bought a boat large enough to live on—not a houseboat, but a thirty-eight-foot cruiser named the "Scalawag."

Elena O'Brien in Houston, 1968.

I sold the Mooney and moved the Scalawag to the Palm Harbor Marina on the mainland side just across the bridge from Palm Beach. It turned out to be a pretty dull place compared to the Marina Travis lived in, that is, except for the occasional late night doings of a certain woman two slips down. However, the marina's proximity to Palm Beach more than made up for the lack of action dockside, because there were tons of pretty women to be found in the city's many lounges and restaurants. The ratio of women to men was better than three to one in my favor—and in my age bracket! This sure made it difficult for a red-blooded male who lived on the water to be lonely.

Ironically, most of the men were looking for women of means, and most of the women were looking for rich men. In a situation such as that you just know someone is always going to be disappointed.

✈ ✈ ✈

On the morning of September 12, 1989, the local TV stations made casual mention that a tropical storm named Hugo was strengthening in the Atlantic. Not thinking too much about it, I went about my normal routine, but a couple of days later Hugo had become a full-blown hurricane. As it approached the northeast Caribbean on September 15, it now had the full attention of folks in Southeast Florida. I discovered that my marina—which was situated on the fairly open waterway between the city of West Palm Beach and the island of Palm Beach—had a policy that if a hurricane was bearing down, everyone had to get their boats out. Apparently sometime in the not too distant past a hurricane had come ashore while some idiot had decided to stay on his boat and ride out the storm. Not a smart move. Needless to say a disaster ensued, and now the owners were rightfully worried about lawsuits.

This posed a huge problem for me. Where in the hell would I take the Scalawag? I knew that the best thing would be to find a sheltered canal and secure it with anchors, but the problem with this was that there were literally hundreds of boat owners in South Florida all looking for the same kind of safe anchorage.

Relieved was not an adequate word to describe how I felt when the storm passed through latitude 26 north and about one hundred miles east of the Palm Harbor Marina. That made it no longer a threat, and everyone breathed big sighs of relief. Ever since that incident, I pay close attention to the weather during hurricane season.

Elena and I remained close and we saw each other several times a week. She had leased a condo on the ocean in South Palm Beach, all in all, a very nice, very chic address. Early one morning, after I'd stayed the night and just as the sun was rising over a flattened sea, we were strolling the beach as gulls hovered over our heads searching for their morning meal when we came upon a baled object. It was not as large as the ones I'd fed to my cattle in Texas, maybe two-thirds the size, but it was strange, nonetheless. A hundred yards further along we came upon another, then another, and then lots of others! It finally dawned on us what we had chanced upon, so we abandoned our walk, went back to her condo and called the authorities. We were somewhat naive in the ways of drug dealers, but we had deduced that these bales contained marijuana.

My pal Travis McGee would have been proud of this boy! When the DEA folks arrived they scooped up a total of thirty-nine bales. One of the officers speculated that the druggies had dropped them off earlier to be collected by a henchman in the dark, or that maybe they'd had to abandon their load when the Coast Guard had come across their boat.

Prior to returning to the condo to do our civic duty, we took a pinch off one of the bales, and that evening we tried a "joint" made from it. Because neither of us had smoked cigarettes, we didn't know how to inhale. (We tried it, we didn't inhale, and we didn't like it!)

A couple of years later Elena decided we should get married, so in April 1990, we did. It was during Easter, which made it possible for my son Ted and his family to come to Florida from Michigan for the big event. My two other children, Carol and Billy had moved to the Sunshine State about the same time as Elena and I, so it was easy for them to make it. We were married aboard the Scalawag then held a second ceremony in Texas a short time later so her children could be witnesses for an exchanging of vows.

Elena stayed with the design firm for a little more than six months then ventured out again on her own. It was not easy trying to build a clientele in a very competitive market, so she began looking around for something else. In the fall of 1991 we opened an antique and consignment shop, and called it True Treasures. We've since opened a second location and the business has been successful beyond our wildest expectations.

We both work sixty hours a week—and for my part it's a night to day change from being a fighter pilot in the Air Force. Elena's a workaholic and the woman expects everyone around her to be the same. I'm constantly telling our friends that if I'd worked as hard in the Air Force as I do now I would have retired as a "ten-star general."

I ran into John Verdi again. Seems he'd recently come across a man in Ft. Lauderdale who owned some rather unusual airplanes, one being an F9F Panther. John was one of a handful of pilots still around who could actually fly this plane, the Navy's first jet, and out of curiosity had contacted the guy to see if he could fly the plane for him. John jumped at the opportunity.

A few months later, while flying the F9F from Houston to Ft. Lauderdale, John disappeared over Louisiana. A weeklong search proved fruitless. Neither John nor the plane was ever found. It deeply saddened me when I learned of his fate. John was a special kind of a guy.

24

Finis

I really enjoy River Rat reunions. Elena and I always time it so as to arrive on Thursday afternoon, take it easy through Thursday evening—just saying hello to old friends and maybe telling a few war stories for the umpteenth time in some quiet corner of a bar before hitting the sheets early. Fridays there's usually some sort of a tour. I've never been much for tours; I've had enough regimentation in the military to last two lifetimes, but Friday night's always a hoot with the flightsuit party. This ritual harks back to the days when most of the guys had fancy suits made by seamstresses in Thailand. Then they slapped all sorts of doodads on them—old squadron patches and/or cute little sayings. Again, not for me. I either showed up in a sport shirt and slacks or an old GI-issue flightsuit—which I still owned because when I closed Perrin AFB I was the last guy standing, which meant there was no one left to turn mine in to.

I remember one particular Friday night's party where I only drank wine, but managed to put away a helluva lot more than I thought. After the main event a bunch of us found our way to the hospitality suite where fellow Rats were taking turns bartending. One handed me a tall glass filled with straight bourbon and a couple of cubes. I quickly upended it and that was all she wrote. Elena managed to get me down to our room with the help of her son Mike and my friend Jack McEnroe, before I had a chance to pull a "Scrappy" and begin insulting someone, or, worse still, starting a fight.

At some point in the wee hours I took one of my two customary walks to the john—that's about the extent of how I get my exercise these days. Anyway, on my way back to bed—and in the pitch dark—I turned right instead of left, and out the damn front door I traipsed. I stupidly let go of the handle just as I woke up enough to realize what I had done, when BAM! the son of a bitch slammed shut! Hotel doors are designed to close automatically when turned loose, but this one was especially swift. And there I stood in the hallway, totally starkers! I'd already made one huge mistake, now I was about to make another. Instead of pounding on the door for Elena to let me in, I started walking the halls. Then it dawned on me that not only didn't I know my room number but that I was thoroughly lost to boot! This is about as sinking a feeling a naked guy with a hangover can get. After what seemed like hours a security guard arrived. He asked me my room number; I had to tell him I didn't know. He asked me my name—luckily I remembered that. He then used his cell phone to call the front desk, escorted me home, unlocked the door and ushered me inside.

What a night! And there were many, many more, but in the words of a song Frank Sinatra made famous, "It was a very good year!"

✈ ✈ ✈

In 2003 I watched one of Oliver North's war stories about the Battle of Britain on Fox television. This gave me the idea to write to the program and suggest that they do one about the bombing of North Vietnam, and in it emphasize how President Johnson and Secretary McNamara screwed it up. I'm proud to say that after about two years of my bugging them I was able to get the job done. The following letter was the start of the campaign.

Dear Colonel North:

After enjoying your showing of the Battle of Britain on Sunday, October 19, the thought occurred to me that the airmen who flew missions into North Vietnam during that war would make a terrific subject for your future "War Stories" show. I am a founder and was the first president of an organization known as The Red River Valley Fighter Pilots Association, which was formed in Thailand in 1967. The name is because of the Red River that flows through Hanoi.

We are nicknamed "River Rats" and as described by Jane Fonda, are the bad guys who flew missions deep into North Vietnam. We have had reunions every year, and are alive and well today. Originally to be a member you had to fly missions into the Hanoi area of North Vietnam. Our members are airmen from the Air Force, Navy, and Marines. This area around Hanoi known as Package VI has been described as the most heavily defended piece of real estate in the history of aerial warfare. It was defended by surface to air missiles, anti-aircraft guns, MiGs and radar, all tied together into an integrated control system.

Many stories have been written about the heroic deeds that these guys performed during this conflict. We can make them readily available to you. There are a lot of film and videos in the Air Force, Navy, and Marine archives.

The River Rats flew missions against targets, which were selected by Robert McNamara, and Lyndon Johnson. I am sure you are aware of their great genius for conducting air warfare. This tight control caused many more losses than would have happened had the commanders in the theatre had more flexibility in dealing with the war. Lyndon Johnson once declared "They don't hit an outhouse in North Vietnam without my approval."

These men fought a difficult war under extremely trying circumstances. It has been stated many times by the American press that the bombing of North Vietnam had no affect on the war, or to bringing the North Vietnamese to the peace table. THAT'S RIGHT, because of the way the war was fought. Had Johnson and McNamara let the guys from the academies, who were trained to run a war do so, it would have been a whole different situation. The story of how these men remained dedicated during these trying times needs to be told.

The disgraceful way the Vietnam air war was fought has left countless scars on so many brave men. Their sacrifices and heroism shown during this unfortunate chapter in American history should not be ignored. By hosting a show and letting the American people know what we did when we were called on, and let them see what we gave when we were asked, you will be doing a great service to so many, some of which do not have a lot of years left. I have attached a sample story (Pardo's Push).

Howard C. "Scrappy" Johnson

I am extremely proud of being instrumental in the founding of the River Rats. It was not something I deliberately set out to do, and in some respects it all kind of just happened, but nonetheless, I consider it one of my greater accomplishments.

It is now November of 2007. I turn 88 in February and I know my days are growing shorter, the shadows longer. And I think back to all those yesterdays.

It's depressing to be an old fighter pilot. Depressing because you can't even swagger good anymore. But it does have its upside, I guess. You can tell better stories, or maybe it seems that way because there are fewer people around who know whether you are lying or not. Which means, pretty soon I'll be able to say such things as, "When I used to play golf I shot under par every round." Or, how about, "When I had my ranch in Texas, I owned half the county." Or what about this for a whale of a tale: "When I was in Vietnam I flew 700 missions—all of 'em in Route Package Six."

Dorie's gone, Danny's gone, Spud's gone, Chappie's gone, Verdi's gone, Walt's gone and Robin's gone. But I'm still hanging in there. And the River Rats are still going strong, too. And that other Kentucky Colonel—the one with the fancy white suits and the cotton candy goatee—well, he might have made a bunch more money than yours truly, but I'll bet the store I've had a helluva lot more fun along the way.

And I've been lucky. I've been a fighter pilot who learned to fly like my cadet days' hero, Colonel Spicer. I've owned a Texas ranch where I was a cowboy like Bob Steele. And I lived on a boat in South Florida, just like Travis McGee. I've also been a successful entrepreneur like Tom Gulick, and I've managed to become a millionaire like Joe Dulin. And now I've written a book like my friend, Ken Bell.

Mine has been anything but a dull life—but you know what?

It ain't over yet!

Biographical Summaries

✈ ✈ ✈

Howard C. "Scrappy" Johnson, Colonel, USAF (Retired). Decorated air-combat veteran, record-breaking pilot and philanthropist, Howard Johnson was born in Knoxville, Tennessee, in 1920. The family moved to Louisville, Kentucky, in 1932 where he attended high school and the University of Louisville. It was there he acquired the nickname "Scrappy," pinned on him by his Sunday School teacher after he got into a fight at a church-sponsored picnic.

Johnson entered the U.S. Army Air Corps in August 1942 as an aviation cadet, and upon graduation in March 1943 was awarded pilot's wings and a commission as a reserve 2nd lieutenant. He spent World War II training aerial gunners at Laredo, Texas, for B-17s, B-24s and B-29s by flying fighters against bombers. He was promoted to captain in 1947, but later accepted a regular commission and reverted to his permanent grade of first lieutenant.

In 1950, Johnson was again promoted to captain. He then flew 87 combat missions in the P-51 fighter plane in Korea, where he was awarded two Distinguished Flying Crosses and seven Air Medals. In 1952, when stationed at Otis AFB, on Cape Cod, he led a flight of four fighters to Thule, Greenland, to protect that base from Soviet reconnaissance overflights. He was promoted to major in April of 1953, and assigned to Hamilton AFB in California.

In 1958, with only 30 hours in the airplane, Scrappy Johnson shattered the world's altitude record in an F-104A by reaching a height of 91,246 feet. He was awarded the Collier Trophy by then–Vice President Richard Nixon for this singular achievement. He was also awarded the West Coast Timer's Trophy, and soon thereafter was promoted to lieutenant colonel.

In 1963, after three years as advisor to the West German Air Force, Johnson was stationed in the 479th Tactical Fighter Wing at George AFB, California. In a squadron deployment that same year, he participated in a historic nonstop flight of F-104s from George AFB to Moron, Spain. The flight lasted more than eleven hours and included six in-flight refuelings. Back at George

AFB, he later served as squadron commander and, after being promoted to colonel, served as Wing Deputy Commander for Operations.

In 1966, he became the Director of Operations for the 388th Tactical Fighter Wing, at Korat Royal Thai Air Force Base, Thailand. Colonel Johnson flew 101 missions over North Vietnam and 17 over Laos, all in the F-105.

In 1967, he founded—and was later the first president of—the Red River Valley Fighter Pilot's Association (The River Rats). He wrote of that inaugural meeting: "Fighter pilots have always thought they were predestined to do things in a big way. We wanted to have a gigantic parade from the flight line to the club, led by three elephants and a band." History records that the parade finally featured six elephants. And thus the River Rats organization was born. It was formally chartered in 1969, and today has over 5000 members. The River Rats have donated hundreds of scholarships to children of POWs and MIAs, as well as many other young people interested in promoting aviation. Scholarship awards have exceeded one million, six-hundred-thousand dollars.

Colonel Johnson is a fighter pilot with over 7,000 hours flown in fifteen different fighter planes. During the course of his career he flew the P-39, P-40, P-47, P-51, P-63, F-80, F-84F, F-84G, F-86, F-94B, F-94C, F-102, F-104, F-105, F-106, as well as various trainers, bombers, transports, and a Mooney. In addition to receiving the Collier Trophy, he has been awarded 2 Silver Stars, 2 Legions of Merit, 7 Distinguished Flying Crosses, 18 Air Medals, and has been inducted into the Kentucky Aviation Hall of Fame.

✈ ✈ ✈

Ian A. O'Connor, Colonel, USAF (Retired). Ian A. O'Connor received his B.A. degree in political science from Benedictine College, Atchison, Kansas, in 1964. Commissioned a second lieutenant in the U.S. Air Force in 1966, he spent five years on active duty during the Vietnam War, then served in various IMA assignments with the reserves. Recalled to active duty for the First Persian Gulf War as a lieutenant colonel, he commanded a squadron in the 31st TFW. He was promoted to colonel and retired after twenty-eight years of continuous active and reserve service. Colonel O'Connor is a graduate of both the Air War College and the Industrial College of the Armed Forces. He is a commercial pilot with single and multi-engine ratings.

Ian A. O'Connor is the author of the novel *The Seventh Seal*. He is a member of Mystery Writers of America and lives in South Florida with his wife, Candice.

Index